Syntax: Generative Grammar

Educational Linguistics - TESOL
University of Pennsylvania
Graduate School of Education
3700 Walnut Street/C1
Philadelphia, PA 19104

by the same authors
Syntax: A Linguistic Introduction
to Sentence Structure

Syntax: Generative Grammar

E. K. Brown and J. E. Miller

HUTCHINSON
London Melbourne Sydney Auckland Johannesburg

Hutchinson & Co. (Publishers) Ltd
An imprint of the Hutchinson Publishing Group
17–21 Conway Street, London W1P 5HL

Hutchinson Group (Australia) Pty Ltd
30–32 Cremorne Street, Richmond South, Victoria 3121
PO Box 151, Broadway, New South Wales 2007

Hutchinson Group (NZ) Ltd
32–34 View Road, PO Box 40–086, Glenfield, Auckland 10

Hutchinson Group (SA) (Pty) Ltd
PO Box 337, Bergvlei 2012, South Africa

First published 1982

© E. K. Brown and J. E. Miller 1982
Illustrations © Hutchinson & Co. (Publishers) Ltd 1982

Set in VIP Times Roman by Preface Ltd, Salisbury, Wilts.

Printed in Great Britain by The Anchor Press Ltd
and bound by Wm Brendon & Son Ltd,
both of Tiptree, Essex

British Library Cataloguing in Publication Data
Brown, E. K.
  Syntax.
  1. Grammar, Comparative and general – Syntax
  I. Title   II. Miller, J. E.
  415   P291

ISBN 0 09 144110 2 cased
     0 09 144111 0 paper

Contents

6 *Syntax: Generative Grammar*

Preface

This volume picks up the major themes from our book *Syntax: A Linguistic Introduction to Sentence Structure* (Brown and Miller 1980) – henceforth BM – and shows how they can be handled in a formalized grammar. BM discusses at length constituent structure and relations between sentences but presents the fundamental ideas of transformational grammar informally. This volume concentrates on the general principles of transformational grammar and on the details of a particular model. Chapters 1–10 provide an account of the standard model, although the treatment of lexical items and complementizers is based on work done after the publication of Chomsky's *Aspects*. Chapters 12–15 offer a revision in the direction of the extended standard model, with special attention to the role of the lexicon. There are no traces and no X-bar notation and the revision is justified by an appeal to distribution and the distinction between morphology and syntax. There are no definitive accounts of any areas of English syntax but possible analyses are worked out and the arguments for them explained. In particular, the chapters on the revised model compare different analyses and criteria.

Like BM, this volume has grown from the need to provide teaching materials for first- and second-year undergraduates. Since existing introductions to generative grammar are either too detailed or cover too much ground in insufficient detail, we have limited the book's scope but gone into just enough detail to give students experience of working with a system of rules.

Chapters 16–23 deal with the treatment of grammatical functions, concentrating on processes and participants. Reflecting current progress in this area of syntax, these chapters are not a highly formalized account but they do attempt to demonstrate that the discussion gains in rigour by being related to a specific framework. The hypothesis at the centre of the discussion is that roles are different from relations, that the latter are best handled localistically and that relations belong to semantics rather than syntax.

An important point is that the discussion of roles and relations in Chapter 21 is independent of generative and interpretative semantics. It is clear from various passages throughout the book that we favour the latter approach but we attempt only to pinpoint the distinctions required and the proper locus for these distinctions in a transformational grammar.

1 Transformational generative grammar

BM introduced a number of concepts that made it possible to discuss constituent structure in a coherent fashion, bringing out general patterns via a statement of the relationships between different constructions. The key concepts were constituent structure rules (chapter 6 of BM), a lexicon (chapter 6, and the account in chapter 8 of the information that might be included in the lexical entries for individual lexemes), transformational relations (chapters 9 and 10), and morphological realization rules (chapters 14 and 15).

This volume explores these concepts in more detail to see exactly what difficulties arise when explicit statements about constituent structure are organized into a single system of rules. As this cannot be done without examining areas of English in some detail, we consider the relation between active and passive sentences, relative clauses, complement structures, and negative and interrogative sentences. Some of these topics figure in Part one of BM, but one or two of the analyses are changed and more attention is paid to the form of the rules and to their interaction.

The type of grammar that we develop is a transformational generative one. The terms 'generative' and 'transformational' were introduced in chapter 4 of BM, but can usefully be examined again. 'Generative' is simple enough: any grammar that is explicit and predicts sentences beyond those in the initial data is generative. The constituent structure grammar of Chapters 4 and 6 in BM is generative.

Chapter 9 of BM discussed active and passive sentences and the need to show that they are related. Such relations are called 'transformational'; a grammar that deals with them is a 'transformational grammar'. If a grammar is both generative and transformational, it is a 'transformational generative grammar'.

For a grammar to be generative and transformational it is not necessary that it handle only syntax. It is perfectly possible to describe the relations between sentences with respect to semantics; a grammar that does so explicitly and with predictive power is still a transformational generative grammar. It so happens that in this introduction relations between sentences are described in syntactic terms.

Another important point is the grounds on which we postulate transformational relations between sentences. It is clear from the discussion of constituent structure in chapters 4, 6 and 9 of BM that we abstract away as far as possible from particular lexical items in particular sentences. For example, the statement about the relationship between active and passive sentences does not mention particular instances like *The cat hated the dog* and *The dog was hated by the cat* but refers to the general structures

NP_1 V NP_2 and NP_2 BE V–pp *by* NP_1.

Although such statements do not mention specific nouns or verbs, we assume that the same lexical items occur in the two constructions related by ⇒ . With respect to the relation described by NP_1 V NP_2 ⇒ NP_2 *was* V *ed by* NP_1, we assume that whatever the verb and nouns are in the construction on the left of the arrow, the same verb and nouns occur in the construction to the right of the arrow: this relates *The cat hated the dog* to *The dog was hated by the cat* but not to *The rat was gnawed by the mouse*.

Semantic considerations have come into play, since the last two examples are not to be related, because the situations they describe differ completely. It is not always so easy to decide which lexical items come into account when a relation between two sentences is proposed. For example, the sentences *The bandits stole money from travellers* and *The bandits robbed travellers of money* seem to describe the same situation; but a form of STEAL occurs in one, a form of ROB in the other. Moreover, the prepositions are different, *from* in the first sentence and *of* in the second.

Because of this distinction between one pair of major lexical items, we do not relate these sentences in our grammar. (Note in passing that the difference in lexical items may reflect a semantic difference: the sentences can be regarded as presenting the 'same' situation from different angles. Either money is seen as being removed from travellers, the view which seems to be expressed by *The bandits stole money from travellers*, or travellers are seen as being removed from their money, which is how one might interpret *The bandits robbed travellers of money*.)

A trickier problem is presented by the sentences *The manage-ment presented the foreman with a watch* and *The management presented a watch to the foreman*. These sentences contain the same nouns and verb but in different orders, and there is a change of preposition. Prepositions do not fit into the dichotomy between major lexical items (nouns, verbs, adjectives, etc.) and minor grammatical items (tense endings, case inflections, plural affixes, etc.). Some linguists relate the two sentences by a transformation, but others take the difference as significant and keep the sentences unrelated by transformation.

Again, there may be a semantic difference. The first sentence of this example can be regarded as saying that the foreman came to be located with a watch, the second as saying that a watch moved to the foreman. The difficulties will be discussed on pages 215–17.

One important property of transformations is illustrated by the sentences **1–8** and the constructions they exemplify.

1	The cat hated the dog	NP_1 V NP_2
2	The dog was hated by the cat	NP_2 *was* V*ed by* NP_1
3	Did the cat hate the dog?	*Did* NP_1 V NP_2
4	The cat didn't hate the dog	NP_1 *did* Neg V NP_2
5	Didn't the cat hate the dog?	*Did* Neg NP_1 V NP_2
6	The dog wasn't hated by the cat	NP_2 *was* Neg V*ed by* NP_1
7	Wasn't the dog hated by the cat	*Was* Neg NP_2 V*ed by* NP_1
8	Was the dog hated by the cat?	*Was* NP_2 V*ed by* NP_1

The relations between the constructions are shown in Figure 1. Instead of being written out in full, each construction is repre-sented by its number.

The list in Figure 1 makes the general principle clear. Every sentence in it is related to every other sentence. In some cases the relation is indirect, e.g. between **3** and **6**, but it is undeniable that there is a relation. Is there a neater way of describing the relations? Does the inelegance of Figure 1 conceal some underlying order?

$$1 \Rightarrow 2 \qquad 2 \Rightarrow 1 \qquad 3 \Rightarrow 1$$
$$1 \Rightarrow 3 \qquad 2 \Rightarrow 3 \qquad etc.$$
$$1 \Rightarrow 4 \qquad 2 \Rightarrow 4$$
$$1 \Rightarrow 5 \qquad 2 \Rightarrow 5$$
$$1 \Rightarrow 6 \qquad 2 \Rightarrow 6$$
$$1 \Rightarrow 7 \qquad 2 \Rightarrow 7$$
$$1 \Rightarrow 8 \qquad 2 \Rightarrow 8$$

Figure 1

Consider the relation between **3** and **6**. What is meant by 'indirect'? Examination of **1** and **3** shows that **3** contains the components in **1** plus an extra item, *did*. Similarly, **6** consists of the components in **2** plus an extra item, Neg. In turn, **2** consists of the components in **1** plus three extra elements, *was, ed* and *by*. Notice that even a discussion of **2** and **6** can refer to **1**. Reference can be made to **1** no matter which pair of sentences is discussed.

This use of **1** as a basic point of orientation allows us to clarify the meaning of 'indirect'. We can proceed from **1** to **2** and then from **2** to **6** by adding items to those in **1** and changing items around, as in the move from **1** to **2**. We can proceed further from **6** to **7** by moving *wasn't* to the front of the construction. All these relations are direct in that we proceed in a straight line through the sequence of constructions. The relation between **3** and **6** is 'indirect': we have to go back to **1** in order to get rid of *did* before going from **1** to **6** by adding and moving items. **3** and **6** are related by their relationship with **1**.

We allow journeys through the sequence of constructions provided that no item is deleted and replaced by another one. We can proceed from **1** to **2** and from **2** to **6**, but having gone from **1** to **2** we cannot then pass on to **3**. That is, there are various routes through the constructions, four in all. These routes are shown in Figure 2. There is no obligation to go to the final point of any route, nor indeed to leave the starting point.

It is possible to retrace one's steps from any point in a route to the starting point, **1**. The representation of the relations in Figure 2 is clearly much simpler than that in Figure 1, and reflects a more orderly view of the relations. This orderly view is that **1**, the least complex construction in English, is the basic, unmarked, neutral construction, the other constructions being more complex and derived from it.

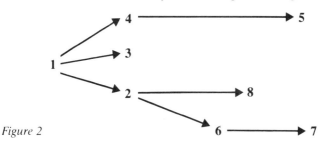

Figure 2

We can now appreciate another part of the meaning of 'transformational'. In the discussion of constituent structure in BM, chapter 4, constituent structure rules (or phrase structure rules) were introduced. These specify simple structures underlying active declarative sentences of English; transformations then transform the simple structures into more complex ones. The term 'phrase structure' or 'constituent structure' is not very informative. A more appropriate term is 'formation rules', which is used in logic. These rules are particularly associated with the logician Carnap and his book *Logical Syntax of Language* (1934). Carnap was concerned with establishing a basic language in which all the propositions of science could be formulated, emphasis being given to the syntax of the language. The formation rules specified the basic sentences, and transformations put the basic sentences in correspondence with other sentences. Carnap might have used the term 'rules of inference' instead of 'transformation rules'. The former term was used by logicians whose business was to establish systems in which complex propositions could be inferred or deduced from a number of basic propositions: the basic propositions were put 'in correspondence' with more complex ones. Carnap, however, used 'transformation rules' to emphasize his interest in the syntax of his sentences, in contrast with their meaning.

It is not logically necessary for a transformational grammar to order the constructions it handles and prescribe certain routes through them, but descriptions set out in that way are neater and reveal regularities that otherwise remain obscure.

Another complexity that accompanies most transformational grammars, though it is not logically necessary, is the distinction between surface syntactic structure and deep syntactic structure. This distinction is found in all transformational grammars, even if it is implicit rather than explicit in the pioneering work of Harris and in Chomsky's early work.

The distinction has already been drawn implicitly in the discussion of the progressive and perfect in chapter 15 of BM, where a satisfactory description of constructions like *is writing* required two levels. On the more abstract level there was a sequence of constituents Tense $-_{\text{Prog}}(\text{BE ing})_{\text{Prog}}-$ WRITE. *Ing* is moved to the right of WRITE, giving WRITE $-ing$ and Tense is moved to the right of BE. The sequence BE $-$ Tense is realized as *is*, WRITE $-$ *ing* as *writing*.

The level on which the sequence Tense $-$ BE *ing* $-$ WRITE appears is the level of deep syntax; the level on which *is writing* appears is the level of surface syntax. Connecting the two levels by transformations explicitly includes in the description the information that *is* and *ing* are closely linked in *is writing*.

A distinction between deep and surface structure also permits explicit statements about the occurrence of tense morphs in the verb sequence in English declarative sentences. By treating Tense as a separate constituent in the deep structure we can state, via affix hopping (see pp. 206–14 in BM), that Tense is added to whatever constituent occurs immediately to its right. We can also capture the relationship between positive and negative sentences and between declarative and interrogative sentences (pp. 94–107). In particular, the occurrence of DO forms can be handled with more insight than is possible with only one level. Finally, not just main clauses but also subordinate clauses share in the illumination, especially relative clauses (pp. 58–67).

The fundamental point is that deep syntactic structures are hypothetical, part of the linguist's description. (From now on, the briefer terms 'deep structure' and 'deep structures' are used.) These hypothetical structures are set up to account for dependencies between morphs or to express other insights into syntactic structure. They are part of a way of looking at sentences that is justified only to the extent that it leads to insights and a clear way of expressing them.

2 Phrase structure rules

In chapter 5 of BM constituent structure or phrase structure rules were introduced to describe the grouping of constituents to form a sentence. This chapter examines these rules in more detail, using the rules proposed in chapter 15 of BM. Since the analyses presented in BM are changed, the set of phrase structure rules in the final description differs from those in **1** below, which are identical with the rules in BM, chapter 14.

i	# S #	$\Rightarrow$	NP VP
ii	NP	$\rightarrow$	Art N Num
iii	Num	$\rightarrow$	$\begin{Bmatrix} \text{sing} \\ \text{pl} \end{Bmatrix}$
iv	VP	$\rightarrow$	Aux V (NP)
v	Aux	$\rightarrow$	T (M) (Perf) (Prog)
vi	T	$\rightarrow$	$\begin{Bmatrix} \text{past} \\ \text{non-past} \end{Bmatrix}$
vii	Perf	$\rightarrow$	HAVE pp
viii	Prog	$\rightarrow$	BE ing
ix	Art	$\rightarrow$	$\begin{Bmatrix} \text{def} \\ \text{indef} \end{Bmatrix}$

Figure 3

Minor changes have been made. *Tense* has been replaced by T, *Modal* by M. The plus signs have been omitted and S is flanked by #, the symbol marking the sentence boundary. As before, optional constituents are inside round brackets; the placing of constituents one above the other inside curly brackets indicates that only one of the constituents is chosen.

In principle there are two sorts of 'phrase structure' rule (henceforth, PS rule). The first, of the form $X \rightarrow Y$, is called *context-free*: no matter what the context of X, i.e. no matter what symbols are to the left and/or right of it, it is rewritten as Y. The other sort is called *context sensitive*, because what X is rewritten as depends on the symbols occurring with it. The rule $X \rightarrow Y/Z\_\_$ is to be read 'rewrite X as Y if X occurs immediately to the right of Z'. The rule $X \rightarrow Y/\_\_Z$ is read as 'rewrite X as Y if X is immediately to the left of Z', and the rule $X \rightarrow Y/Z\_\_W$ is read as 'rewrite X as Y if X occurs immediately to the left of Z and immediately to the right of W'.

These three rules can be expressed in the form $ZX \rightarrow ZY$, $XZ \rightarrow YZ$ and $ZXW \rightarrow ZYW$. Context-free rules can be expressed in the same form as the last context-sensitive rule, with the proviso that the context is immaterial: e.g., $AXB \rightarrow AYB$, where A and B are any constituents or none. (Because these rules rewrite symbols, a more general name than PS rule is simply 'rewrite rule'.)

S is known as the *initial symbol*. It is given. All the other symbols are *derived* from the initial symbol by applying the appropriate rules. $\rightarrow$ here means 'is rewritten as'. The rules generate a derivation as follows. Consider the rules in Figure 3. To S is applied rule **i**, which yields a second line consisting of NP and VP. These are written below S. The third line in the derivation can be obtained by applying rule **iv** to VP or rule **ii** to NP. (The numbering of the rules is purely an aid to recognition.) The lines of the derivation obtained by applying the rules are set out in Figure 4. The numbers on the left indicate the number of each line in the derivation.

line 1	# S #
line 2	# NP VP #
line 3	# NP Aux V NP # *or* # Art N Num VP #

Figure 4

There are two possibilities for line **3** because either the NP or VP can be rewritten. The symbols that are not rewritten are repeated in the next line.

The derivation contains information about the constituent structure of sentences, information which has to be dug out of the derivation. The digging-out is done by constructing a *phrase marker*. Take the partial three-line derivation in Figure 4–partial, because most of the symbols in **3** can be rewritten by rules in Figure 3. To construct a phrase marker we first write down the initial symbol in the derivation. In the second line of the derivation there are no difficulties, since only the symbol S in the first line can be rewritten. The symbols in the second line are written below S, each being joined to S by a line.

The third line is then compared with the second. We take the first possibility – NP Aux V NP. The rightmost symbol in **3** is checked against the rightmost symbol in **2**, which reveals that **3** has NP where **2** has VP. The leftmost symbols in **3** and **2** are then compared. Since in both lines this symbol is NP, we infer that the NP in **2** has not been rewritten. As there are only two symbols in **2**, we also infer that VP has been rewritten (the procedure is intended to be so explicit that a mindless robot could work through it).

We then proceed thus. Having verified that the leftmost symbols are identical in any two lines of a derivation, we compare the next symbol in from the left in one line with the corresponding symbol in the other. In this instance we find Aux in **3** but VP in **2**. Since we have already found that the rightmost symbols are different we know that everything from Aux to the end of **3** has been derived from VP. We take NP and write it below NP in the phrase marker, joining the two NPs with a line. The Aux V NP sequence is written out below VP and joined to it by a line. The resulting phrase marker is shown in Figure 5.

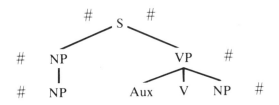

Figure 5

If we run through the derivation of Figure 4 choosing the second possibility for **3** the resulting phrase marker is that of Figure 6.

The different partial derivations yield different phrase markers; but suppose rule (**ii**) is applied to the first occurrence of NP in the first alternative for **3**. This yields a fourth line containing Art N Num Aux V NP and the derivation is of the form of Figure 7.

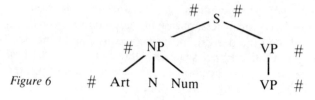

Figure 6

line	1	# S #
line	**1**	# S #
line	**2**	# NP VP #
line	**3**	# NP Aux V NP #
line	**4**	# Art N Num Aux V NP #

Figure 7

Suppose now that rule **(iv)** is applied to the second alternative for **3**. This yields a fourth line with Art N Num Aux V NP and the derivation is of the form of Figure 8. Although the fourth lines in

line	**1**	# S #
line	**2**	# NP VP #
line	**3**	# Art N Num VP #
line	**4**	# Art N Num Aux V NP #

Figure 8

the partial derivations of Figures 7 and 8 are identical, the partial derivations are different, witness **3** of each. Corresponding to Figure 7 is the phrase marker of Figure 9 and corresponding to Figure 8 the one of Figure 10.

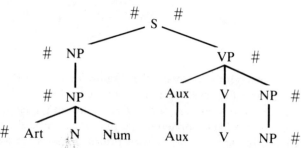

Figure 9

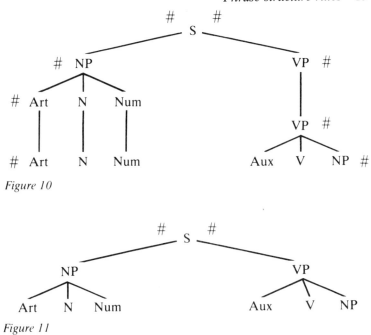

Figure 10

Figure 11

By convention, if a phrase marker contains more than one occurrence of the same node joined by lines all occurrences except the highest are deleted. This convention applied to the phrase markers of Figures 9 and 10 yields the phrase marker of Figure 11.

Linguists always work with the sort of simplified phrase marker of Figure 11; although corresponding to more than one derivation, it represents clearly and unequivocally the information needed about the constituent structure of a sentence. This particular phrase marker corresponds to only two derivations but if all the rules of Figure 1 applied in different orders many equivalent derivations would correspond to a single phrase marker.

A phrase marker can be defined as a graph with the general name *tree diagram*. The graph consists of a root node and other nodes connected by lines called *branches*. The branches must not cross each other and there must be a unique path from the last node on each branch to the root node. Since each node is labelled, tree diagrams are also called *rooted labelled graphs*. These graphs are put to many uses by mathematicians and scientists, and linguists have merely borrowed them to represent constituent struc-

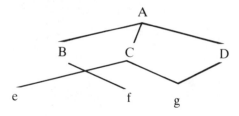

Figure 12

ture. Figures 9–11 fit the definition but the tree of Figure 12 does not.

In the tree in Figure 12 the branches from B to f and from C to e cross and there are two paths from g to A. The conventions for tree diagrams, although established by mathematicians, make sense in syntax. If the labels in Figure 12 are replaced by labels from constituent structure analysis the graph is nonsensical. Of course, no linguist would want to devise such a description of syntactic structure, but remember that our aim is a mechanical method that could be followed by a mindless robot (see Figure 13).

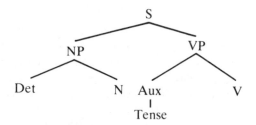

Figure 13

The nodes in a phrase marker are said to be in a relation of dominance with each other. If there is a path from a node Y to a node Z, Z '*dominates*' Y. If there is no node between Y and Z, Z '*immediately dominates*' Y. In the phrase marker of Figure 11 S dominates all the nodes below it but it immediately dominates only NP and VP. The dominance relation, as is clear from chapter 5, allows us to express the notion of an X being a Y, e.g., of Art, N and Num being an NP.

From Figures 7 and 8 it is plain that a derivation is a sequence of strings, each line a string of symbols. The symbols are put together by an operation called *concatenation* that is usually binary (applying to two symbols at a time) and associative but non-commutative, though its binary nature is not always observed. The descriptive nature of the operation makes syntactic sense: it does not matter whether an Aux is added to the left of a V and then an NP added to the left of Aux, or vice versa; but it does matter whether, for instance, an NP is put to the left of V or the right of V, as different constructions result, which is why the operation is non-commutative.

Concatenation is denoted by the symbol ⌒, e.g. NP ⌒ VP, but the symbol is omitted where no confusion can arise and is left out of the PS rules here.

A derivation is not just any sequence of strings. There must be more than one string in the sequence, and each string must differ from the string that immediately precedes it, in that one symbol in the previous string is replaced by one or more symbols in the given string. The initial string is exempt from this restriction. The replacement of a symbol in one line by one or more symbols in the following line must be in accord with the rules of the grammar. From all these remarks it follows that a derivation is an *ordered sequence* of strings.

Compare now the rules in Figure 3 and the derivation in Figure 7. The last line of Figure 7 contains symbols, Aux and NP, that can be rewritten by a rule in Figure 3 and the derivation is said to be *unterminated*. If the last line were def N sg past M V, none of the symbols could be rewritten by a rule of Figure 3 and the derivation would be *terminated*. The last line of a terminated derivation is called the *terminal string*.

The grammar is provided with a vocabulary that consists of the symbols, S, ⌒, VP, past, etc. Symbols that can be rewritten by some rule of the grammar constitute the *non-terminal vocabulary*, and symbols that cannot constitute the *terminal vocabulary*.

The terminal vocabulary in Figure 3 consists of syntactic terms, but the discussion in chapter 3 of BM makes it clear that these can be rewritten as lexical items. Strictly speaking they are not terminal vocabulary, and a distinction is drawn between syntactic and lexical vocabulary; only the syntactic is affected by the above remarks about terminal and non-terminal vocabulary.

Relative to the transformational grammar explained here, a more subtle distinction can be drawn between *non-terminal, pre-terminal* and *terminal strings*. *Non-terminal strings* contain non-terminal syntactic vocabulary, *pre-terminal strings* contain terminal syntactic vocabulary, and *terminal strings* contain lexical vocabulary.

Only one restriction on PS rules has been mentioned (page 21) but there are several.

Restriction 1: only one symbol can be rewritten at a time.

Rules of the form A → xy are allowed, but not rules like AB → xyz or AB → xyzj. Suppose we have the grammar of Figure 14. One derivation produced by these rules is in Figure 15.

i	A	→ BC
ii	B	→ DE
iii	C	→ FG
iv	DE	→MNP

Figure 14

line 1	A
line 2	BC
line 3	DEC
line 4	DEFG
line 5	MNPFG

Figure 15

The procedure for constructing phrase markers can be applied as far as **4**. It breaks down at the comparison of **4** and **5** – is D rewritten as M or MN, or is E rewritten as N or NP? All is clear if only one symbol is rewritten at a time – hence this restriction.

Restriction 2: No symbol can be deleted.

Without this restriction it is impossible to construct a single phrase marker corresponding to a derivation. Suppose rule **iv** of Figure 14 is D → ∅. The rule means that D is deleted. The rules now produce a derivation in which the first four lines are the same as in Figure 15, but the fifth line is EFG. It is necessary that each line in a derivation be at least as long as the preceding one, but the rule D → ∅ yields a fifth line one symbol shorter than the fourth. The lowest occurrence of D should dominate another symbol; as there is no other symbol D must be connected to E, F or G. But it cannot be joined to F or G, as branches would cross, and it cannot be joined to E as there would be no unique path from E to A. Consequently the construction of the phrase marker comes to a halt.

Restriction 3: No permutations are allowed.

There are no rules of the form AB → BA nor any sequence of rules that lead to the permutation of symbols, albeit in several steps. If such rules were allowed the 'is a' relation could not be expressed by phrase markers. Suppose there is the set of rules of Figure 16.

  i A → BC
ii BC → CB

Figure 16

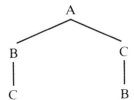

Figure 17

The derivation generated by these rules corresponds to the phrase marker in Figure 17. This phrase marker expresses the absurdity that a B is a C and a C is a B. A parallel linguistic absurdity would be to say that a noun phrase is a verb or an Aux is an NP.

Restriction 4: (NB. This restriction applied in the earliest models of transformational grammar but was abandoned in connection with the improved treatment of relative clauses. The matter receives further comment in chapters 5–8 below.) No symbol can be rewritten as itself or as a sequence of symbols containing itself.

That is, there are no rules A → A or A → BCAD. Without this restriction derivations can be infinite and there is no finite procedure for constructing phrase markers. For example, the rules A → Ab and A → a generate the derivation of Figure 18.

line 1 A
line 2 Ab
line 3 Abb
      etc.

Figure 18

A vital piece of information about the procedure for constructing derivations is that the procedure does not refer to the PS rules themselves. For the moment let us simply accept that this is so, since the topic is not of immediate concern, but we will return to it in chapter 14.

Context-sensitive rules, mentioned early in the chapter, make it possible to achieve the effect of a permutation. A further restriction can be placed on PS rules to ensure that no permutations occur but it is too strong to be met by grammars of natural languages. The operations performed by context-sensitive rules can also be carried out by transformational rules (chapters 8, 9 and 14 of BM) but the latter do not apply until a derivation with its associated phrase marker has been generated by the context-free PS rules. In this fashion the grammar is given a solid starting point.

Technical terms

context-free PS rule
context-sensitive PS rule
derive
initial symbol
phrase marker
tree diagram
branch
node
rooted labelled graph
dominate
immediately dominate
concatenation
unterminated derivation
terminated derivation
terminal string
non-terminal string
pre-terminal string
non-terminal syntactic vocabulary
terminal syntactic vocabulary
terminal vocabulary

Exercises

1

Study the following set of PS rules and answer questions (a) and (b).

   i   X → MN(Z)
   ii M →DE
   iii N → FG
   iv Z → ST
   v   E → PQ
   vi S → KL

(a) Are the following strings terminal or non-terminal? What symbols constitute the terminal vocabulary?

    MNZ, DEFG, DPQFG, DPQN, DPQFGST

(b) Which of the following strings can be generated by the above rules?

    EFG, DNKLT, PQFGKLT, DPQNZ, DPQFGT, MNKLT, EKLT

2

Construct a derivation showing one possible sequence of strings generated by the rules in (1). Convert the derivation to a phrase marker.

3

Write PS rules that generate the English sentences below. Since the rules are to generate only the given constructions and word forms, you can ignore, e.g., the fact that English noun phrases can contain more than one adjective and the fact that there are present tense verb forms (*plays*) and past tense forms (*played*). The same advice applies to the noun forms: i.e. one of the rules is N → {*paintings, gardens, . . .*}. Your rules should generate sentences with correct syntactic structure, though some will be peculiar with respect to their meaning.

    The paintings fascinate the students
    The famous paintings fascinate the visitors
    The statues in the gardens attract visitors

Exciting matches attract spectators
The pictures in the museums are beautiful
The statues are very unusual
The very beautiful paintings attract visitors

4

Using the PS rules on page 15, write derivations for the structure
of the following sentences:

Bill has written a poem
The painting is priceless
The bridge may have collapsed

3 Transformations

It is unfortunate that the precise, neat system of rules in chapter 2 is inadequate to describe natural language. It suffices if we merely want to say that verb phrases in English consist of, e.g., Modal + Past Tense − HAVE − BE + pp − V + *ing*, as in *might have been playing*. But this description does not relate BE to *ing* or HAVE to *pp*, nor does it express the generalization that the tense morph is affixed to the first constituent in the verb phrase in a declarative sentence of English.

As is shown in chapter 14 of BM, the desired statements can be made if deep syntactic structures are postulated in which the related items occur together and in which Tense is treated as a separate constituent. The rules on page 208 of BM generate a derivation corresponding to the phrase marker in Figure 19. In order to place the constituents in the order in which the corresponding surface morphs occur, *ing* has to be put on the right of SLEEP, *pp* to the right of BE and Past to the right of MAY. This involves the permuting of constituents, which PS rules are not allowed to do. As the distinction between deep and surface

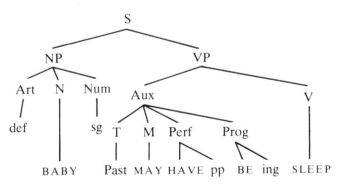

Figure 19

structure permits us to state the relationships, we are obliged to introduce rules that can permute constituents.

Our description also deals with relations between sentences, or, in the terms used earlier, prescribes a route through the set of constructions (cf. page 12). One way to prescribe a route is in terms of constituents being added or permuted, which needs rules that can add new constituents to phrase markers as well as permuting already existing constituents. A third necessary operation is deletion. These complications make the grammar capable of handling relations between sentences, one of the most important achievements of transformational grammar, and of handling discontinuous constituents.

The rules that can adjoin, delete and permute are called transformations (T-rules). In this chapter their properties are listed; following chapters provide examples of their application in the description of English.

T-rules are more complex than PS rules. They consist of two parts, a *structural analysis* or *description* – SA for short – and a *structural change* – SC for short. The SA specifies the sort of phrase marker to which the T-rule can apply. Suppose the SA of a given T-rule contains the symbols A B C. The rule applies to a phrase marker in which all the nodes can be analysed into subsets such that one subset is dominated by A, another by B and a third by C, and such that there are no nodes not dominated by A, B or C. If a phrase marker can be analysed according to the SA of a T-rule, it is said to be *analysable with respect to that rule*. The concept of *structural analysability* is perhaps the central notion in transformational grammar. (Note that since the SA of a T-rule specifies one or two constituents in a phrase marker, leaving others unspecified, T-rules apply to a set of phrase markers.)

The structural change in a T-rule specifies how the phrase marker is affected by it. The concepts of the SA and SC are illustrated in the following paragraphs on deletion, adjunction and permutation.

Deletion

Suppose the phrase marker in Figure 20 is to be mapped into the phrase marker in Figure 21. The T-rule effecting the deletion is stated in Figure 22.

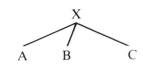

Figure 20 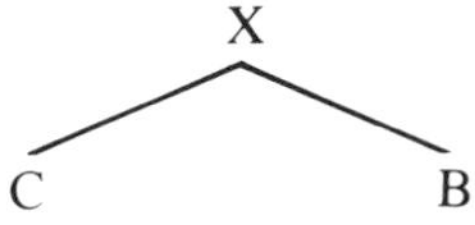   Figure 21

SA: A   B   C
      1 – 2 – 3
SC: 1 – 2 – Ø

Figure 22

The symbols in the SA are assigned numbers because they can be more complex that those in Figure 22 and the use of numbers simplifies the statement of the rule. Ø indicates that whatever was in that particular position is deleted. The dashes show that A, B and C are *sisters*, i.e. are all immediately dominated by the same node.

The phrase markers in Figures 20 and 21 are relatively simple. The deletion rule may apply to a more complex phrase marker and the symbols in its SA may correspond to non-terminal nodes.

If a non-terminal node is deleted, all the nodes it dominates are also deleted. In Figure 23 C is deleted and H and I also disappear.

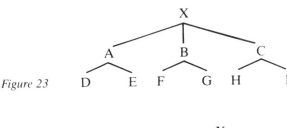

Figure 23

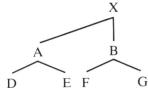

Figure 24

Adjunction

Adjunction is the addition of a new node to a tree. There are three types of adjunction. The first, *sister adjunction*, maps the tree of Figure 25 on to the tree of Figure 26 and the tree in Figure 25a on to the tree of Figure 26a.

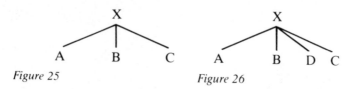

Figure 25   *Figure 26*

The T-rule that sister adjoins D is stated in Figure 27.

SA: A   B   C
      1   2   3
SC: 1   2–D   3

Figure 27

The dashes in the SA tell us that A, B and C are sisters; the dashes between 2 and D and between D and 3 tell us that D is adjoined as a sister to B and C, i.e. is attached to X.

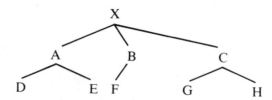

Figure 25a

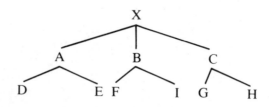

Figure 26a

The T-rule that adjoins I is stated in Figure 27a.

```
SA:   A    F    C
      1    2    3
SC:   1   2–I   3
```

Figure 27a

The dash after 2 in the SC indicates that I is adjoined as a sister constituent of F, i.e. it is attached to the node immediately dominating F.

The second type of adjunction is *Chomsky adjunction*, exemplified in the mapping of the tree of Figure 28 on to the tree of Figure 29.

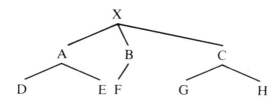

Figure 28

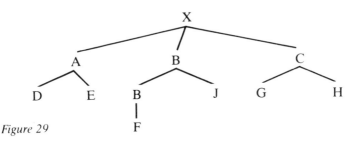

Figure 29

The relevant T-rule is stated in Figure 30.

```
SA:   A    B    C
      1    2    3
SC:   1   2+ J  3
```

Figure 30

The + sign indicates that Chomsky adjunction is involved. In this operation a node N is detached from the node N_1 that dominates it. The detached node is copied, the copy being added to the tree in such a way that it immediately dominates N and is immediately dominated by N_1. The + sign in the SC is placed immediately next to the constituent that is copied, in this case B. If J was attached to the left of B the SC would read 1 J +2 3.

The third type of adjunction is *daughter adjunction*, which attaches a constituent to a node in the tree. The adjoined constituent is a *daughter* of the node it is attached to. Consider Figures 31 and 32.

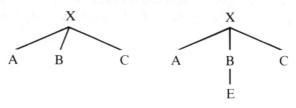

Figure 31   Figure 32

The T-rule effecting daughter adjunction is stated in Figure 33. The / sign indicates daughter adjunction, the constituent to the right of / becoming the daughter of the constituent to the left of / .

SA: A   B   C
     1   2   3
SC: 1   2/E   3

Figure 33

The adjunctions exemplified above involve the addition of a node that does not occur in the tree operated on by the T-rule.

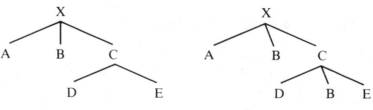

Figure 34   Figure 35

It is also possible to add a copy of a node already in the tree. This type of adjunction is *copying*, cf. Figure 34 and 35, and the T-rule of Figure 36.

SA:	A	B	D	E
	1	2	3	4
SC:	1	2	3–2–4	

Figure 36

The SC states that constituent 2 is repeated and that the second occurrence is a sister of 3 and 4.

Permutation

This operation is illustrated by the trees in Figures 37 and 38.

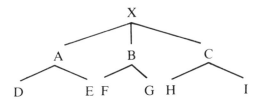

Figure 37

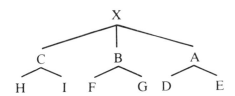

Figure 38

The T-rule that permutes A and C is stated in Figure 39.

SA:	A	B	C
	1	2	3
SC:	3	2	1

Figure 39

When a non-terminal node is deleted, the nodes it dominates are also deleted. The same, *mutatis mutandis*, applies in the permuting of constituents: when A and C are permuted the nodes they dominate are carried along.

Permuting can be thought of as a complex operation consisting of copying – adjunction and deletion. For instance, we can think of A in Figure 37 as being copied to the right of C and the original node A being deleted. Similarly, C in Figure 37 can be copied to the left of B and the original C deleted. In the interests of simplicity, however, we continue to talk simply of constituents being permuted.

A T-rule can be applied to a phrase marker if the latter is analysable with respect to the T-rule, but it does not follow that the T-rule has to apply. A distinction can be drawn between *optional* and *obligatory T-rules*. The passive T-rule in chapter 8 of BM is optional: it need not apply to a phrase marker even if the latter is analysable with respect to it. This reflects the fact that sentences in English can be active or passive, the choice being free. On the other hand, since certain embedded sentences (see chapter 9 of BM) have to be mapped into relative clauses, the various relative clause T-rules are obligatory.

PS rules differ from T-rules in that the optional-obligatory distinction is not usually applied to them. A PS rule applies whenever the last line at any stage in a derivation contains a symbol that appears to the left of the arrow. This brings up another distinction between PS rules and T-rules, namely *ordering*. The PS rules in Figure 3 (page 15) do not need to be ordered, because some rules cannot apply until others have – e.g. rule (**ii**) cannot apply before rule (**i**) – and because it does not matter which order the rules apply in when there is a choice. Either rule (**ii**) or rule (**iv**) could apply to **3** of the derivation in Figure 4 (page 16), but the last line of the derivation and the corresponding phrase marker are the same no matter which rule applies first.

Context-free PS rules are usually *intrinsically ordered:* (the rules order themselves) but T-rules are sometimes *extrinsically ordered*, the reason being that in the derivation of complex sentences many T-rules apply. To generate correct sentences the linguist may have to decree arbitrarily that one T-rule applies before another. The ordering of T-rules is implicit in the description of English in chapters 6–9 and is discussed in chapter 10.

There are two more distinctions between T-rules and PS rules.

One is that the application of a PS rule to a symbol in the lowest line of a derivation yields a new line without affecting the other lines further up the derivation: T-rules apply to one whole phrase marker to derive another whole phrase marker, as shown by Figures 20–35.

The other distinction is that PS rules operate on constants, whereas T-rules operate on variables. Consider the PS rules of Figure 3 (page 15) and the phrase marker of Figure 19 (page 27). A PS rule merely rewrites a given symbol as another symbol and the rewritten symbol is necessarily constant. T-rules, however, delete, permute and adjoin. As we will see later, some T-rules add constituents to Aux. This happens no matter whether Aux contains only Tense, or Tense and Perf, or Tense and Prog, or Tense, Perf and Prog. Only Aux is mentioned in the SA, but Aux, varying with respect to the constituents it dominates, is a variable. (The term *variable* is used in a different connection in chapter 10).

The deep structure deemed necessary for an adequate description of main verbs and auxiliaries in English is shown in Figure 11 (cf. chapter 14 of BM). If HAVE and *pp*, BE and *ing* are sister constituents in the deep structure it is necessary to move *pp* and *ing* into the positions occupied by the corresponding surface morphs. Tense, too, has to be moved to the right of the immediately following constituent.

On page 208 of BM the movement of affixes was described thus: 'Any affix which is found to the left of a verb is to be moved to the right of that verb. An affix may hop a verb only once.' This rule does not specify its output exactly. For instance, the movement of *ing* to the right of SLEEP in Figure 19 could result in the two trees shown in Figures 40 and 41.

The structure of Figure 40 results from sister adjunction of *ing* to SLEEP, that of Figure 41 from Chomsky adjunction. One advantage offered by the latter is that, once the lexemes have been

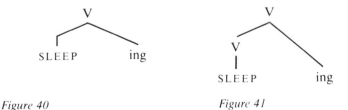

Figure 40   *Figure 41*

mapped into orthographic forms, it can be shown that the form *sleeping* consists of the two morphs *sleep* and *ing*, that these two morphs together make up a verb form and that *sleep* itself is a verb form to which an affix has been added. If the morpheme being moved is *pp*, Chomsky adjunction shows that, e.g., *played* consists of *play* and *ed* and that *play* itself is a verb. Similarly, Tense can be Chomsky adjoined to the immediately following constituent.

A formal statement of affix hopping is given in Figure 42.

Affix hopping

SA:	X	Af	Vb	Y
	1	2	3	4
SC:	1	3+	2#	4

Conditions: i Af = T, pp, ing

ii Vb = V, Perf, Prog, or M

iii Y may be null

Figure 42

Af and Vb are cover symbols, necessary because the rule applies to different constituents. Y represents whatever constituents are to the right of the main verb, Prog, etc. It is null if Vb represents an intransitive verb. The T-rule applies from right to left across a phrase marker and the # sign, in addition to functioning as a word boundary marker, prevents an affix being moved more than once.

Suppose a phrase marker contains HAVE – pp BE – ing V. Affix hopping moves *pp* and *ing* to yield HAVE BE – pp V – ing (ignoring the details of Chomsky adjunction). There is nothing in the SA to prevent the rule from moving *pp* to the right of V, since *pp* is an Af to the left of a Vb (V). This undesirable consequence is eliminated by inserting #, the rule yielding the structure HAVE BE – pp # V – ing #, in which *pp* is not immediately to the left of V.

Figure 41 illustrates the effect of Affix Hopping when Af is *ing* and Vb is V. Its application to the other instances of Af and Vb in Figure 19 differs only in the labels of the nodes.

We conclude this chapter with the notion of *derived constituent structure* and *derived phrase marker*. The PS rules, together with the lexical insertion rules (discussed in the next chapter) constitute the *base component* of the grammar and the structures they generate are the *basic constituent structure*, displayed in *base phrase markers*.

The application of T-rules yields *derived constituent structure*, displayed in *derived phrase markers*. The surface structure, arrived at with the application of the last possible T-rule, is the *final derived structure*, displayed in a *final derived phrase marker*.

Technical terms

base component
base phrase marker
basic constituent structure
Chomsky adjunction
constant
copying
daughter
daughter adjunction
deletion
derived constituent structure
derived phrase marker
extrinsically ordered
final derived phrase marker
final derived structure
intrinsically ordered
obligatory T-rule
optional T-rule
permutation
sister
sister adjunction
structural analysability
structural analysis
structural change
variable

Exercises

1

Which of the transformations below can apply to the phrase marker? What effect do the applicable transformations have on the phrase marker?

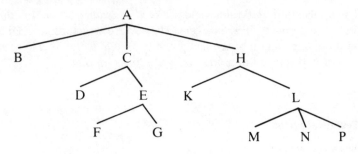

i	SA:	B	C	H		
		1	2	3		
	SC:	1	Ø	3		
ii	SA:	B	C	K	L	
		1	2	3	4	
	SC:	1	2	3	Ø	
iii	SA:	B	C	L		
		1	2	3		
	SC:	1	2	Ø		
iv	SA:	B	D	F	M	
		1	2	3	4	
	SC:	1	2	3–Z	4	
v	SA:	B	C	K	L	
		1	2	3	4	
	SC:	1	2	3	4–S	
vi	SA:	B	C	K	L	
		1	2	3	4	
	SC:	1	2	3+ S	4	
vii	SA:	B	D	R		
		1	2	3		
	SC:	2	1	3		
viii	SA:	B	D	E	K	L
		1	2	3	4	5
	SC:	Ø	2	S+ 3	4	5

2

State the transformations that map phrase marker **1** into the phrase markers **2–5**.

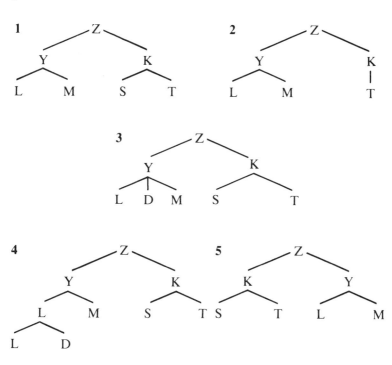

3

In (a) below are sentences and a partial analysis. In (b) are sentences transformationally related to those in (a). Write transformations that derive the structure of the sentences in (b) from the structures in (a).

(a) The policeman found some loot in the cellar

   NP(THE POLICEMAN) VP(past FIND NP(SOME LOOT) PP(IN THE CELLAR))

   The dog chased cats in the park

   NP(THE DOG) VP(past CHASE NP(CAT) PP(IN THE PARK))

You will find the diamonds in a box in the attic

$_{NP}$(YOU) $_{VP}$(non-past WILL FIND $_{NP}$(THE DIAMOND) $_{PP}$(IN $_{NP}$($_{NP}$(A BOX) $_{PP}$(IN THE ATTIC))))

We go to Brighton regularly

$_{NP}$(WE) $_{VP}$(non-past GO TO BRIGHTON $_{ADV}$(REGULARLY))

Bill climbs mountains quite often

$_{NP}$(BILL) $_{VP}$(non-past CLIMB MOUNTAIN $_{ADV}$(QUITE OFTEN))

(b)   In the cellar the policeman found some loot
In the park the dog chased cats
In a box in the attic you will find the diamonds
We regularly go to Brighton
Bill quite often climbs mountains

4 The lexicon

Chapter 7 of BM contains a long discussion of the information about lexemes that has to be included in any comprehensive syntax of a language. The conclusions of that chapter are formalized here.

Each lexeme has an entry in the lexicon that specifies, firstly, the syntactic class it belongs to. This information is expressed by features, [+N] for nouns, [+V] for verbs, [+A] for adjectives, [+P] for prepositions. When a lexeme is considered for insertion into a phrase marker the lexical insertion rule attaches to a node labelled V only a lexeme with the feature [+V], and similarly for nodes labelled N, A or P. These features are *lexical category features*.

Another essential bit of information relates to the syntactic classes with which a lexeme can co-occur. Some verbs can occur without an NP to their right but other verbs require such an NP. For example, a verb like SLEEP has in its lexical entry the feature [+[__#]] and a verb like HIT has the feature [+[__NP]]. The + sign indicates that the lexeme can be inserted into a phrase marker containing the environment represented inside the inner pair of brackets. The features are *strict subcategorization features*.

The above two types of feature express the information crucial to the success of any syntactic description, but other information is also thought appropriate. This relates to the different classes of noun that can be distinguished, especially those differences that affect syntax (see pages 85–91 in BM).

Included in the lexicon are *syntactic features* such as [±Animate] [±Human], [±Concrete], [±Common] and [±Count]. To save space not all the features are listed in every entry, as from the presence of some features other features can be predicted. For example, a noun that is [+Human] is also [+Animate], and a noun that is [+Animate] is also [+Concrete]. A noun that is [+Concrete] and [+Type] (e.g. BUTTER in the sense of 'kind of butter') is [+ Count], which does not imply that only these nouns are count nouns. Implication relations between features are expressed by rules that apply to every lexical entry before a lexeme is inserted into a tree. The rules, exemplified in Figure 43, are called *redundancy rules* because they specify what is predictable and therefore redundant if repeated in every lexical entry. The arrows of Figure 43 can be read as 'implies'.

$$[+\text{Human}] \rightarrow [+\text{Animate}]$$
$$[+\text{Animate}] \rightarrow [+\text{Concrete}] \qquad \left(\begin{array}{c} [+\text{Concrete}] \\ [+\text{Type}] \end{array} \right) \rightarrow [+\text{Count}]$$
$$[-\text{Concrete}] \rightarrow [-\text{Animate}]$$

Figure 43

The effect of the redundancy rules can be illustrated by the lexical entry for BOY. This lexeme is [+Human], [+Animate], [+Concrete], [+Common] and [+Count]. The entry specifies [+Human], [+Common] and [+Count]; [+Animate] and [+Concrete] are added by the redundancy rules.

The syntactic features and the lexical category features constitute the set of *inherent subcategory features*, so called because the features are held to be inherent in lexemes.

A fourth type of information has to do not with single lexemes but with combinations of nouns and verbs. Traditional terms described a verb like ADMIRE as requiring an animate subject (depending on one's attitude to animals other than Man) and a verb like FRIGHTEN as requiring an animate object. This information can be captured by *selection frames* or *selectional features*, as they are generally known in generative grammar.

The lexical entry for FRIGHTEN contains the feature $[+[\_\_(\text{Det})$ $_N[[+\text{Animate}]]_N]$, and the entry for ADMIRE contains $[+[(\text{Det})$ $_N[[+\text{Animate}]]_N$ $X\_\_]]$. Selectional features are employed in various ways. Chomsky uses them to prevent the grammar from generating sentences like *The thunder frightened the sea*, as follows. As suggested in chapter 9 of BM, the traditional statement that a particular verb has to co-occur with particular types of noun is captured by having a verb lexeme inserted first into the matrix sentence in a given phrase marker, with the information in the selectional feature for the verb being copied on to the appropriate noun.

For example, FRIGHTEN is inserted into a phrase marker with two NPs. Since the verb is inserted first, neither of the N nodes has a lexeme attached to it. When FRIGHTEN is attached to the verb node, the feature [+Animate] is copied from the selectional feature and attached to the N node to the right of the verb. When a noun lexeme is attached to that node, the features in its lexical entry must match the items in the phrase marker for insertion to be possible. In the example here, not only does the entry have to contain [+N] corresponding to the N node but it also has to contain [+Animate] corresponding to the feature copied on to the N node when the verb is inserted. If the entry for the noun contains [−Animate], there is a mismatch and the noun is not inserted.

The discussion in chapter 7 of BM indicated that this use of selectional features is controversial. A sentence like *The thunder frightened the sea* is not hopelessly wrong. It is impeccable in word order, word structure and subcategorization. Only with respect to the situation it describes do we have doubts. How far should meaning enter into a description of syntax? A complete description of a language (or at any rate one that has pretensions at covering more than the grossest facts) must discuss the sound system, the structure of words, the structure of sentences and meaning; and 'meaning' certainly includes statements about sentences describing situations that are anomalous with respect to the laws of physics and biology in our world.

Semantically anomalous sentences occur in myths, folk-tales and science fiction, where they are accepted by readers without their syntactic credentials being questioned. Everyday practice suggests that a grammar intended to handle the largest possible range of sentences should be constructed so that sentences like *The thunder frightened the sea* are generated.

The term 'grammar' is used both in the sense of a complete description of a language and in the narrower sense of a description of the syntax. In the following chapters 'grammar' is used in this second sense. At the same time the syntactic component of the complete description is to interlock with the semantic component.

This distinction bears on the status of selectional features. Either they are accorded no status at all and kept out of the lexicon; or they are kept and used not to prevent sentences being generated but to provide information necessary if the semantic component is to handle semantic anomalies. In the syntactic description of *The thunder frightened the sea* SEA has the inherent syntactic feature

[−Animate] and FRIGHTEN has the selectional feature [+[__Det $_N$[[+Animate]]]]. If the generation of this sentence proceeds in spite of the features, the mismatch recorded by the semantic component constitutes the grounds for deciding there is an anomaly in the meaning.

How are lexemes with their features to be inserted into phrase markers? It is assumed that each of the nodes, N, A, V and P dominates a dummy symbol Δ, which is replaced by a lexeme. The dummy symbol is introduced by a set of rules N → Δ, V → Δ, A → Δ. The rules that insert lexemes are transformations, in that they have a structural analysis, consisting of the various bits of information encoded in features, and a structural change, the insertion of a lexeme. A given lexeme is inserted only if the phrase marker, or part of the phrase marker, is analysable with respect to the lexical entry. The lexeme insertion rules are called *local transformations*, by which is meant that they apply to a single node in a phrase marker.

Some examples of lexical entries are given in Figure 44, though they are intended merely as a summary of the discussion here and in Chapter 7 of BM. In the next chapter lexical entries are extended and given a bigger role, but the material of Figure 44 still constitutes the core of each entry.

BOY	FACT
[+N]	[+N]
[+[Det__]]	[+[Det__S]]
[+Common]	[+Common]
[+Human]	[−Concrete]
[+Masc]	[+Count]

SLEEP :	FRIGHTEN
[+V]	[+V]
[+[__#]]	[+[NP__]]
[+[[+Animate] X__]]	[+[__Det $_N$[[+Animate]]]]

Figure 44

In Figure 44, the entry for BOY has the feature [+Masc]. Any entry with the feature [+Human] can have either [+Masc] or [−Masc]. This feature has a part to play in the description of English syntax, since it is relevant to the choice of *himself* or *herself* (chapter 5). The small number of features in the lexical entries is increased by the redundancy rules of Figure 43 (page 42). BOY requires the addition of [+Animate], [+Concrete] and [+Count] and FACT acquires [−Animate]. The symbol X in the selectional feature for SLEEP is explained in the next chapter.

Technical terms

dummy symbol
lexical category feature and syntactic feature (= inherent
   subcategory feature)
lexical insertion rule
local transformation
redundancy rule
selection frame/selection feature
strict subcategorization features

Exercises

1

Write lexical entries for:
   COOK, PUT, SCATTER, BENEFIT, PREGNANT,
   COLLIDE, PEOPLE, CLERGY

2

What English lexemes can be paired with the following lexical entries? What features can be added by redundancy rules?

(i) [+N]   (ii) [+V]
[−[Det ___]]   [+[___ NP   (A)]]
   [+def]
   [−Concrete]
   [−Count]

(iii) [+A]

 [+[___ PP]]

 [+[[N, +Animate] ___]]

(iv) [+N]

 [+[Det ___]]

 [+Mass]

 [−Human]

(v) [+V]

$$\left\{ \begin{array}{l} [+[\ \underline{\qquad}\ \#]] \\ [+[\ \underline{\quad}\ NP\ ]] \end{array} \right\}$$

 [+[N,[−sg] ___]]

(vi) [A]

 [+[Prog__]]

(vii) [+V]

$$\left\{ \begin{array}{l} [+[\_\#] \\ [+[\_NP\ PP]] \end{array} \right\}$$

5 The standard model

The model of description offered in the preceding chapters is known as the standard model. 'Basic model' would be a more appropriate term, as nobody ever took it as a standard, but all work in generative grammar over the past fifteen years has taken that model as a starting point. The following chapters formalize the description of the passive construction and relative clauses presented in chapters 5–6, add a description of complements (chapter 8) and interrogatives and negatives (chapter 9) and discuss the interaction of T-rules (chapter 10). Thereafter we will discuss how the standard model can be modified to permit simpler analyses, with the proviso that simplifying one part of a description often complicates other parts.

The PS rules (page 15) are not adequate for the analyses that are to come. They do not specify phrase markers containing more than one S, although pages 137–43 in BM present a view of relative clauses as sentences embedded inside other sentences. The sequence *the book which you are reading* contains an NP, *the book*, and a residue, *which you are reading*. For reasons given in chapter 6 this residue is treated as a sentence, and an example like *the book which you are reading belongs to me* is analysed as $_S$(The book $_S$(which you are reading) belongs to me). This analysis has to be incorporated in the PS rules. As *the book* in the above example is itself an NP and as the whole sequence *the book which you are reading* occupies an NP position, the structure required is $_{NP}$($_{NP}$(the book) $_S$(which you are reading)$_S$)$_{NP}$, which is generated by the rule NP → NP S.

A symbol which appears on both the left and the right sides of an arrow in a PS rule is *recursive*. Making S and NP recursive violates Restriction 4 (page 23) but the violation is necessary to circumvent other problems (pages 108–9). Recursive S also has a part to play in the description of complements (chapters 7–8).

In *We knew that the machine wouldn't work* the sequence *that the machine wouldn't work* is regarded as a sentence complementing the verb *knew*. At the same time the embedded sentence is regarded as a nominal, since it occurs in positions occupied by NPs. The rule expressing this view is NP → S.

Sentences can also occur as the complements of nouns, as in *He accepted the fact that he had lost the election*. The sequence *that he had lost the election* is seen as a sentence functioning as the complement of *fact*, and the whole sequence *the fact that . . .* is analysed as an NP with the constituents Det N S. Notice the difference between the $_{NP}($ NP S $)_{NP}$ analysis of relative clauses and the $_{NP}($ Det N S $)_{NP}$ analysis of noun complements. The rule generating this structure is NP → Det N S.

Other modifications to the PS rules relate to the immediate constituents of S. Consider again the sentence *We knew that the machine wouldn't work*; what is the function of *that*? One answer is that it marks the following sequence as a sentence reduced in status to a subordinate clause complementing the main verb of the matrix sentence. This view is expressed in the name 'complementizer' given to *that*. It is reflected in this description by a node COMP that is generated alongside NP and VP under the S node.

The COMP node is also relevant in describing relative clauses. Consider relative clauses such as *The athlete who won the prize is a complete novice* and *The house which he is selling has dry rot*. Relative clauses may contain constituents such as *who*, *which* and *whom*, known as relative pronouns because they relate the clause in which they occur to a preceding NP and because they can be thought of as replacing full nouns. They do not occupy positions that can be occupied by full nouns (at least in neutral sentences) but they share with the pronouns a distinction between human and non-human forms (*who/whom* versus *which*) and a distinction between subject and object forms (*who* versus *whom*).

Relative pronouns also indicate that the sequence in which they occur complements a noun. To capture this fact it is assumed here that every subordinate clause, i.e., every embedded sentence, contains a node COMP. This constituent is useful in the statement of selectional restrictions between verbs and complementizers (pages 74–5).

The surface structure of *The house which he is selling has dry rot* is shown in Figure 45.

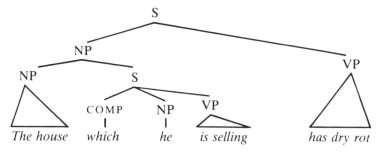

Figure 45

Although in the surface structure only certain clauses contain a COMP constituent, all clauses derive from deep sentences and it is impossible to ensure that only embedded sentences contain a COMP. Surface structures like ₛ(COMP *He watched television*) are not correct but are easily dealt with. There is a convention, invoked in the discussion of relative clauses and complements, that an empty node, i.e. a node dominating no constituents, is deleted. This convention applies to empty NPs, VPs and Ss and applies naturally to empty COMP nodes. COMP nodes unaffected by the convention are those dominating relative pronouns, complementizers (see chapter 7) and interrogative pronouns in *Who did you meet* or *Tell me who you met*.

There are two types of COMP, one with the feature $[+Q]$ for interrogative sentences and one with the feature $[-Q]$ for other sentences. The feature is specified by a PS rule COMP $\rightarrow [\pm Q]$. If $[+Q]$ is chosen the interrogative rules apply (pages 98–104) and COMP either comes to dominate a *wh* word or is deleted during the derivation of yes–no interrogatives. If $[-Q]$ is chosen, COMP dominates a relative pronoun or a complementizer or is deleted if it is in a main clause.

The treatment of negative constructions requires a third change in the PS rules. In both interrogative and negative constructions considerations of meaning play a part. Although one of the basic assumptions of this book is that syntax should be described in its own terms, at the same time a description of a language is not complete until an account of its syntax is linked with an account of the meaning expressed by the various syntactic constructions.

How is a link-up to be achieved in transformational grammar? How are the meaning of a sentence and the meaning of words to be represented? Is the link-up to take place at the level of deep or surface syntax? The first choice in the development of transformational grammar was the level of deep structure and this entailed a change in deep syntax.

One aim of a transformational grammar is to express relationships between different syntactic constructions, among which are declarative and interrogative structures, whether positive or negative (see 1–8 on page 11). With respect to meaning one fundamental assumption is that sentences like *The dog hated the cat*, *Did the dog hate the cat?* and *The dog didn't hate the cat* share a central portion of meaning. They all relate to a dog, a cat and hating. The sentences differ in meaning with respect to whether the speaker is asserting or denying the existence of the situation and with respect to whether the speaker is making an assertion or asking a question.

Suppose that the deep structures of these sentences are all of the form NP VP and that the T-rules that derive interrogative and negative sentences are optional. If these rules apply, they not only map a deep structure into a derived one but add an extra piece of meaning, which will be missed in the link-up with semantics, as the latter takes place at the level of deep structure before any T-rules apply.

To overcome this difficulty it was once proposed that deep structures optionally contain either Q or Neg as well as NP and VP. Q and NEG are peculiar constituents, but their function is to make all relevant information available to the semantic link-up. Q, which is here replaced by COMP, signals that the speaker is asking a
$$[+Q]$$
question; Neg signals that the speaker is either asking a question with negation or is making a denial. (Although the original motivation for the introduction of COMP and Neg was semantic, these
$$[+Q]$$
constituents have a role to play in selectional restrictions, since forms like *ever* occur after pronouns only in interrogative or negative sentences, at least in modern English.)

These constituents in the deep structure make the interrogative and negative T-rules obligatory, as they have to apply if a phrase marker contains COMP or Neg. The initial PS rule is now
$$[+Q]$$
S → COMP (Neg) NP VP.

Like the interrogative and negative T-rules, the Passive too can be made obligatory. Instead of the Passive T-rule introducing the Passive constituent (page 125 in BM), *Pass* is introduced as an optional constituent in the base (see Aux rule in **1** below) and the Passive T-rule applies if *Pass* is present. This treatment assigns verbs like WEIGH and SEEM that do not occur in the passive construction the strict subcategorization feature [−[PASS__]].

The PS rules (page 15) have now been altered considerably, but there remain three further changes.

The first affects the rule introducing *Num*. Instead of having a separate number constituent, we can represent number as a feature on the noun. Any noun with [+Count] in its lexical entry also has [±sg]. This feature is taken into the phrase marker along with noun lexemes and is copied into T, and when T is moved by affix hopping the number feature is also moved to the right of HAVE, BE or V. (Compare the agreement rules on pages 53–4.) If number is represented as a feature on nouns, the feature has to be turned into a separate constituent, since words like *boys*, *bushes* and *oxen* consist of two morphs. However, only [−sg] need be converted to a constituent, as [+sg] is not realized by any morph in the surface structure.

The second change affects the constituents *def* and *indef* which, like number, are demoted to features on the determiner. THIS is [+Dem] (for 'demonstrative'), [+Def] (for 'definite'), THE is [−Dem], [+Def] and A is [−Dem], [−Def]. The distinction between *this* and *these*, *a* and *some* indicates number agreement between determiner and noun. This is handled by a T-rule of Determiner Number Agreement that copies [±sg] onto the determiner.

The final change in the PS rules arises from the comment (page 44) that the nodes N, V, A and P dominate a dummy symbol that is replaced by a lexeme and its attendant features. The revised set of PS rules is given in **1**.

1

$$S \rightarrow COMP \ (Neg) \ NP \ VP$$

$$COMP \rightarrow [\pm Q]$$

$$VP \rightarrow Aux \ V \left\{ \begin{matrix} A \\ \overline{NP} \end{matrix} \right\}$$

$$NP \rightarrow \left\{ \begin{matrix} (Det) \ N \ (S) \\ NP \quad S \end{matrix} \right\}$$

$$Aux \rightarrow T \ (M) \ (Perf) \ (Prog) \ (Pass)$$

$$T \rightarrow \begin{Bmatrix} \text{past} \\ \text{non-past} \end{Bmatrix}$$

$$\text{Perf} \rightarrow \text{HAVE} \quad \text{pp}$$

$$\text{Prog} \rightarrow \text{BE} \quad \text{ing}$$

$$\text{Pass} \rightarrow \text{BE} \quad \text{pp}$$

$$N \rightarrow \Delta$$

$$V \rightarrow \Delta$$

$$A \rightarrow \Delta$$

This chapter can usefully be concluded by stating the T-rules mentioned so far and adding the T-rule that derives reflexive pronouns. The latter may seem a peculiar bedfellow for passive, verb number agreement, etc. but all these rules have the common feature that they apply within simple sentences and do not involve embedding or recursion (pages 134–9 in BM).

2   Passive (obligatory)

SA:	NP	X	Pass	V	NP
	1	2	3	4	5
SC:	5	2	3	4	$_{PP}[_P[\text{BY}]_P 1]_{PP}$

This rule maps, e.g., the phrase marker in Figure 46 on to that in Figure 47, applying whenever a phrase marker contains *Pass*. The X between 1 and 3 in the SA represents whatever constituents come between them, there being various possibilities, T, T M, etc.

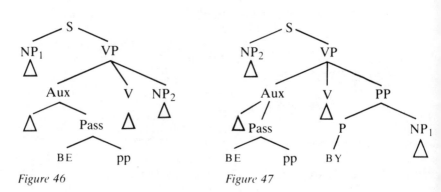

Figure 46   Figure 47

Verb number agreement 1 (obligatory)

SA: X   N   non-past   Y

$$\begin{bmatrix} [+F] \\ \cdots \\ [+sg] \end{bmatrix}$$

    1   2   3   4

SC: 1   2   3 − [+sg] 4

Condition: the leftmost constituent of Y ≠ M

This rule states that V or any constituent in Aux except a modal verb agrees in number with the subject noun if tense is non-past and number is singular: *is, plays, has*. The cover symbol Y is used as it is only necessary to specify that the constituent immediately following non-past cannot be a modal verb. If Y is a modal verb the rule does not apply.

Verb number agreement 2 (obligatory)

SA: X   N   non-past   BE   Y

$$\begin{bmatrix} [+F] \\ \cdots \\ [-sg] \end{bmatrix}$$

    1   2   3   4   5

SC: 1   2   3 − [−sg] 4   5

The import of this rule is that if the subject noun is plural and the tense is non-past, only HAVE and BE have special forms: *have* (versus *has*) and *are*.

Verb number agreement 3 (obligatory)

SA: X   N   past   BE   Y

$$\begin{bmatrix} [+F] \\ \cdots \\ [\alpha sg] \end{bmatrix}$$

    1   2   3   4   5

    1   2   3 − [αsg] 4   5

In this rule α in the SC and SA is a cover symbol for $+$ and $-$. The rule says that if the tense is past and if the constituent immediately to the right of past is BE, then the number feature, $[+\text{sg}]$ or $[-\text{sg}]$, is copied from the noun. BE is the only lexeme with special singular and plural past tense forms: *was* and *were*.

The verb number agreement rules apply to matrix and embedded sentences and derive the sort of configuration in Figure 48.

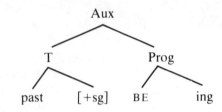

Figure 48   past $[+\text{sg}]$ BE   ing

Affix hopping

This rule is stated on page 36.

Determiner number agreement

SA: Det   N
$$\begin{bmatrix} [+\text{F}] \\ \ldots \end{bmatrix} \qquad \begin{bmatrix} [+\text{F}] \\ \ldots \\ [\alpha\text{sg}] \end{bmatrix}$$
          1   2

SC: 1   2
$[\alpha\text{sg}]$

This rule says that whatever the number on N, it is copied on to the determiner.

Number constituent

SA: $_{\text{NP}}[$ (Det)   N$]_{\text{NP}}$
$$\begin{bmatrix} [+\text{F}] \\ \ldots \\ [-\text{sg}] \end{bmatrix}$$
              1   2

SC: 1   2+ $[-\text{sg}]$

This rule derives a phrase marker in which [−sg] is a separate constituent. The above two rules derive the sort of structure in Figure 49.

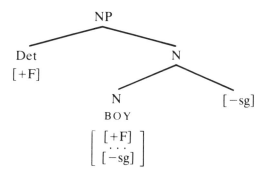

Figure 49

Reflexive

SA: ₛ[X   NP Y NP   Z]ₛ
       1   2   3 4   5
SC: 1   2   3 4   5
                 [+Refl]
      Condition: 2 = 4

This rule says that if there are two identical NPs in a simple sentence, [+Refl] is added to the second NP. We assume that the feature is added to the N, though this is not actually specified by the rule. This rule is the first stage in mapping the structure of *The boy blamed the boy* on to the structure of *The boy blamed himself*, the mapping being completed by orthographic rules that replace the constituents of the NP by the appropriate form: *himself, herself, itself* or *themselves*.

In this version of the standard model the final set of rules, applying after all other T-rules, is the orthographic rules that spell out lexemes and grammatical morphemes as morphs. Some examples are given below. The central principle is that for each category, N, V, etc., the rules specify the irregular forms one by one, with a general rule for all the regular forms at the end.

Orthographic rules

$$_M[CAN]_M - {_T[past]_T} \Rightarrow could$$

Affix hopping creates the structure $_M[_M[CAN]_M \ _T[past]_T]_M$.

The orthographic rule replaces CAN, past, the M and T nodes with *could*, thereby deriving $_M[could]_M$.

$$_{Perf}[HAVE]_{Perf} - {_T[[non\text{-}past] - [+sg]]_T} \Rightarrow has$$
$$V - {_T[past]_T} \Rightarrow V - ed$$
$$MAN - [-sg] \Rightarrow men$$
$$OX - [-sg] \Rightarrow OX - en$$
$$N - [-sg] \Rightarrow N - s$$

Although few in number, these T-rules illustrate the problem of extrinsic ordering (page 34). Suppose verb number agreement 3 applies to the structure $_S[$THE MONGOOSE past $_{Pass}[$BE EN$]_{Pass}$ [+sg] ATTACK THE SNAKE] to derive $_S[$ ... past[+sg] ...]. [−sg] Passive now derives the structure $_S[$THE SNAKE past [+sg] [−sg] $_{Pass}[$BE EN] ATTACK BY THE MONGOOSE]. Eventually the [+sg] grammar derives the surface sentence *The snakes was attacked by the mongoose*,[1] which is correct for some dialects of English but not the one described here. The rules have to be extrinsically ordered so that Passive permutes the NPs before a verb number agreement rule applies.

Similarly, as the reader can verify, if Reflexive applies before Passive, the grammar generates sentences like *Himself is admired by Bill* instead of *Bill is admired by himself (but not by anyone else)*. The ordering has to be Passive, then Reflexive, though it does not matter whether Reflexive applies before affix hopping or vice-versa.

---

1 Here and throughout the book an asterisk (*) indicates an ungrammatical sentence.

Technical terms

complement
complementizer
COMP deletion
orthographic rules
passive

recursive
reflexive
standard model
verb number agreement

Exercises

1

To each of the following deep structures apply the transformations of Verb Number Agreement and affix hopping and the appropriate orthographic rules. Apply the Passive to (c) and (d) and Number Constituent to (b), (c) and (d).

(a)   A STUDENT past BE ING WRITE THE   ESSAY
        [+sg]   [+sg]

(b)   THE NOBLE non-past HAVE pp BE ING
          [−sg]   CHASE ROBIN

(c)   THE OUTLAW past Pass CATCH A NOBLE
          [−sg]   [+sg]

(d)   THE MONSTER past Pass CAN HAVE pp EAT A
        [+sg]
                                        TOURIST
                                        [−sg]

2

For each of the sentences below draw a phrase marker showing the deep structure, state the transformations that derive the surface structure and draw a phrase marker showing the surface structure. Students with spare time can draw phrase markers showing the structure derived by each transformation.

1   The essays were written by the students
2   The car has been repaired by the mechanic
3   Coleridge might have been disturbed by a person
4   Some poets have won the Nobel Prize
5   Some people deceive themselves

6   Relative clauses

This and the next three chapters are concerned with embedding and recursion, concepts that were introduced in chapter 9 of BM. This chapter makes precise the various T-rules and modifies the deep structures.

Before we proceed to the analysis of relative clauses one caveat is required: the rules proposed here do not handle all types of relative clause in English. Of relative clauses with *wh-* forms they describe only *restrictive* ones (**1a**), not *non-restrictive* ones (**1b**).

1a   I love those books which are historical novels
1b   I love those books, which are historical novels

1a asserts that the only books the speaker loves are historical novels; **1b** draws attention to some books, which happen to be historical novels.

The rules also fail to handle relative clauses introduced by *that*. These clauses differ in syntax and morphology so much that it is doubtful whether *that* should even be labelled 'relative pronoun'.

Another point that requires explanation is the analysis of *the house which he is selling* as $_{NP}[NP\ S]_{NP}$ and not $_{NP}[Det\ N\ S]_{NP}$. The reason for this can be seen from the structure in Figure 50.

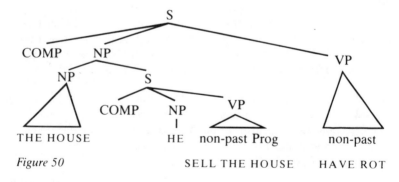

Figure 50

A crucial stage in a transformational account of relative clauses (page 65) is the replacement of a noun phrase in the embedded sentence that is identical with the head noun phrase, i.e. the NP that is the sister of the embedded S. In Figure 50, as the NP *the house* occurs both as the head NP and as the object NP in the S, relativization can proceed. If the Det N S analysis were adopted, relativization would not proceed, because the NP in the embedded S would contain a Determiner (optionally) and an N, whereas the head NP would contain a Determiner, N and S.

In chapter 11 of BM there is a single relative clause rule that identifies the NP in the embedded S identical with the head NP and replaces it with a constituent $\begin{bmatrix} \text{rel} \\ \text{pro} \end{bmatrix}$ that is moved to the front of the embedded S. This rule is now split into two rules, relative pronoun formation and relative pronoun movement. Nouns are inserted into phrase markers along with at least their inherent features and determiners, too, have features. Although the features play a part in relativization, the comparison of NPs taking in both lexemes and their associated features, the latter are not included in the rules and diagrams that follow.

2 Relative pronoun formation (obligatory)

$$
\begin{array}{lllllllll}
\text{SA:} & X & {}_{NP}[{}_{NP}[\text{Det N}]_{NP} & Y & {}_{S}[W & {}_{NP}[\text{Det N}]_{NP} & Z]_{S}]_{NP} & U \\
& 1 & 2\quad 3 & 4 & 5 & 6\quad 7 & 8 & 9 \\
\text{SC:} & 1 & 2\quad 3 & 4 & 5 & \emptyset\quad 7 & 8\quad 9 \\
& & & & & [+\text{wh}] \\
\end{array}
$$

Condition: 2 = 6 and 3 = 7

U, Y or Z may be null

The outermost brackets labelled NP enclose the brackets labelled S, which shows that the structure to which the rule applies is an NP containing an S. Inside the NP is another NP, to the left of S. Constituent 1, X, is a cover symbol standing for any structure to the left of the relative clause and the NP it modifies. X always includes COMP but there may be other structure, as in *I knew that the book he wanted cost £10.* 2 and 3 are the constituents in the NP modified by the relative clause, and 4 indicates that the embedded sentence containing the NP identical with the modified NP may not be adjacent to the latter, as in *I saw the house which you said Bill liked.* This has the deep structure $_S$[I saw $_{NP}$[the house $_S$[you said $_S$[Bill liked the house]$_S$]$_S$]$_{NP}$]$_S$.

6 and 7 are the Det and N identical with the Det and N in the modified NP; 5 and 8 are cover symbols showing that the NP is not the first constituent in the embedded S and need not be the last one.

9 is another cover symbol to show that there may be structure to the right of the relative clause, as in Figure 50.

Applied to Figure 50, the rule merely adds [+wh] to the N in the NP THE HOUSE inside the embedded sentence.

Relative pronoun movement moves the NP with [+wh] to the front of the embedded S. It has two SAs and three SCs, for the reasons mentioned on pages 138–40 in BM.

3a   Relative pronoun movement (obligatory)

SA: X $_{NP}$[NP $_S$[COMP Y   NP W]$_S$]$_{NP}$ Z
                                 [+wh]

1	2	3	4	5	6	7
SC: 1	2	3/5	4	∅	6	7

Condition: X or Z may be null
                  Y may be null
(3/5 indicates that 5 becomes the daughter of 3)

3a applied to the structure in Figure 50 derives that in Figure 51.

3b   Relative pronoun movement (obligatory)

SA: X $_{NP}$[NP $_S$[COMP Y $_{PP}$[P   NP]$_{PP}$]$_S$]$_{NP}$ Z
                                        [+wh]

1	2	3	4	5	6	7
SCi: 1	2	3/$_{PP}$[5 6]$_{PP}$	4	∅	∅	7
SCii: 1	2	3/6	4	5	∅	7

The SA in **3b** is different in that the moved NP is inside a PP, as in $_S$[I found $_{NP}$[$_{NP}$[the knife]$_{NP}$ $_S$[She stabbed her lover $_{PP}$[$_P$[with]$_P$ $_{NP}$[the knife]$_{NP}$]$_{PP}$]$_S$]$_{NP}$]$_S$. In the structures generated by this grammar any PP is always at the end of the embedded sentence, which is why there is no variable W between the PP and the boundary of the sentence. SCi states that the whole PP becomes a daughter of COMP, while SCii states that only the NP does. The output of SCii is shown in Figure 52.

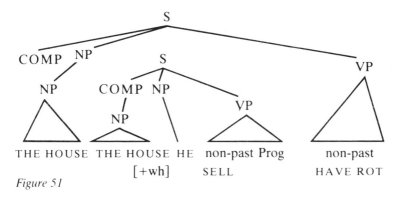

Figure 51

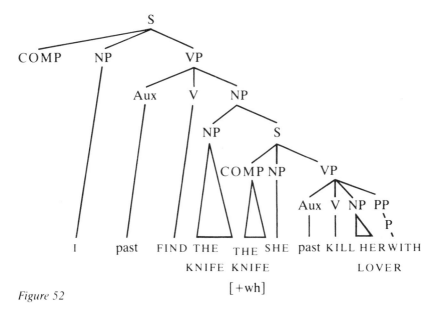

Figure 52

Relative clauses in English can occur with no relative pronoun, as in *The house he is selling has dry rot* and *I found the knife she stabbed her lover with*. Following the account on pages 141–2 of BM we will state a T-rule deleting the NP marked [+wh] if there are two NPs at the front of the embedded S.

4   Relative pronoun deletion (optional)

$$\text{SA:} \quad X \ _S[NP \ NP \ Y]_S \ Z$$
$$\qquad\quad 1 \quad 2 \quad 3 \quad 4 \quad 5$$
$$\text{SC:} \quad 1 \quad \emptyset \quad 3 \quad 4 \quad 5$$

As the sequence of two NPs occurs only in embedded sentences after relative pronoun movement (at least in the set of sentences generated by this grammar), the SA is relatively simple. When the NP is deleted, COMP is empty, and is deleted under the convention that empty nodes are deleted.

On pages 142–4 of BM it was proposed that *the man scratching his head, the man run over by a bus* and *the music on the piano* derived from deep structures containing embedded sentences, e.g. $_{NP}$[the man $_S$[The man is/was scratching his head]$_S$]$_{NP}$. The key to the description of these sentences is that the subject noun and some form of BE can be deleted – compare **5**. (BE, whether a main verb, or Progressive or Passive, has the feature [+Cop].)

5   Relative clause reduction (optional)

$$\text{SA:} \quad X \ _{NP}[NP[_S \ \underset{[+wh]}{NP} \quad \underset{[+Cop]}{W} - T \ Y] \ _S]_{NP} \ Z$$
$$\qquad\quad 1 \qquad 2 \quad 3 \qquad 4 \quad 5 \ 6 \qquad 7$$
$$\text{SC:} \quad 1 \qquad 2 \quad \emptyset \qquad \emptyset \quad \emptyset \ 6 \qquad 7$$

As before, X is null if the head NP is the subject of the matrix sentence and Z is non-null; and vice-versa if the head NP is the object in the matrix sentence. Y shows there is some structure to the right of   W   .
$\qquad\quad$ [+Cop]

On page 143 of BM it was suggested that the relationship between adjectives and relative clauses could be captured if adjectives originated in embedded sentences that were reduced by relative

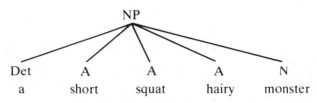

Figure 53

clause reduction, the adjective being shifted into the NP that is the sister of the embedded S. One problem not mentioned earlier is that NPs can contain more than one adjective, as in *a short squat hairy monster*. The structure for this sequence is that in Figure 53.

This structure is difficult to generate by the usual PS rules, because any number of adjectives can occur in an NP. PS rules rewrite a symbol as a definite number of other symbols, not as some unspecified number; attempts to handle the occurrence of more than one adjective by a PS rule have generated structures that are too complex. The rules in **6** generate the structure in Figure 54.

6   1   NP → (Det) (Adj) N

     2   Adj → A (Adj)

     3   A → {SHORT, HAIRY, ...}

     4   N → {MONSTER, ...}

     5   Det → {A, ...}

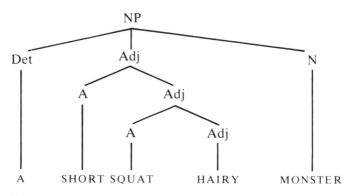

Figure 54

The structure in Figure 53 can, however, be generated by T-rule, since any number of embedded sentences can be generated and reduced to adjectives that are then moved into the head NP. Figure 55 shows the output of relative clause deletion applied to a structure S[NP[The book S[The book is old]S]NP is a novel]S. Adjective shift moves the A into the NP that is the sister of the embedded S.

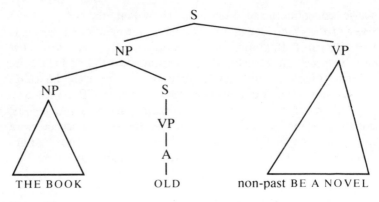

Figure 55

7   Adjective shift (obligatory)

SA: X $_{NP}[_{NP}[^Y$ $N]_{NP}$ $_S[^A]_S]_{NP}$ Z
SC: 1   2   3   4   5

          1   2 – 4 – 3   Ø   5

4 becomes a sister of 2 and 3, as in Figure 56.

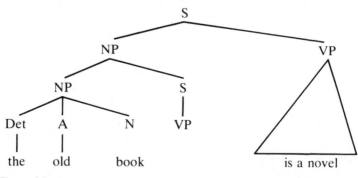

Figure 56

The empty VP, and then the empty S, are deleted by the general convention that nodes dominating nothing are deleted. The NP immediately dominated by S is also deleted, since it no longer dominates two nodes but only another NP.

This description of attributive adjectives does not apply with equal success to every adjective in English. Some adjectives, like

ILL, occur only in predicative position (*The man is ill*) and others only in attributive position (**This crisis is major*). However, the description does apply to many adjectives and can be offered in a general introductory work.

The grammar can handle adjectives like ILL and MAJOR if the lexical entries contain rule features indicating that a particular adjective blocks the application of a T-rule or that it requires the T-rule to apply. For example, ILL could have the feature [−Adj. Shift], which prevents the Adjective Shift rule from applying and MAJOR could have the feature [+Adj. Shift], which ensures the application of Adjective shift to any relative clause containing MAJOR. Although a number of linguists have invoked rule features, it must be understood that their use is controversial. Transformations are supposed to apply to general syntactic structure without mentioning individual lexemes but rule features break this convention by allowing individual lexemes to play a part without being mentioned in the SA of the transformation. It is reasonable to conclude that the definitive generative analysis of adjectives in English has yet to be developed.

To round off this account here are the rules that substitute *who* or *which* for an NP. The rules make crucial use of the inherent features [+Human] and [−Animate].

$$\textbf{8a} \quad NP\begin{bmatrix} X \\ [+\text{Human}] \\ [+\text{wh}] \end{bmatrix}_{NP} \Rightarrow {}_{NP}[\text{who}]_{NP}$$

$$\textbf{8b} \quad NP\begin{bmatrix} X \\ [-\text{Animate}] \\ [+\text{wh}] \end{bmatrix}_{NP} \Rightarrow {}_{NP}[\text{which}]_{NP}$$

Technical terms

adjective shift	relative pronoun formation
non-restrictive relative clause	relative pronoun movement
relative clause	relativization
relative clause reduction	restrictive relative clause
relative pronoun deletion	rule feature

Exercises

1

For each of the following sentences draw a phrase marker showing the deep structure. State the transformations that derive the surface structure and illustrate the effect of each transformation.

1 The book John was reading is a novel
2 The textbook you found the information in is recommended by the professor
3 The old stamps are priceless
4 The castle bought by the architect has advanced dry-rot

2

Relative clauses in English can be introduced by *that*. Examine the data below and answer the questions that follow it.

Data

1a	the house that Jack built	**2a**	the house which Jack built
1b	the man that I met	**2b**	the man who/whom I met
1c	the people that came	**2c**	the people who came
1d	the book that I found the picture in	**2d**	the book which I found the picture in
1e	*the book in that I found the picture	**2e**	the book in which I found the picture
1f	that ilk cock that Peter heard him crow	**2f**	the same cock which Peter heard crow
1g	a knight that he loved chivalry	**2g**	a knight who loved chivalry
1h	the man that his wife died	**2h**	the man whose wife died

Note: (**1f, 1g, 1h**) represent a relative clause construction that was current in earlier stages of English and still occurs in various dialects, though not the literary one.

Questions

(i) Describe the surface syntax and morphology of **1f–1h**, comparing them with the surface syntax and morphology of **2f–2h**.

(ii)   What other constituents introduce relative clauses in English, though not in the literary dialect?

(iii)   Does *that* occur in other constructions? Is it appropriately described as a 'relative pronoun'?

(iv)   Devise a transformational account of **1a–1h**.

7 Complement structures: their distribution

This chapter and the next are devoted to complement structures in English, examples of which are given in italics in **1**.

1a Everyone knew *that the new leader would lose the election*
1b *That he didn't get in touch for a whole month* dismayed and annoyed her
1c I want *to see this new film*
1d *To give up now* would be mad
1e I hate *handing money to the taxman*
1f *His making a din* shows a lack of concern for others

Complement structures – subordinate noun clauses, infinitives and gerunds – occur as the subject of verbs (**1b, 1d, 1f**) or the object (**1a, 1c, 1e**). Subordinate noun clauses are introduced by *that* (**1a, 1b**), gerunds are signalled by *-ing* or *'s . . . ing* (**1e, 1f**) and infinitives are signalled by *to* or *for . . . to*, as in **2**.

2 *For him to make such a claim* shows that he has no solution

The *-ing* forms look like participles but they differ in syntax: *the child was weeping*, with participle, correlates with *the weeping child*, but *making a din* does not correlate with **a din was making*.

Traditional grammars say merely that gerunds, etc. are subjects or objects of verbs; an account that draws a distinction between constituents and functions has to decide what gerunds, etc. are by way of constituents as well as stating their function as subject or object. All complement structures are treated here as nominals, since they occur in positions that can also be occupied by noun phrases. Moving from **1a** to **1f** in sequence, we see that the complements can be replaced by ordinary NPs, e.g. *his car, this attitude, a bigger house, his plan, that man, your proposal*.

Subordinate noun clauses occur also in subject position in passive sentences, while gerunds occur in both subject and object position – **3**.

> **3a** *That he would lose the election* was suspected by everyone
>
> **3b** *Handing money to the taxman* is avoided by everyone with a good accountant
>
> **3c** A lack of concern is shown by *his making a din*

Infinitives do not typically occur in these positions in passive sentences and never after prepositions. Gerunds occur freely with prepositions – *We blame it on his not paying attention* – but noun clauses tend not to, although there are instances: *In that he went hill walking alone he was very foolish.*

The data in **1** to **3** is undisputed but other data is less straightforward. Some verbs like RELATE and SHOW, can be followed by an NP and a PP, as in *They related their adventures to all the children, They showed their slides to all the visitors.* It is easy to form the impression that infinitives and noun clauses introduced by *how* or *that* do not occur as the NP between such verbs and a PP: **The children promised to behave themselves to their mother, *He said that the building was decayed to Peter, *They showed how to build a kite to their children.*

There are however grounds for supposing that the limitations on distribution are not the general sort that would cast doubt on the analysis of complements as nominals; **4a–4e** are of the same structure as the last three examples but are acceptable.

> **4a** They explained how to build a kite to all the children in the street
>
> **4b** He said that you were wrong not just to me but to everyone
>
> **4c** He described how he crossed the Amazon jungles to hall after hall of enthralled audiences
>
> **4d** He emphasized that it was essential to have good data to all the many students who studied under him
>
> **4e** Rip would relate how he had met Hendrick Hudson and his crew in the Catskills to anyone who was prepared to listen

The limitation appears to attach to specific verbs; it is difficult, for instance, to devise acceptable sentences with TEACH or PROMISE. With some verbs sentences like those in **4** are incorrect even when the verb is followed by an ordinary NP: *She related Peter the story*. Acceptability also depends on stylistic factors. The sentences in **4** have longer NPs after *to* than the unacceptable sentences in the preceding paragraph. Even a sentence with TEACH can be brought to the borders of acceptability if the NP after *to* is long enough: *He had taught that it was essential to have good data to the many generations of students who had studied under his guidance*.

Another argument against the analysis of complements as nominals rests on the sentences in **5** and **6**.

5a   That cigarette smoke causes cancer is believed by doctors

5b   For a visa to be necessary would be highly inconvenient

6a   *That that cigarette smoke causes cancer is possible is believed by doctors

6b   *For that you have a visa to be necessary would be highly inconvenient

The general structure of **5a**, **6a** is X – *is believed by doctors*. In **5a** X is *that Y causes cancer*, Y being *cigarette smoke*. In **6a** X is *that Y is possible*, but Y, unlike Y in **5a**, is not an ordinary NP but another complement – *that cigarette smoke causes cancer*. When one construction is embedded in another construction of the same type, the resulting *self-embedding* is very difficult to interpret. The unacceptability of **6a** can be attributed to the self-embedding of the noun clause and need not have any consequences for the analysis of *that* clauses as NPs. Indeed, exactly the same problem arises with respect to sentences in which one relative clause is embedded in another: *The boy the teacher the headmaster reprimanded chased had broken a window*.

The structure of **5b** is X – *would be highly inconvenient*, where X is *for – Y – to be necessary*, Y being an ordinary NP, *a visa*. The structure for **6b** is the same, except that Y is a noun clause – *that you have a visa*. It is arguable that **6a** is worse than **6b**, since **6b** is more easily interpreted because the two complements are set off from each other by the contrast between *for* and *that*. If so, the unacceptability inherent in self-embedding can be mitigated by relatively small stylistic factors, which fits with the suggestion that the difficulties are perceptual and can be discounted.

Another factor is that the self-embedding occurs at the beginning of **6a**, **6b** but is more acceptable in other positions. For instance, the sentences in **7** have been accepted by undergraduate students (who did not know what was at stake) and by educated native speakers without training in linguistics. The examples either are identical with or are based on sentences that were held incorrect by a linguist attacking the analysis of infinitives and noun clauses as NPs, and illustrate the importance of obtaining verification of one's intuitions.

7a He protested against the decision that for the bill to be marked 'paid' meant nothing and that he would have to pay the whole sum whether he liked it or not

7b John was happy when he learned that to own a car didn't disqualify you

7c He exercises so rarely that to lift those bricks is bad for his heart

7d I don't believe that for you to study history hurts you

7e I don't believe that to study history is a waste of time

Another objection directed against the analysis of *that*-clauses and infinitives as NPs is that they cannot be conjoined with ordinary NPs. The examples used are *She used to like watching television and to play volleyball*, *She used to like to watch television and physical exercise*, and *She used to like physical exercise and to watch television*. But are these examples bad with respect to syntactic structure or just clumsy in style? One sentence in which an ordinary NP is conjoined with a noun clause, was accepted by the informants without question: *He proposed a 20 per cent reduction for the elderly and that the office be moved to the suburbs*.

Note that only infinitives and noun clauses cause problems, as the distributional evidence supports the analysis of gerunds as NPs (**8**).

8a We reported his going off without permission to our commanding officer

8b He explained his not arriving on time to the team manager

8c That John's smoking could harm others is perfectly possible

8d He maintained that his son's being a member of the team was pure coincidence

To say that complements are analysed as NPs is to give only one part of the picture. The treatment of noun clauses, for instance, has to be more complex, since they are equivalent to full sentences. Infinitives too can be equivalent to full sentences, as in **9**.

9a   For all the students to fail the exam means the teaching was at fault

9b   For the exam to be failed by all the students is distressing

The infinitive phrases in **9** contain subject and object nouns and a verb and can be active or passive (**9b**). Moreover, perfective and progressive morphs occur in infinitives (**10**).

10a   For all the students to have failed the exam is distressing

10b   For all the students to be failing the exams is distressing

An infinitive construction like that in *I want to see this film* might seem to pose a problem, as it has no subject noun, but the paradigm in **11** suggests an answer.

11a   I want you to see the film   **11a′**   He wants me to see the film

11b   I want him to see the film   **11b′**   He wants you to see the film

11c   I want to see the film   **11c′**   He wants to see the film

When the person who has the desire is not the person who is to do the seeing, there is a noun between the main verb and the infinitive form. The noun is missing from the last pair of sentences describing situations in which the same person has the desire and is to do the seeing. The paradigm is handled here by deriving the structure of *I want to see the film* from the structure of *I want me to see the film*. As utterances corresponding to the last sentence are to be heard, the T-rule that derives the structure is optional.

Gerunds correspond to sentences in the same way as infinitive phrases.

Noun clauses, infinitives and gerunds are derived here from

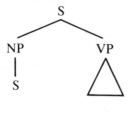

Figure 57

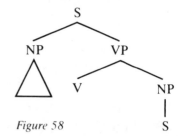

Figure 58

sentences that are constituents of NPs. This treatment rests on the assumption that *that, to, for . . . to* and *'s . . . ing* are minor grammatical morphs; their only role is to signal that the sequence they precede or occur in is a complement and functions syntactically like a noun. The deep structure for **1b, 1d, 1f** is shown in Figure 57, the deep structure for **1a, 1b, 1e** in Figure 58.

Other complement structures that the grammar should handle are exemplified in **12**.

12a Everyone knew it that he would lose the election
12b I love it that he's so happy here
12c The fact that he came at all surprised everyone

12a, 12b are not regarded (in Britain at least) as good written English but they are to be heard regularly in spoken English. In **12** the complement is the complement of a noun – *it* in **12a, 12b** and *fact* in **12c**. **12a, 12b** require the deep structure of Figure 59, **12c** – that of Figure 60.

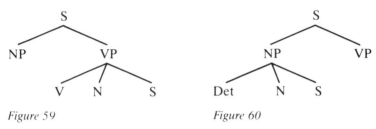

Figure 59   *Figure 60*

In Figure 59 the N is IT and in Figure 60 it is FACT. In many transformational accounts even the structure of sentences like **1a** is derived from the structure in Figure 59, the IT being deleted; but since all the data indicates that the various complements are NPs and not unspecified constituents of NPs that are complements of IT, **1a** and **12a** are here derived from different deep structures. The latter are generated by the PS rules on page 51, supplemented by subcategorization frames in lexical entries. For example, the entry for FACT shows that it can be inserted into the frame Det__S and the entry for QUESTION shows that it can be inserted between a Det and a [+Q], even though the [+Q] is in a different sentence.

Exercises

See page 91 for exercises to chapter 7 and 8.

8 Complement structures: their derivation

The first stage in the derivation of complement structures is to introduce the constituents from which derive the *complementizers*, *that*, *'s . . . ing* and *for . . . to*. The required deep structure constituents, THAT, FOR TO and POSS ING, are stored in the lexicon and attached to COMP by a lexical insertion rule. Various dependencies between verbs and complementizers have to be handled and the insertion rule is controlled by features added to the COMP node from verb lexemes, just as features are added to N nodes. The dependencies are exemplified in **1** to **4**.

1a   He reported that the manager had resigned
1b   He reported the manager's having resigned
1c   *He reported for the manager to have resigned

2a   That he resigned is certain
2b   ?His resigning is certain
2c   *For him to resign is certain
2d   For him to resign is astonishing

3a   It appears that he has resigned
3b   *It appears his having resigned
3c   *It appears for him to have resigned

4a   That he reacted in that way means that he is suspicious
4b   *That he reacted in that way means for him to be
         suspicious
4c   For him to react in that way means that he is suspicious

Which complementizer occurs depends on the main verb or adjective in the matrix sentence. For instance **2** shows that CERTAIN does not take a FOR TO complement and **4** shows that MEAN does. A sample of selectional features is given in **6**, with the lexical entries for the complementizers in **5**.

5

THAT	POSS ING	FOR TO
$\left\{\begin{array}{c}[+COMP]\\ [+1]\end{array}\right\}$	$\left\{\begin{array}{c}[+COMP]\\ [+2]\end{array}\right\}$	$\left\{\begin{array}{c}[+COMP]\\ [+3]\end{array}\right\}$

REPORT

6a

$$[+[\_\_{}_S[COMP\ X]_S]]$$

$$\left\{\begin{array}{c}[+1]\\ [+2]\end{array}\right\}$$

ASTONISHING

6b

$$[+[_S[COMP\ X]_S\ \ Y\ \ V\ \_\_]]$$

$$\left\{\begin{array}{c}[+1]\\ [+2]\end{array}\right\}\quad[+Cop]$$

MEAN

6c

$$[+[_S[COMP\ X]_S\quad Y\_\_\quad{}_S[COMP\ W]_S]]$$

$$\left\{\begin{array}{c}[+1]\\ [+2]\\ [+3]\end{array}\right\}\qquad\left\{\begin{array}{c}[+1]\\ [+2]\end{array}\right\}$$

X in the selectional features stands for the other constituents with COMP; Y stands for constituents between the complement S and the main verb or adjective – *His resigning was astonishing* and *His resigning would have been astonishing*. What has to be specified is that ASTONISHING is immediately preceded by a form of a copula verb like BE or APPEAR, hence the feature [+Cop]; [+1], for instance, indicates that the complementizer with that feature can be inserted – THAT. Two features inside curly brackets show that either of the designated complementisers can occur: *They reported that he had resigned/his having resigned*; only

COMP in embedded complement sentences receives a feature. Although POSS, ING and TO have to be moved from COMP into the correct surface structure position, there are advantages in attaching them to COMP. Selectional features can be stated more easily and the T-rules of tense-modal deletion (T/M deletion) and equi-NP-deletion are simplified. The latter rule plays a major part in the description of complements.

Various tidying-up rules relate to the derivation of complements. Since tensed verb forms and modal verbs do not occur in infinitives and gerunds (*For my brother to can afford such a car is astonishing*, *His finished first was not unexpected*), Tense and M have to be eliminated from deep structures, which is done by a rule called T/M deletion – **7**.

7 T/M Deletion (obligatory)

$$\text{SA:} \quad \underset{1}{X} \left\{ \begin{matrix} \text{POSS} & \text{ING} \\ \text{FOR} & \text{TO} \end{matrix} \right\}_{2} \underset{3}{\text{NP}} \underset{4}{\text{T}} \underset{5}{\text{(M)}} \underset{6}{Y}$$

$$\text{SC:} \quad 1 \quad 2 \qquad 3 \quad \emptyset \qquad \emptyset \quad 6$$

The rules that move TO, ING and POSS away from COMP are stated in **8**. ING is moved into the first position in VP, becoming the left sister of whatever was previously the first constituent – Prog, Perf, Pass or V but not T or M, which are deleted before ING is moved. ING is subsequently hopped around the constituent to its right by affix hopping. TO is moved into first position in the VP, where it stays, and POSS is attached to the right of the subject N by Chomsky-adjunction. POSS is not moved until equi-NP-deletion has applied (cf. p. 78).

8a ING movement (obligatory)

$$\text{SA:} \quad \underset{1}{X} \quad \underset{2}{\text{POSS}} \quad \underset{3}{\text{ING}} \quad \underset{4}{\text{NP}} \quad _{\text{Aux}}[\underset{5}{Y}] \quad \underset{6}{Z}$$

$$\text{SC:} \quad 1 \quad 2 \quad \emptyset \quad 4 \qquad 3\text{–}5 \qquad 6$$

8b TO movement (obligatory)

$$\text{SA:} \quad \underset{1}{X} \quad \underset{2}{\text{FOR}} \quad \underset{3}{\text{TO}} \quad \underset{4}{\text{NP}} \quad _{\text{VP}}[\underset{5}{Y}]_{\text{VP}} \quad \underset{6}{Z}$$

$$\text{SC:} \quad 1 \quad 2 \quad \emptyset \quad 4 \qquad _{\text{COMP}}[3]_{\text{COMP}} - 5 \quad 6$$

8c POSS movement

	X	POSS	Y	N	U
SA:	1	2	3	4	5
	1	2	3	4	5
SC:	1	∅	3	4+ 2	5

Condition: Y does not contain NP

Once POSS and ING have been moved, COMP is empty and is deleted under the convention that empty nodes are pruned from phrase markers. One important point in connection with TO movement is that VP comes to dominate a node COMP, which in turn dominates TO.

It was earlier proposed (pages 72–3) that infinitives be derived from full sentences and that even examples like *I want to see this film* should be derived from a deep structure [I WANT [I SEE THIS FILM]]. This analysis can be extended to gerunds, with sentences like *I hate writing essays* being derived from the deep structure [I HATE $_{NP}[_S[$I WRITE ESSAY$]_S]_{NP}]$. Just as there are infinitives with two NPs and a verb – *For you to reject the offer would make me unhappy* – so there are gerunds with two NPs and a verb – *I resented your learning these rules* which supports the derivation of gerunds from sentences.

The major rule involved in the derivation of infinitives and gerunds is equi-NP-deletion. Consider the underlying structure of *My brother wants to buy this book* (Figure 61). TO movement has applied.

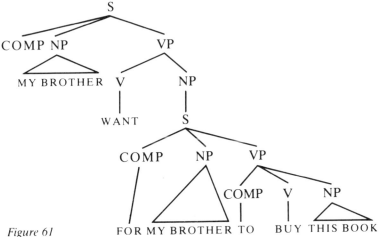

Figure 61

Equi-NP-deletion, stated in **9**, deletes the occurrence of MY BROTHER in the embedded S and FOR.

9 Equi-NP-deletion (obligatory)

$$\text{SA:} \quad \underset{1}{X} \quad \underset{2}{NP} \quad \underset{3}{Y} \quad {}_S[\left\{\begin{matrix} \text{POSS} \\ \text{FOR} \end{matrix}\right\} \underset{4}{} \quad \underset{5}{NP} \quad \underset{6}{VP}]_S \quad \underset{7}{Z} \quad \underset{8}{NP}$$

$$\text{SC:} \quad \underset{1}{1} \quad \underset{2}{2} \quad \underset{3}{3} \quad \underset{\emptyset}{} \quad \underset{\emptyset}{} \quad \underset{6}{6} \quad \underset{7}{7} \quad \underset{8}{8}$$

Condition: either 2 or 8 is null but not both
either 2 = 5 or 5 = 8
X and Y may be null or W may be null

This T-rule maps the structure of Figure 61 into that of Figure 62, and derives the structure in Figure 64 from that of Figure 63.

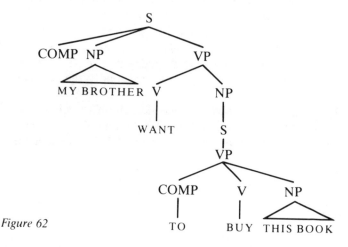

Figure 62

The crucial information in the SA of equi-NP-deletion is that it applies to a structure containing an embedded S introduced by FOR (Figure 61), or POSS (Figure 63). In both cases there is no structure to the right of the embedded S and 7 and 8 in the SA are null, but X (= COMP) and Y (= WANT/RESENT) are not null. In both cases 2 = 5. For a structure in which 1, 2 and 3 are null and 5 = 8, consider the phrase marker of Figure 65, which shows the structure for *Learning this rule depressed the students*. Note that ING movement has applied.

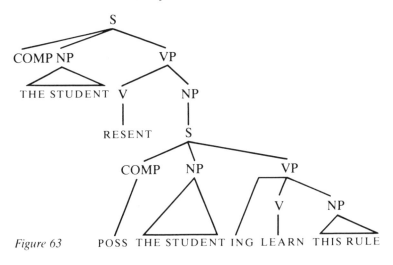

Figure 63

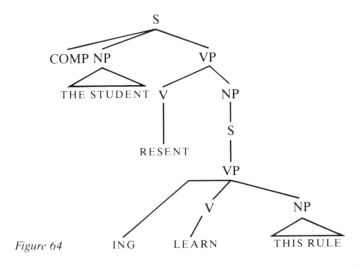

Figure 64

Arguments relating to the syntactic component of a transformational grammar support structures like the ones in Figures 61–65. There is also an enormous advantage for the semantic component: it is clear from the syntactic deep structure whether or not the person with the desire and the person to do the buying (Figure 61) are

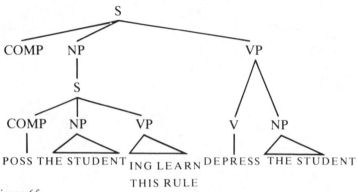

Figure 65

one and the same. That the subject noun in the complement is deleted has no relevance for the semantic component in the standard model, since syntactic structures are interpreted at the level of deep structure, before any constituents are deleted.

One syntactic argument for equi-NP-deletion is based on co-occurrence restrictions. ELAPSE, for example, does not co-occur with animate subject nouns (indeed with any noun other than one denoting a unit of time), and this restriction applies both to simple sentences – *Tom elapsed* – and to sentences with infinitives – *Tom wanted to elapse*. The restriction is exactly the same in both cases but would have to be stated twice if the infinitive were not derived from a complete sentence. In the 'complete sentence' analysis the restriction is stated once only, before the sentences are reduced to infinitives or gerunds. The restriction also applies to sentences where the infinitive has an overt subject noun (*Bill wanted Tom to elapse*) but still has to be stated only once.

The remarks on selectional restrictions (pages 44–5) show that arguments like the one above are not irresistible, but there are stronger syntactic arguments. For instance, a peculiar sentence like *Shaving himself annoyed me* would, on the analysis proposed here, derive from a deep structure $_S[_S[$ HE$_i$ SHAVE HE$_i]_S$ ANNOY ME$]_S$. On the other hand, the acceptable sentence *Shaving myself annoyed me* derives from $_S[_S[$ I SHAVE I$[_S[$ ANNOY I$]_S$. The unacceptability of the first sentence seems connected with the subject of SHAVE not being the object of ANNOY, which it is in the second. With gerunds deriving from complete deep sentences, it should be possible to have a single T-rule that handles both [BILL RESENT

[BILL HAND MONEY TO THE TAXMAN]] and [[I SHAVE I]
ANNOY I].

Another argument rests on the claim that if in a clause there are two coreferential NPs (NPs referring to the same object in the world) one of the NPs can contain OWN, but not otherwise: (*Fortunately) Fred crashed his own car* but not **Fred crashed my own car*. *Own* also occurs in complements without a subject where the subject has been deleted by equi-NP-deletion, e.g. *Crashing my own car made me furious*. However, a sentence like *Crashing your own car made Fred furious* is impossible. If the latter derives from S(NP(S(FRED CRASH MY CAR)) MAKE FRED FURIOUS), OWN cannot be inserted, since FRED refers to one person and MY (= OF I) to another. That is, the same restriction applies in the derivation of sentences with and without infinitives and gerunds.

(The argument of the preceding two paragraphs is not entirely endorsed by the authors; it is given as an example of the arguments used by linguists who accepted the 'complete sentence' analysis.)

The second major T-rule in the derivation of complements is subject raising, which applies when the subject NP in the matrix sentence is not identical with the subject NP in the embedded S. The structure underlying *I want my brother to buy this book* is shown in Figure 66.

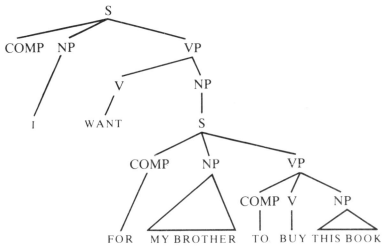

Figure 66

Obviously FOR has to be deleted but the mapping has another step, witness examples like *I want him to buy this book. Him, her, us, me* and *them* occur to the right of a verb or a preposition in English, in object position. *Him* in the preceding example will fit the pattern if it too is the object of WANT, but in Figure 66 the whole embedded S is the object of WANT. The way round this difficulty is to raise the subject NP of the complement sentence into object position in the matrix sentence, for which we need the raising rule in **10**.

10   Subject to object raising (obligatory)

$$\text{SA:} \quad X \quad V \quad _{NP}[_S[FOR \quad NP \quad Z]_S]_{NP}$$
$$\qquad\quad 1 \quad 2 \qquad 3 \qquad 4 \quad 5$$
$$\text{SC:} \quad 1 \quad 2 \; - \; 4 \; \emptyset \; \emptyset \; 5$$

The output of this rule is shown in Figure 67.

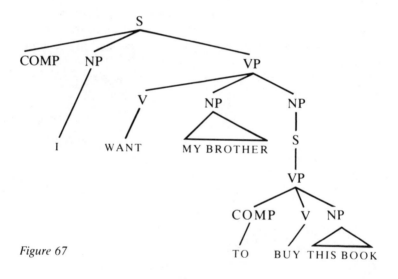

Figure 67

Constituent 4 in the SA is now the object of WANT and the embedded S looks peculiar in that it contains only a VP. Under the convention governing the 'cleaning up' of phrase markers, S nodes that do not branch are deleted; it seems plausible that an NP node dominating a VP should also be deleted. These operations leave a single S dominating two VPs.

In order to generate sentences like *His father is likely to be ill* a T-rule is needed that raises NPs from subject position in an embedded S to subject position in the matrix S. The rule, stated in **11**, maps the structure of Figure 68 into that of Figure 69.

11   Subject to subject raising (optional)

$$SA: \quad X \quad _{NP}[_S[\text{FOR} \quad NP \quad Z]_S]_{NP} \quad VP$$
$$ 1 \phantom{X _{NP}[_S[\text{FOR}}} 2 \quad\;\; 3 \quad\; 4 \phantom{]_S]_{NP}} 5$$

$$SC: \quad 1 \quad\;\; 3 \;-\; _{NP}[_S[\emptyset \quad \emptyset \quad 4]_S]_{NP} \quad 5$$

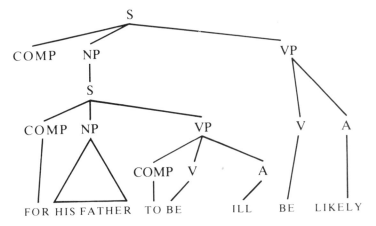

Figure 68

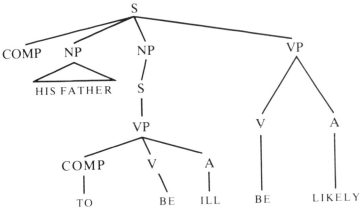

Figure 69

In order to generate *His father is likely to be ill* the embedded S is moved to the right-hand side of the tree by a major T-rule, extraposition. This rule, whose name is not another example of generative jargon but goes back to the 1930s, was first devised to handle sentences like *It was announced by the Chairman that the company was bankrupt*, whose structure is shown in Figure 70.

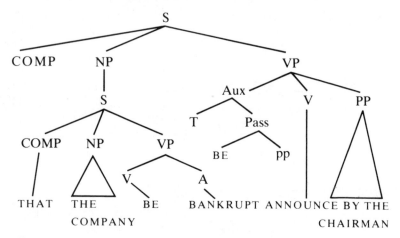

Figure 70

The embedded S is detached from the immediately dominating NP node, moved to the right of VP in the matrix sentence and attached to the matrix S node. The rule of extraposition is stated in **12**.

12   Extraposition (optional)

$$\text{SA:} \quad \underset{1}{X} \quad {}_S[\underset{2}{\begin{Bmatrix} \text{FOR} \\ \text{TO} \\ \text{THAT} \end{Bmatrix}} \quad \underset{3}{Y]_S} \quad \underset{4}{Z}$$

$$\text{SC:} \quad 1 \quad \emptyset \quad \emptyset \quad 4 - {}_S[2 - 3]_S$$

Condition: Z may be null

In Figure 70, Z corresponds to BE pp ANNOUNCE BY THE CHAIRMAN and its associated structure and X is COMP. If the example were *He knew that the fact that the company was bankrupt was announced by the Chairman*, X would represent the structure of *He knew the fact*, and extraposition would move the embedded S to derive the structure of *He knew the fact was announced by the Chairman that the company was bankrupt.*

With respect to Figure 69, X corresponds to COMP HIS FATHER and Z to the VP in the matrix S. Extraposition maps the phrase markers of Figures 69 and 70 into those of Figure 71 and 72.

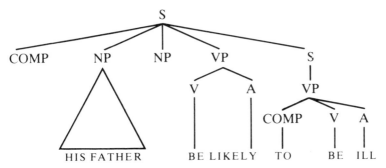

Figure 71

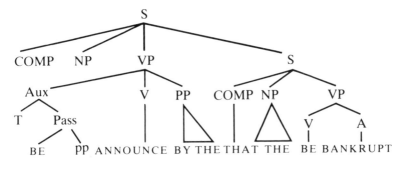

Figure 72

The empty node in Figure 72 is not deleted. In English there must always be a noun in subject position and the empty node is filled by the 'dummy' noun IT. Since there is a convention that empty nodes are deleted (cf. page 64), the convention has to be qualified to allow one exception: an empty subject node in the topmost sentence of a phrase marker is not deleted. The rule inserting IT is formulated in **13**.

13   IT insertion (obligatory)

SA: X $_S[_N[$ $]_N$ Y$]_S$ Z
  1   2   3

SC: 1 $_N[$IT$]_N$ − 2   3

The essential factor is that an empty NP lies to the immediate right of a sentence boundary, which means that the rule does not apply to the empty N in Figure 71, which is deleted.

The embedded S in Figure 68 could have THAT as its COMP. In that case subject to subject raising would not apply, since its SA mentions FOR, but extraposition and IT insertion would apply to derive *It is likely that his father is ill*. Other lexemes that occur in these structures are CERTAIN (**14**) and APPEAR (**15**).

14a   He is certain to come
14b   It is certain that he will come
14c   That he will come is (by no means) certain

15a   It appears that our team has won
15b   Our team appears to have won

The rules formulated so far do not specify relatively simple sentences like *To write novels is easy* and *Writing a poem is difficult*. Such sentences do not specify who is doing the writing and it might be supposed that the subject noun phrase does not dominate any lexeme at all. However, (stilted) English sentences like *For one to write novels is easy* and *One's writing a poem is difficult* provide, for the 'complete sentence' analysis, a way of capturing the relation between infinitives with no subject noun and those with *one*. We assume that a lexeme ONE is inserted into deep structures and optionally deleted if it is preceded by FOR. The rule of ONE deletion is stated in **16**.

16   ONE deletion (optional)

SA: X $_S[\begin{Bmatrix} \text{FOR} \\ \text{POSS} \end{Bmatrix}$ NP   Y$]_S$ Z
  1   2   3   4   5

SC: 1   ∅   ∅   4   5

Condition: 3 dominates ONE

This rule maps the tree of Figure 73 on to the tree of Figure 74.

The extraposition rule in **12** does not apply to all POSS ING complements: this appears correct, given the peculiarity of *It is certain

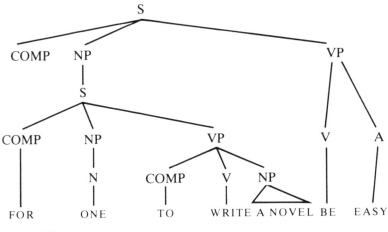

Figure 73

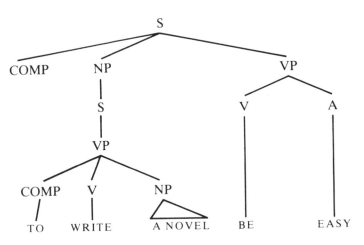

Figure 74

the manager's having embezzled the money. Although it is usually assumed without comment that extraposition does not apply to any POSS ING complements, this assumption is incorrect. Examples like the above are indisputably unacceptable but the following are good: *It is easy writing poetry, It was fun learning to drive, It is exhilarating skiing down the mountain.*

These examples are frequent in spoken English and can be interpreted as arising from two stretches of utterance that coalesce: e.g., the utterance corresponding to *it is easy* followed by the utterance corresponding to *writing poetry*, which is added to explain the reference of *it*. It is interesting that this suggestion gains plausibility from a recent change in the English perfect construction, which used to be, and indeed still is, described as not allowing specific time adverbs like *last Tuesday* or *this morning*. In spite of the descriptions, speakers produce utterances, with breaks in intonation, corresponding to *I have seen him – on Thursday* and utterances like *I have seen him on Thursday*, without any pause or break in intonation, are now to be heard regularly. (These utterances are not used to place emphasis on any constituents but are equivalent to *I saw him on Thursday*. It is not clear what the end-point of this change will be, but it is worth noting that the simple past forms of the verb were replaced by the perfect forms in spoken French, in many Slav languages and in south German.)

One question is whether sentences like *It was fun learning to drive* should be handled by rules (as yet to be developed) describing appropriate discourse (conversation or written text). In the absence of an answer to this question the construction under consideration will be treated as containing an extraposed gerund, though the study of actual conversation may entail a reappraisal of this analysis. Extending the data to these extraposed gerunds has one immediate advantage: since any complement can be extraposed, a simpler rule is possible that mentions just COMP instead of the individual complementizers. Such a general rule allows *It is fun their being here for a whole month*, whose status is indeterminable for the simple reason that extraposed gerunds are typical of spoken English and full POSS ING complements are typical of written English but occur rarely in speech.

It will be assumed that the gerunds derive from deep sentences with ONE as the subject NP, as this permits us to relate the above examples to *Writing an essay is easy*, etc. The general rule of extraposition is stated in **17**.

17   Extraposition

$$\begin{array}{lcccc} \text{SA:} & X & {}_S[\,\text{COMP} & Y]_S & Z \\ & 1 & 2 & 3 & 4 \\ \text{SC:} & 1 & \emptyset & \emptyset & 4 \quad {}_S[2 \ 3]_S \end{array}$$

Apart from ING, the mapping is identical with that from Figure 69 to Figure 71. As before, IT is inserted into the empty subject NP and the non-branching extraposed S node is pruned, leaving an NP dominating a VP. So in *John seems to be happy, to be happy* is treated as a VP.

An additional device implicit in the foregoing paragraphs is the control of T-rules by lexemes (cf. page 65). For example, extraposition does not apply if the complement is dependent on CERTAIN and if it has the POSS ING complementizer. (Note that extraposition with TO is necessary to derive *John is certain to win*.) The required information can be stored in the lexical entry for CERTAIN: [−Extrap., if $_S[_{NP}[_S[(\text{POSS NP}) \text{ ING Y}]]Z$ CERTAIN]]. Z allows for various combinations of auxiliary constituents and the POSS NP in brackets allows for a full sentence complement. Extraposition applies freely if the complement is dependent on a lexeme such as FUN, EASY, EXHILARATING.

Another rule controlled by lexemes is Subject to Subject Raising. If this rule is obligatory, the grammar does not generate sentences like *For Bill to misunderstand the question is not very likely*, but if it is optional a problem arises with respect to SEEM. The deep structure of *The lion seems to be contented* is shown in Figure 75.

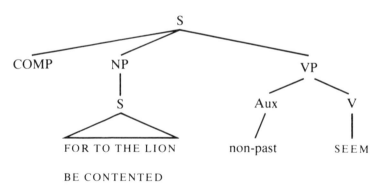

Figure 75

If subject to subject raising does not apply, the grammar generates **For the lion to be contented seems*. SEEM and (APPEAR) require the application of subject to subject raising. They also require the application of extraposition, otherwise the grammar generates *That the company is bankrupt appears.* Some lexical entries are given in **18**.

18

SEEM

$[+V]$

$[+[_S[COMP \quad X]_S \underline{\quad}]]$
    $[+wh]$

   $[+ \quad Extrap.]$

$[+[_S[COMP \quad X]_S \underline{\quad}]]$
    $[+3]$

  $[+ \quad sub.\ to\ sub.\ raising]$

  $[+ \quad Extrap.]$

EASY

$[+A]$

$[+[_S[COMP \quad X]_S \underline{\quad}]]$
    $[+3]$

PROBABLE

$[+A]$

$[+[_S[COMP \quad X]_S \underline{\quad}]]$
    $[+1]$

SURPRISING

$[+A]$

$[+[_S[COMP \quad X]_S \underline{\quad}]]$

$\left\{ \begin{array}{c} [+3] \\ [+1] \end{array} \right\}$

$[- sub.\ to\ sub.\ raising]$

CERTAIN

$[+A]$

$[+[_S[COMP \quad X] \underline{\quad}]]$

$\left\{ \begin{array}{c} [+1] \\ [+2] \end{array} \right\}$

$[+ \quad Extrap.]$ if

$_S[_{NP}[_S[(POSS\ NP)\ ING\ Y]\ Z$

$CERTAIN]]$

The features for SEEM are split into two sets, since extraposition is obligatory only if the COMP is THAT; subject to subject raising only if the COMP is FOR TO. EASY requires FOR TO but allows extraposition and subject to subject raising to apply optionally: compare *To confuse the students is easy, It is easy to confuse the students, The students are easy to confuse.*

SURPRISING requires THAT or FOR TO as COMP – compare *That Bill passed his driving test is surprising. For Bill to pass his driving test is surprising*, but **Bill is surprising to pass his driving test*. The last sentence is prevented by the rule feature forbidding the application of subject to subject raising.

As was said on page 65, rule features are attractive. They permit general T-rules and solve the problems raised by the analysis of complements but represent a significant increase in the power of the grammar. As we will see, this undesirable increase is to be avoided (pages 133–70).

Technical terms

complementizer
equi-NP-deletion
extraposition
ING movement
IT insertion
ONE deletion

POSS movement
rule feature
subject to object raising
subject to subject raising
T/M deletion

Exercises to chapters 7 and 8

1

(a), (b) and (c) each contain a partial deep structure and a list of transformations. Apply the transformations to the deep structure and say what surface structure is derived. The *etc*. at the end of each list relates to obligatory rules such as affix hopping and verb number agreement.

   (a) $_S$(COMP THE REPORTER Past Pass STATE $_{NP}$($_S$(THAT THE FIRM Past HAVE MAKE A LOSS)))
        passive (applies to the matrix S), extraposition, IT insertion, etc.

   (b) $_S$($_{NP}$($_S$(FOR TO THE HYENA non-Past BE ING GNAW A BONE)) Past BE CERTAIN)
        subject raising, extraposition, etc.

   (c) $_S$(THE STUDENT Past WANT$_{NP}$($_S$(FOR TO THIS UNIVERSITY Pass ACCEPT THE STUDENT)))
        passive (applies to the embedded S), equi-NP-deletion, etc.

2

For each of the following sentences draw a phrase marker showing the deep structure and state what transformations derive the surface structure. Draw phrase markers showing the surface structure and, time permitting, the effect of each transformation.

1 Taking notes exhausted my friend
2 Bill wants the report to indicate that the contract is certain to be won by us
3 The accountant's threatening to resign persuaded the chairman to accept the proposal

3

(i) There are restrictions on the co-occurrence of complementizers and the verb in the matrix sentence containing the complement. Into the frame *Everyone* _____ insert one of the verb forms in (a) followed by one of the sequences in (b). Which combinations of verb form and complement are possible?

(a)   *regretted, conjectured, ignored, minded, resented, assumed, forgot (about)*
(b)   *his being completely incompetent, that he was completely incompetent, for him to be completely incompetent*

(ii) Consider the verb forms *proves, means, implies, shows*. Each verb form can be preceded and followed by a complement. Use the following set of complements to find out whether there are any restrictions on which type of complement can precede or follow the verbs:

> *for the machine to break down so soon*
> *for the quality inspection to be shoddy*
> *that the machine broke down so soon*
> *that the quality inspection is shoddy*
> *the machine's breaking down so soon*
> *the quality inspection's being shoddy*

Can you think of other verbs that share the co-occurrence restrictions?

(iii) Which of the adjectives in (a) can be inserted into the frames in (b)?

(a)   *distressing, puzzling, certain, probable, astonishing, crazy*
(b)   *It is _____ for Bill to have won the competition*
       For Bill to have won the competition is _____

Notes

1   Two distinctions are relevant to the above questions. The first is the classification of verbs as factive or non-factive. KNOW is factive, and *You knew he was wrong* implies *He was wrong.* The implication holds even if the first sentence is negative or interrogative: *You didn't know he was wrong* and *Did you know he was wrong?* both imply *He was wrong. Factive* is derived from *fact.* Compare *I was aware (of the fact) that he was wrong.*

The second distinction is between adjectives describing effects on people's emotions and other adjectives, e.g. *exciting, spooky, surprising* as opposed to *green, large, uninteresting.*

2   Speakers of English have different intuitions about the verbs and adjectives in this exercise. This fact is interesting in itself but equally important is how the data is handled by the transformational model under discussion. Write lexical entries incorporating the necessary information.

9 Sentence negation and interrogatives

Consider the examples of yes–no interrogatives in **1**.

1a Can you visit us next week?
1b Is he playing football these days?
1c Has he returned the book he borrowed?
1d Was the car stolen yesterday morning?
1e Did he come to see you?

The structure of **1a–1d** is straightforward; it is the same as that of the corresponding declarative sentences, except that the first V in the VP has been moved into initial position in the sentence. **1e** is not so easily described because it contains *did*, which does not occur in the corresponding declarative sentence *He came to see you*. Other constructions in which DO forms occur are shown in **2**.

2a He doesn't like swimming
2b Doesn't he like swimming?
2c He does like swimming
2d John plays football and so do I

DO forms occur in negative and interrogative sentences, in declarative sentences but bearing special stress, and as pronominal forms (**2d**). Even with special stress they do not occur before forms of the Perfective HAVE or BE or a modal verb, and they do not occur in declarative sentences at all except with special stress or before an NP.

Transformational descriptions normally generate deep structures without DO and introduce DO where necessary with a T-rule (pages 121–7 in BM). It is true that the deep structure of positive declarative sentences is taken as the basic one from which other structures are derived and it is true that in many dialects of English non-emphatic declarative sentences do not contain a DO form. On the other hand, DO forms occur in all other constructions, and there are dialects in which even non-emphatic declarative sentences contain DO forms before main verbs and before BE.

These facts suggest the desirability of generating DO as a constituent of the base, but where should it be generated? It is not a main verb. (Constructions like *do the crawl* are ignored here. The DO in them is a main verb – *Did he do the crawl?*) DO does not express perfectiveness or progressiveness, co-occurring with BE in some dialects. It does, however, behave syntactically like a modal verb, occurring before *not* or *n't* (*He can/does not tolerate fools gladly*), in first position in interrogatives (*Can/does he eat meat?*) and with emphatic stress (*I 'do play chess, I 'can play chess*).

The above facts suggest that DO is a modal verb, even though it may seem that DO is not a modal verb semantically, since it does not express possibility, prediction, volition or necessity. This objection can be met by two reminders: the label 'modal' is assigned on distributional criteria, and active declarative sentences with no modal verb express a 'factual' modality. This modality is neutral and unmarked in the literal sense that it is not expressed by a special verb unless it is emphasized that something is indeed a fact, in which case DO forms occur.

Before writing a T-rule to derive the structure of yes–no interrogatives we have to look at the distribution of *not* and *n't*, as the rule should handle positive and negative interrogatives. The distribution is illustrated in **3**.

3a He does not/doesn't play chess
3b He isn't/is not playing chess
3c He hasn't/has not been playing chess
3d He can't/can not play chess

Not and *n't* occur after the first constituent in the VP. Forms like *didn't* are usually regarded as constituting one word, and we will write rules that contract *not* to *n't* if Neg becomes part of the preceding constituent.

Not occurs in positions where *n't* never does (**4** and **5**).

4a For John not to have written is ridiculous
4b *For John n't to have written is ridiculous

5a John's not having written is ridiculous
5b *John's n't having written is ridiculous

The grammar does not handle sentences like *John's having not written is ridiculous* or *He might have been not working*, which are instances of constituent negation, not sentence negation.

4 and **5** show that *n't* does not occur in infinitive or gerund phrases. In these constructions we find *not* rather than *n't*, but in a position different from that which it occupies in full sentences: **John not has written.*

Since Neg is generated to the left of the subject NP by the PS rules, it has to be moved into the appropriate position. Two rules are required. The first moves Neg into first position in Aux, where it stays if the constituent to its right is TO or ING. Otherwise Neg moves to the right of the next constituent. The first rule is stated in **6**.

6   Neg movement (obligatory)

SA: COMP   Neg   NP $_{Aux}[$ Y$]_{Aux}$ Z
        1   2   3   4   5

SC: 1   ∅   3   2 − 4   5

The output of this rule is illustrated in Figure 76.

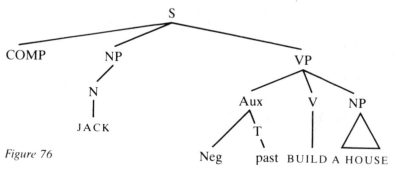

Figure 76

The second rule is stated in **7**.

7   Neg placement (obligatory)

SA: X $_{Aux}[$Neg   Y   Z$]_{Aux}$ W
        1   2   3   4   5

SC: 1   ∅   3 − 2   4   5

Condition: Y = first constituent following Neg but not TO or ING

This rule moves Neg into second position in Aux provided that Aux is not in a complement sentence. It applies after affix hopping.

We have already seen that Neg is realized by *not* or *n't*. We assume that Neg, if it remains an independent constituent, is realized as *not* but that it is realized as *n't* if it becomes part of another constituent. After Neg has been moved into second position in Aux, an optional rule, Neg attraction, moves it into the first constituent in Aux. The rule is stated in **8** and its output shown in Figure 77.

8 Neg attraction (optional)

$$\text{SA:} \quad X \quad {}_{Aux}[Y \quad Neg \quad (Z)]_{Aux} \quad W$$
$$\phantom{\text{SA:} \quad} 1 \quad\quad 2 \quad 3 \quad 4 \quad\quad 5$$
$$\text{SC:} \quad 1 \quad\quad 2/3 \quad\; 4 \quad\quad 5$$

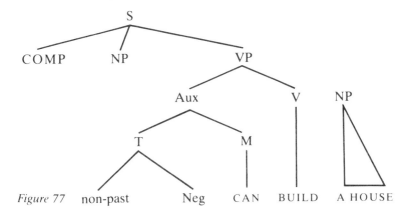

Figure 77

Let us return to DO. The grammar generates sentences like those in **9** and **10** but not the asterisked ones.

9a   He reads books
9b   He does read books
9c   He has read books
9d   *He does have read books
9e   He is reading books
9f   *He does be reading books
9g   He has a book
9h   He does have a book
9i   He is tall
9j   *He does be tall

10a   *He reads not books
10b   He doesn't/does not read books
10c   He hasn't/has not read books
        etc.

Most transformational descriptions of English fail to notice that the DO forms are not obligatory, since sentences like *He came not to the castle* and *Came he to the castle?* are archaic or literary rather than hopelessly unacceptable. In only two environments in literary English must DO be deleted (remembering that in complements DO is deleted by T/M deletion): before BE and before the Perfective HAVE – *He does have written a novel* but *He does have a Stradivarius*. If DO occurs it must be stressed in a declarative sentence: *He 'does play chess.* DO deletion is stated in **11**.

11   DO deletion (obligatory)

$$\text{SA:} \quad \underset{1}{X} \quad _{Aux}[\underset{2}{Y} \quad \underset{3}{DO} \quad \begin{Bmatrix} Perf \\ BE \end{Bmatrix} \quad \underset{4}{Z}]_{Aux} \quad \underset{5}{} \quad \underset{6}{U}$$

SC: 1   2 $\emptyset$ 4   5   6

Condition: Z may be null

On the assumption that affix hopping applies before the rule that derives the structure of yes–no interrogatives, all we need is a rule that moves either the first constituent in VP or the first constituent and Neg (not incorporated but independent). This rule, subject–verb inversion, is stated in **12** and derives sentences like those in **13**.

12   Subject–verb inversion (obligatory)

$$\text{SA:} \quad \underset{1}{\underset{[+Q]}{COMP}} \quad \underset{2}{NP} \quad _{VP}[\underset{3}{X} \quad \underset{4}{(Neg)} \quad \underset{5}{Z}]_{VP}$$

SCi: 1 3   2 $\emptyset$ 4   5

SCii: 1   3   4   2 $\emptyset$ $\emptyset$ 5

13a   Could John not leave tomorrow?
13b   Couldn't John leave tomorrow?
13c   Could not John leave tomorrow?

If Neg attraction has not applied then **13a** is derived. If Neg attraction has applied then **13b** is derived. **13c** is derived by SCii. The rules also generate **14**.

14 Wrote John a poem?

And this is not so much wrong as archaic. Another interrogative structure in English is shown in **15**.

15a Who bought the estate?
15b Which programme did you watch?
15c Where have you left your gloves?
15d What is he doing in Nemphlar?

As with negative and yes–no interrogatives, the deep sources of **15** are structures that would otherwise be mapped into declarative sentences. The interrogative pronouns derive from indefinite pronouns on the assumption that **15** and **16** are parallel.

16a Someone bought the estate
16b You watched a/some programme
16c You have left your gloves somewhere
16d He is doing something in Nemphlar

The indefinite determiner SOME has [+wh] and [−wh] in its lexical entry. If [+wh] is chosen, SOME is inserted into a phrase marker containing COMP, though there may be several sentence $[+Q]$
boundaries between COMP and SOME, as in the deep structure of $[+Q]$ $[+wh]$
What book did Bill say that Tom persuaded Fred to buy? The relationship between [+wh] and the categorization feature $[+[COMP (X)\_\_]]$ can be expressed by a redundancy rule. (For a $[+Q]$
discussion of redundancy rules see pages 41–2 and 139–43.) If [−wh] is chosen, SOME is inserted into any phrase marker but SOME ONE is not realized as *who* or *which* or *what* and is not moved to the front of the sentence. The deep structure of **15a** is shown in Figure 78, the deep structure of **15c** in Figure 79.

The deep structure of **15a** contains SOME and COMP. If the $[+wh]$ $[+Q]$
deep structure contained COMP and SOMEONE, the rules would $[+Q]$ $[−wh]$
derive the surface structure of *Did someone buy the estate*? The

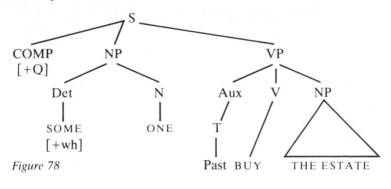

Figure 78

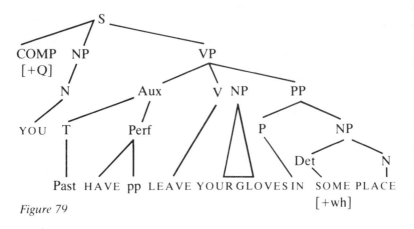

Figure 79

orthographic rules realize SOMEONE as *who, which, what one*
[+wh]
or *which one*. The derivation of **15a** is simple in that no constituents are permuted, in contrast with **15b–15d**. There is, however, one movement in the derivation of **15a**: SOME ONE, the NP,
is detached from S and reattached to COMP. This movement takes
place in matrix and embedded sentences, e.g. in the description
both of *Who phoned?* and *Tell me who phoned?* In the second, the
complementizer function of *who* comes out clearly, as it signals
the beginning of an indirect question.

What facts does the grammar have to account for in its description of *wh* interrogatives? In addition to the movement of the
[+wh] constituent, there is the movement of the first V in the VP.
This is handled already by subject–verb inversion; one compli-

cation is that these movements do not take place in the derivation of every *wh* interrogative, as shown by **17**.

17a You watched which programme?
17b You've left your gloves where?
17c He's doing what in Nemphlar?

These sentences are not completely equivalent in meaning to **15b–15d**, since the speaker is either asking for confirmation of what has perhaps been misheard or of a surprising bit of information. The word order is accompanied by an extra-prominent stress on the *wh* word. These important facts are not immediately relevant for our purposes, the essential fact being that **17a–17c** are related to **15b–15d**.

Whereas there is no movement of constituents in **17**, the sentences in **18** demonstrate that the first verb in the VP can be moved to the left of the subject NP without the *wh* word being moved. As in **17**, the *wh* word carries an extra-prominent stress. Utterances corresponding to these sentences are produced when the speaker has not heard the whole of the previous utterance (e.g. *Did they watch 'Tomorrow's World? – Did they watch what?*) but enough to realize that a question is being asked about the watching of a programme. The important task of stating the conditions under which **17** and **18** are appropriate belongs to another component of the general grammar.

18a Did they watch which programme?
18b Have you left your gloves where?
18c Is he doing what in Nemphlar?

In addition to subject–verb inversion the derivation of *wh* interrogatives requires a rule to move [+wh] constituents to the front of the sentence to become the daughter of COMP. The sentences in **19** show that if the   NP   is inside a PP, either the whole PP is
                                     [+wh]
moved or the NP alone is moved, leaving the preposition 'stranded' at the end of the sentence.

19a In what book did you find this information?
19b What book did you find this information in?

The analysis of relative clauses in chapter 6 also involved the movement of an NP with [+wh] to become the daughter of COMP and, as in **19**, an NP inside a PP could be moved leaving the preposition behind or the whole PP could move. Our present instruments for viewing the syntactic landscape lead us to suppose that there is a generalization to be captured: any constituent with [+wh] can become a daughter of COMP. The question is complicated, however, by the fact that in relative clause structures the [+wh] constituent has to move. The facts might be accommodated in one rule by including a condition that the rule is obligatory if COMP is [−Q], which it is in the relative clause structure but not in the interrogative one: compare **20**.

20　[+wh] movement A

SA:　COMP　X　NP　Y
　　　　　　　　　　[+wh]

　　　　　　1　　2　3　　4

SC:　　1/3　　2　∅　　4

Condition: X or Y may be null

21　[+wh] movement B

SA:　　COMP　X　$_{PP}$[P　NP]　Y
　　　　　　　　　　　　　[+wh]

　　　　　　　1　　2　　3　4　　5

SCi:　　$^1/_{PP}$ [3　　4] 2 ∅　∅ 5

SCii:　　1/4　2　　3 ∅　5

Condition: X or Y may be null

These two rules replace the rules of relative pronoun movement in chapter 6 and handle *wh* interrogatives as well. Notice that rules **(20, 21)** and several previous rules have not been characterized as optional or obligatory. This is because the interaction of these rules is complex and they are subject to stylistic and dialectal variation. Some of these problems are mentioned in the following paragraphs. One way of handling them is by filters, which are discussed on pages 165–6.

With respect to the special features of interrogatives, note that the derivation of *You found this information in what book?* involves only the orthographic rule that realizes SOME as *what*.
　　　　　　　　　　　　　　　　　　　　　[+wh]
What book did you find this information in? requires the application of subject–verb inversion, [+wh] movement B – SCii, and the orthographic rules. *Did you find this information in some*

book? and *Did he find the information in what book*? require only subject–verb inversion.

A second complication arises from the generation of COMP in $[+Q]$ embedded sentences. The obvious answer is that embedded sentences with COMP map into indirect questions such as *Tell me $[+Q]$ what he said* or *I asked what was on the agenda*, and indeed the grammar generates this type of sentence by the application of $[+wh]$ movement A without subject–verb inversion. One difficulty, however, is that subject–verb inversion and $[+wh]$ movement have to be independent of each other, which means that the grammar generates *What book you bought*?, which is correct as an indirect question but not as an independent interrogative. A second difficulty is that the rules generate *Tell me he said what*, which is an incorrect indirect question.

A third complication is that the proper analysis of indirect questions is unclear. The standard type to be found in grammars of English is, e.g., *Tell me what he said*, but many indirect questions in spoken English have the same form as direct questions, without any break in rhythm or change in intonation to indicate that these questions might be less dependent on the main verb than 'genuine' indirect questions. (Incidentally, the very term 'indirect question' is based on certain assumptions about the analysis of these constructions that may not be justified – see the next paragraph.) Examples are: . . . *from the point of view of how can we improve things* (radio programme), *Could you tell us are there any after-school clubs*? (questioner at a meeting), *One important consequence is to answer the question why does this construction exist*? (from written English).

The existence of these 'direct indirect' questions raises problems that go far beyond the scope of this book but the issues at stake can usefully be stated: is, e.g., *Could you tell us are there any after-school clubs* an instance of a genuine 'indirect' or 'dependent' question, and are sentences like *I knew what house he had bought* to be given an analysis $_S[I$ knew $_{NP}[_{NP}[$what house$]_{NP}$ $_S[$He had bought it$]_S]_{NP}]_S$? If the latter analysis can be supported it will at least account for the difference in word order between the direct, independent question *What house had he bought*? and the indirect, dependent question . . . *what house he had bought*. The latter would not be a question at all.

Failing answers to the above questions, the rules of [+wh] movement are left as stated in **20** and **21** in spite of the incorrect structures they generate. For the moment we are caught in a dilemma: how can we have a general statement of [+wh] movement and prevent incorrect structures? Fortunately an exit from the dilemma is indicated by the discussion of surface filters on pages 165–6. Suffice it to say now that the surface filters save the general statement and allow us to remove the condition that [+wh] movement is obligatory when COMP is [+Q].

Another T-rule that has to be mentioned is tag formation, used in deriving sentences like those in **22**.

22ai	You returned the book, didn't you?
22aii	You didn't return the book, did you?
22bi	He will come to the party, won't he?
22bii	He won't come to the party, will he?
22ci	He can play poker, can't he?
22cii	He can't play poker, can he?

With respect to meaning these sentences are different from ordinary yes–no questions. If someone asks *Did you return the book*? the speaker makes no assumptions but asks for information. In contrast, when someone asks *You returned the book, didn't you*? the speaker assumes that the reader did return the book but asks for confirmation of that assumption.

The essential point for a description of syntax is that if the main sentence is positive, the tag is negative, and vice versa. **22b** and **22c** are straighforward in that the modal verb in the main sentence is repeated in the tag. It is usually assumed that tags are formed by copying the appropriate constituents by a rule called tag formation (or some similar name) along the lines of **23**.

23　Tag formation

$$\text{SA:} \quad \text{X} \quad \text{NP} \quad \text{Z} \quad \begin{array}{l}\langle\emptyset\rangle_1 \\ \langle\text{Neg}\rangle_2\end{array} \quad \text{Y}$$

$$\phantom{\text{SA:} \quad} 1 \quad\;\; 2 \quad\;\; 3 \quad\;\; 4 \quad\quad\;\; 5$$

$$\text{SC:} \quad 1 \quad 2 \quad 3 \quad 4 \quad 5 \quad 3 \; \begin{array}{l}\langle\text{Neg}\rangle_1 \\ \langle\emptyset\rangle_2\end{array} \; \text{Pron}$$

$$\phantom{\text{SC:}}\quad\quad\quad\quad\quad\quad\quad \text{Condition:} \; \text{Z} = \text{M, Perf, Prog, Pass}$$

The copying is fairly complex. The significance of the angled numbered brackets is that if the sentence has nothing between Z and Y (i.e. is positive), the copied constituent is followed by Neg, but if the sentence contains Neg, the copied constituent has nothing between it and the pronoun. Positive sentences acquire negative tags and vice-versa, at least in the data we are dealing with. Another twist is that unless the NP contains a pronoun it is replaced by a pronoun in the tag. Note that tag formation applies before DO deletion; otherwise **22a** would not be generated.

The structure derived by tag formation is shown in Figure 80.

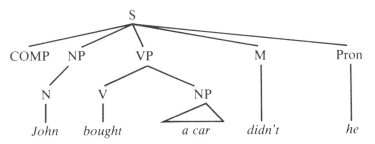

Figure 80

Tag formation generates the desired sequence of constituents but it may not generate the most appropriate structure. Another possibility is that the tag question derives from a separate sentence. Utterances related to declarative sentences are typically used for making statements and utterances related to interrogative sentences are typically used for asking questions. However, utterances related to **22** can be seen to express a statement followed by a question, a view captured in Figure 81.

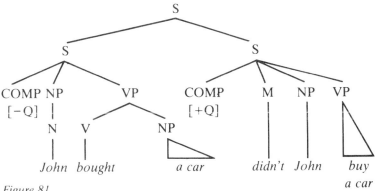

Figure 81

With respect to this structure, tag formation is deletion not copying, and *John* in the second S could be pronominalized by a separate rule applying after tag formation. As there is no space to explore the alternative analyses, the choice is not made, though it must be said that the second analysis makes more sense in relation to semantics.

Technical terms

DO deletion
Neg attraction
Neg movement
Neg placement
subject–verb inversion
tag formation
[+wh] addition
[+wh] movement A
[+wh] movement B

Exercises

1

To each partial structure below apply the transformations listed and the appropriate orthographic rules. What surface structures are derived?

(a) COMP BILL Past HAVE EN FIND SOME THING
     [+Q]   [+wh]

     affix hopping, subject–verb inversion, [wh] movement

(b) COMP Neg THE DOG Past BE ING CHASE THE CAT
     [−Q]

     affix hopping, Neg movement, Neg placement, Neg attraction

(c) COMP TOM Past SAY S(COMP Neg JOHN Past BUY
     [+Q]   [−Q]

     SOME BOOK
     [+wh]

     affix hopping, Neg movement, Neg placement, Neg attraction, [wh] movement

2

For each sentence below draw a phrase marker showing the deep structure and state what transformations derive the surface structure. Illustrate the effect of each transformation.

    1   Didn't Maria attract Henry?
    2   What did you say Julia could have been doing?
    3   Where was Edmund intending to live?

3

Collect tag questions from conversation and printed matter. Apart from DO, is the auxiliary verb in the tag always the same as the auxiliary in the main clause? Does the tag always contain an auxiliary verb? Are tags always attached to declarative sentences?

10 The cycle, rule ordering and constraints

The grammar developed in the preceding chapter has a set of base rules (PS rules), a set of lexical entries, and a set of transformations. Implicit in the application of T-rules are certain principles that are now to be drawn out and made explicit. The first is the *transformational cycle*.

The development of this principle dates from early transformational grammar when the principle was strictly adhered to that a symbol on the left-hand side of a PS rule could not appear on the right-hand side. This meant that each phrase marker contained only one S, the root node. So that the grammar could handle sentences like *He knew that she wouldn't come back*, which derives from a structure with two sentences, special T-rules embedded one S in another S or conjoined two or more Ss. These rules were *generalized transformations*.

Difficulties were caused by sentences like *The plan devised by the general was stated by the colonel to be useless*. The deep structure of this sentence is shown in Figure 82.

Not only is S_2 embedded inside S_1, but S_3 is embedded inside S_2. The Passive applies to S_3 and again to S_1, but the embedding of S_2 in S_1 has to take place before the second application of Passive. These difficulties constituted the *traffic rules problem*: how to apply the T-rules in the right place and in the right order.

These difficulties were handled by relaxing one of the restrictions on PS rules and allowing S to appear on both sides of the arrow; that is, S became recursive. This change made generalized T-rules unnecessary, as Ss were embedded in their proper position by the PS rules. There remained the problem of T-rules that applied more than once in a derivation – such as the double application of Passive to the structure in Figure 82 – but this was solved by adopting the convention that T-rules apply first to the lowest S in

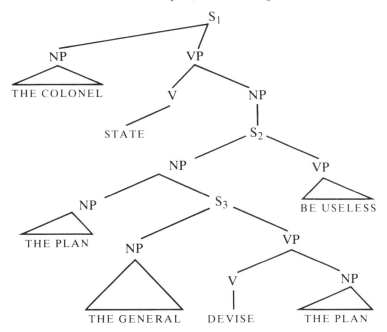

Figure 82

a phrase marker, then the next S up, and so on until the highest S is reached.

This convention, the *transformational cycle*, ensures that Passive applies twice to the phrase marker in Figure 82 and in the appropriate places. Although there are few overt arguments for the principle of the cycle, it did solve the traffic rules problem and simplifies the task of describing the syntactic structure of sentences with a number of subordinate clauses. It has been suggested that, with S recursive, the cycle is not necessary and that, e.g., the Passive be allowed to apply to a phrase marker like that in Figure 82 as often as possible, and that other rules be allowed to apply as often as possible. Such a description is perfectly possible, but since none has been developed along these lines it is not known what problems would be created by the absence of the cycle. Given these unknown factors, and the intuitive appeal of the cycle, it has been employed in this grammar.

One complexity is that not all T-rules apply on every cycle. Tag formation, for example, does not apply to embedded sentences –

consider the unacceptability of *I asked whether he wrote to you, didn't he*. One way of preventing the generation of such sentences is to allow tag formation to apply only to the highest S in a phrase marker, i.e. on the last cycle. T-rules restricted in this respect are *last cyclic*.

The second principle is *rule ordering* (mentioned on pages 34 and 56), which has been applied covertly in the description of English syntax, for instance in relation to the rules generating negative and interrogative structures. The fact that PS rules are unordered causes no difficulties, as the same phrase marker is generated no matter what the order of application, but a lack of ordering between T-rules in the description offered here can be a source of embarrassment. Consider the phrase marker of Figure 83.

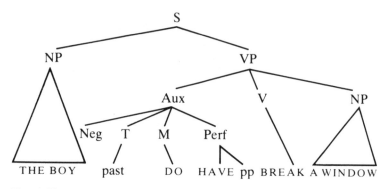

Figure 83

This is the underlying structure of *The boy hasn't broken a window*. Three rules apply to this structure: DO deletion, affix hopping and Neg placement.

If Neg placement applies first, Neg is moved to the second position in Aux, producing the phrase marker of Figure 84.

DO deletion applies, since DO occurs to the left of Perf, and we would then expect affix hopping to apply. This expectation is only partially fulfilled, because while *pp* can move to the right of BREAK, T cannot move to the right of HAVE. Affix hopping applies to an Af and Vb that are adjacent but Neg placement makes T and Perf no longer adjacent. To generate the required structure the three rules have to be applied in the order: DO deletion, affix hopping and Neg placement, which ensures that

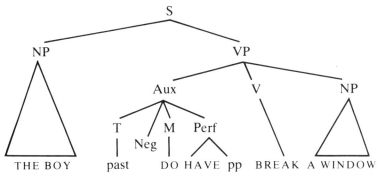

Figure 84

Neg is not moved to the second position in Aux until *pp* has been moved to the right of BREAK.

With respect to Figure 84, if affix hopping applies before DO deletion, DO is separated from Perf by T, and DO deletion does not apply.

Although the preceding paragraphs argue that Neg placement, affix hopping and DO deletion have to be ordered, the ordering applies only in the description of English offered here. In another description DO deletion might be reformulated to apply before or after affix hopping, or affix hopping might be stated so as to apply before or after Neg placement. The complexity of T-rules without ordering has to be balanced against the relative simplicity of T-rules with ordering.

The crucial point is that ordering is imposed on rules to avoid a breakdown in derivations. A common misunderstanding is occasioned by statements like the following (to be found in introductions to generative grammar): the order of transformations involved in the generation of *It was stated that a spectre was haunting Europe* is extraposition and IT insertion.

Such statements do not impose an order on these rules. In fact, there are two interpretations: one relating to the derivation of a particular sentence in the lecture room, say, and one relating to generative grammar as a device that specifies potential sentence structures. With respect to the particular sentence, the interpretation is that if it is to be generated the rules apply in a particular order, which is not the same as saying that those rules have to be specified as always applying in that order.

The grammar can be thought of as a one-armed bandit. Many different sequences of symbols can be specified but it cannot be predicted which sequence of symbols will be specified on any one run of the machine. On one run the grammar could generate *That a spectre was haunting Europe was stated by Marx*, on another run – *Marx stated that . . .* , and on a third run *It was stated by Marx that . . . .* Or the grammar will generate none of these structures on any given run. The essential point is that it has the potential to specify each of the three structures without extraposition and *It* insertion being ordered relative to each other in the list of T-rules.

The reason these rules do not need to be ordered is that *It* insertion cannot apply unless extraposition has operated. It is of course true that if the grammar does generate *It was stated by Marx that a spectre was haunting Europe* extraposition will have applied first, creating the conditions for the application of *It* insertion. What is needed is *partial* ordering of the rules.

The cycle and rule ordering – in particular, the need to order rules only to avoid a derivational breakdown – can be further illustrated by the mapping of the structure of Figure 85 into *I believe myself to be honest*.

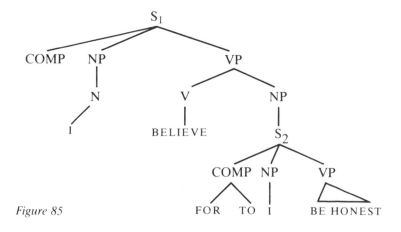

Figure 85

Subject to object raising moves the subject NP from S_2 into S_1, and reflexivization replaces the raised NP with *myself.* Do these rules need to be ordered relative to each other? They do not. Reflexivization is stated so that it applies within simple sentences.

(This reflects the accepted view of the distribution of reflexive pronouns, which does not encompass sentences like *The Prior of St Andrews, Hepburn, persuaded the canons to vote himself into the Archbishopric*.) Reflexivization cannot apply to the structure in Figure 85 as one occurrence of *I* is in S_1 and the other in S_2. Subject raising can apply and indeed creates the conditions for the operation of reflexivization.

Another, perhaps rather contrived, example demonstrates how reflexivization can apply both before and after subject to object raising. The example, taken from a textbook on transformational grammar, is: *I believe myself to have defended myself well*. The deep structure is in Figure 86.

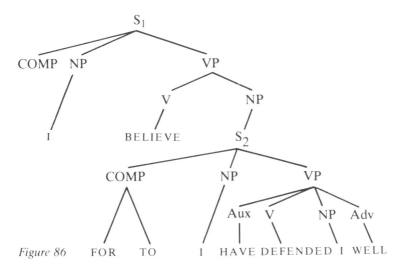

Figure 86

On the S_2 cycle reflexivization replaces the occurrence of *I* in the VP with *myself*. On the S_1 cycle subject to object raising moves the subject NP *I* from S_2 into S_1 and reflexivization replaces the raised NP with *myself*. Without the cycle it would be impossible to ensure that the two reflexive pronouns were generated, since subject raising could raise the subject NP into S_1 before S_2 had acquired its reflexive pronoun. Imposing an ordering would also be impossible, as one rule applies both before and after the other. Reflexivization could be specified to apply both within a single sentence and across sentence boundaries, but the more general or complex a rule, the greater the danger that incorrect structures will be specified. From this morass we are saved by the cycle.

A final word on the cycle and rule ordering. The two principles are independent of each other, and the amount of ordering required in a grammar depends on the analyses employed. One that uses affix hopping and the Passive T-rules requires a lot of ordering but a grammar without these rules requires very little.

Rules that have ordering imposed on them by the linguist are *extrinsically ordered*. Rules whose application is controlled by themselves are *intrinsically ordered*. For example, the PS rules on page 51 can apply only in a certain order. Rules 2, 3, etc. cannot apply before rule 1, which introduces the symbols on which they operate. After rule 1, either rule 2 or rule 3 can apply – the order is not important. The T-rules examined above, extraposition and *It* insertion, can also apply only in one order and are intrinsically ordered.

A third principle needed in transformational grammars is that of constraints on T-rules. Consider the structure of Figures 87 and 88. The structure in Figure 87 underlies *The book which my friend mentioned Tom wrote is excellent.* This relative clause structure is more complex than those on pages 61–3, for the NP identical

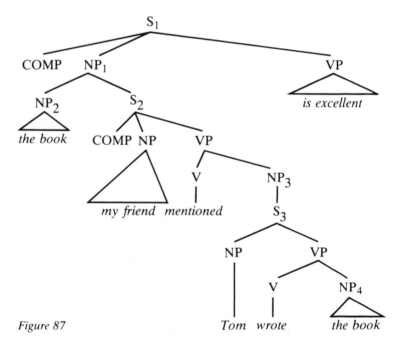

Figure 87

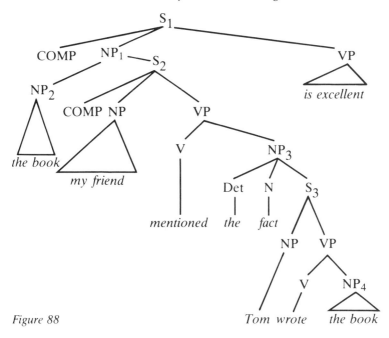

Figure 88

with the head NP, NP$_2$, is separated from it by two S nodes, S$_2$ and S$_3$. In spite of the extra S node, the relative clause T-rules derive a correct surface sentence.

The structure in Figure 88 looks the same, with the NP identical with NP$_2$ separated from it by two S nodes. One difference, however, turns out to be significant. S$_3$ is not the only constituent of the object NP in S$_2$ but is in apposition to *the fact, fact* being the head of the NP. When this structure is mapped into a surface structure, the latter is incorrect: **The book which my friend mentioned the fact that Tom wrote is excellent.*

To avoid the generation of such incorrect structures the *complex NP constraint* has been proposed. It runs: 'No element contained in a sentence dominated by a noun phrase with a lexical head noun can be moved out of that noun phrase by a transformation.' The constraint applies to the structure in Figure 88: in order to relativize the NP *the book*, that NP has to be moved out of S$_3$ to the front of S$_2$. As S$_3$ is dominated by an NP node and the head of the NP is the lexical noun *fact*, the NP *the book* is stuck in S$_3$.

Another example of a structure to which the complex NP constraint applies is: $S_1[_{NP_1}[_{NP_2}[\textit{the car}]_{NP_2}\ _{S_2}[\textit{I believed}$ $_{NP_3}[\textit{the claim}\ _{S_3}[\textit{the thief was driving the car}]_{S_3}]_{NP_3}]_{S_2}]_{NP_1}$ *was a Jaguar*$]_{S_1}$

The structure in Figure 89 presents a different problem.

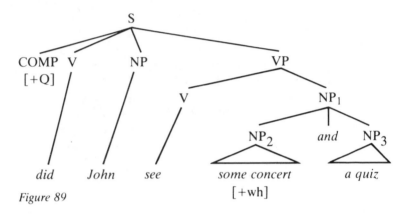

Figure 89

If the *wh* movement applies to NP_2 and moves it into the domination of COMP, an incorrect structure is generated: **Which concert did John see and a quiz?* An incorrect structure results too from the movement of NP_3 to the front but if NP_1 is moved the output is correct: *Which concert and which quiz did John see?* The constraint is the coordinate structure constraint: if there are two or more conjoined constituents (NP_2 and NP_3 in Figure 89), any rule applying to one of the conjoined constituents must also apply to the other.

The constraint applies to relative clauses. In the structure $S_1[_{NP_1}[_{NP_2}[\textit{the concert}]_{NP_2}\ _{S_2}[\textit{John saw the concert and a}$ *quiz*$]_{S_2}]_{NP_1}$*was marvellous*$]_{S_1}$ the head NP in the relative clause structure is NP_2 and the NP identical with it is conjoined with another NP: *the concert and a quiz.* If the relative clause T-rules apply, they generate a structure **The concert which John saw and a quiz was marvellous.*

It might be possible to formulate the interrogative or relative clause T-rules so that a conjoined constituent is never moved out of a coordinate structure. But this would bury among various T-rules an interesting property of all coordinate structures. It is to bring this property out into the open and to state it once and for all for every transformational rule that the coordinate structure constraint is retained.

A third constraint relates to *bounding*. Consider the structure in Figure 90.

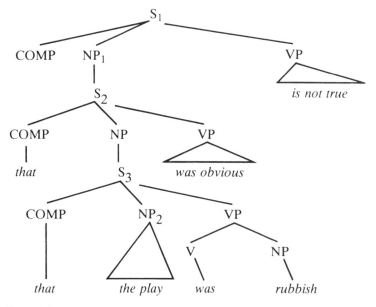

Figure 90

This tree, with one complement embedded in another, maps into the surface structure *That it was obvious that the play was rubbish is not true*. As part of the mapping, extraposition moves S_3 to the end of S_2 and the empty NP_2 node is filled by *it*. The problem is that extraposition could move S_3 to the end of S_1, deriving the incorrect **That it was obvious is not true that the play was rubbish*.

Extraposition has to be constrained so that it moves complement sentences only to the end of the next sentence up; the complements are *upward-bounded*. In a detailed account of English syntax the bounding constraint would be stated with an indication that there are constituents across which a sentence can be extraposed. Since the exact nature of these constituents does not need to be specified in all details, they would be represented by a variable, on condition that the variable does not correspond to a sequence containing more than one sentence boundary. Looked at in this way, upward bounding (and the other constraints) are constraints on variables.

The constraints mentioned in this chapter apply to the movement of constituents upwards in a phrase marker (not the coordinate structure constraint). One general intrinsic constraint, following naturally from the type of operations carried out by T-rules, is that no rule can move constituents into an S higher than the S reached at a given point in the transformational cycle. For example, the relativization rules cannot apply to the tree in Figure 87 until the cycle reaches S_1, because only there is it clear which noun in S_2 or S_3 is to be relativized.

Even when this intrinsic constraint does not apply, because a suitably high S has been reached, the upward movement of constituents is limited by the complex NP constraint and upward bounding. This aspect of transformational grammar illustrates well how several particular statements are replaced by a single general statement in the development of a theory, for these two constraints can be subsumed under a principle of *subjacency*.

It turns out that upward bounding, applying to the movement of constituents across sentences, is a particular instance of subjacency, which encompasses movement across NPs as well. The necessity for including NP nodes is demonstrated by structures like the one in Figure 91.

If no movement takes place, the structure is mapped into the structure of *The only example which this gallery possesses of Dürer's*

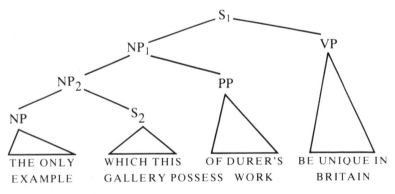

Figure 91

work is unique in Britain. If S_2 is moved out of NP_2 into NP_1, we derive the structure of *The only example of Dürer's work which this gallery possesses . . .*, but if S_2 is moved beyond NP_1 to be attached to S_1 to the right of VP we derive the incorrect structure **The only example of Dürer's work is unique in Britain which this gallery possesses.* The difficulty is that embedded Ss can be moved out of an NP and attached to the next S up in precisely this way. Consider the tree in Figure 92.

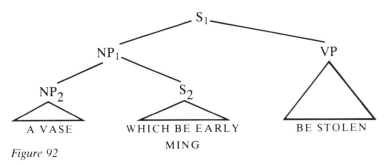

Figure 92

If no sentence is moved, we derive the structure of *A vase which was early Ming was stolen*, but S_2 can be moved out of NP_1 and attached to S_1 to the right of VP to derive the structure of *A vase was stolen which was early Ming*. That is, a sentence movement that derives incorrect structures with respect to Figure 91 derives a correct structure with respect to Figure 92. The only difference appears to be that in Figure 91 the embedded S is moved out of one NP (NP_2), then up past a second NP (NP_1) to be attached to S_1, whereas in Figure 92 the embedded S is moved out of one NP but does not ascend past any other NPs.

If NP as well as S is taken as crucial for the subjacency principle – as a *subjacency node* – a general constraint can be stated that embraces both extraposition and the rule of relative clause shift that moves S_2 in Figure 92:

1 *subjacency constraint* – a constituent cannot be moved over more than one subjacency node. S and NP are subjacency nodes.

What is interesting is that this principle can be extended to the structure in Figure 88, provided the condition is added that the configuration $_{NP}[S]_{NP}$ is ignored. In Figure 87 the NP *the book* is raised out of S_3 past NP_3 into S_2 to derive *The book which my friend mentioned that Tom wrote.* In Figure 86, however, the same movement derives **The book which my friend mentioned the fact that Tom wrote.* In Figure 87 NP_3 dominates only S (the configuration is $_{NP}[S]_{NP}$), but in Figure 88 NP_3 dominates Det N (the configuration is $_{NP}[$Det N S$]_{NP}$). Our proposed condition, 'Ignore $_{NP}[S]_{NP}$' gets rid of an extra constraint, the complex NP constraint, and avoids the awkward task of defining 'lexical head noun' in a way which can be understood by a rule, not just by a sympathetic reader.

The above constraints operate whenever a T-rule applies. It has been suggested that in addition *deep structure constraints* are required that apply to deep structures before any T-rules and *surface structure constraints* that apply to surface structures. Both these types of constraints are known as *filters*.

If constructions like *John wrote not* and *Came John to the masque?* are to be excluded rather than marked as archaic, the exclusion could be performed by either a deep or a surface structure filter. The deep structure filters are stated in **2**, the surface structure ones in **3**.

2 $*_S[($COMP$($Neg$)$ NP   V   X$]_S$
           [+Q]

3a $*_S[$COMP   V   NP   (Neg)   X$]_S$
           [+Q]

3b $*_S[$ NP   V   Neg   X$]_S$

The single deep filter is possible because the crucial constituents are adjacent, thereby enabling us to use the intersecting brackets to indicate that either COMP or Neg or both are present. As these
                    [+Q]
constituents are not adjacent in the surface structure, two filters are needed at that level. Anticipating the discussion on pages 165–6, we can say that in fact it is the surface filters that are seen as most promising because they permit significant simplification of the transformational component.

Technical terms

bounding
complex NP constraint

constraints on variables
deep structure constraint/filter
extrinsically ordered
generalized transformation
intrinsically ordered
relative clause shift
rule ordering
subjacency
subjacency node
surface structure constraint/filter
transformational cycle
traffic rules problem
upward bounding

Exercises

1

Assume the deep structures in (a) and the transformations in (b). In what order do the transformations apply to generate the structure of *Susan was shown a painting by John*?

(a) $NP(BILL) \, VP(Aux(Past\ Pass) \, V(WRITE) \, NP(THIS\ BOOK))$
 $NP(JOHN) \, VP(Aux(Past\ Pass) \, V(SHOW) \, NP(A$
 $PAINTING) \, PP(TO\ SUSAN))$

(b) Passive SA: NP   X   Pass   V   NP
 1   2   3   4   5

 SC: 5   2   3   4 $PP[P[BY]1]$

 Dative shift SA: NP_1 Aux   V   NP $PP(P(TO)$ $NP_2)$
 1   2   3   4   5   6

 SC: 1   2   3   6   4 $\emptyset$

2

Keeping in mind the principle adopted here that transformations are extrinsically ordered only if incorrect structures would otherwise be generated, consider the transformations proposed so far and determine which of them require extrinsic ordering.

11 The psychological and mathematical connections

The previous chapters treated transformational grammar as a sophisticated instrument for the description of syntax. We may not accept that the syntax of sentences should be handled solely in terms of constituents and we may be drawn towards semantics rather than pure syntax, but if we want to investigate recursion in natural language – the embedding and conjoining of sentences – we have to employ a description along the general lines developed by Harris and Chomsky.

Many linguists do not regard transformational grammar as merely a descriptive device for the use of linguists. From the beginning Chomsky has been inspired not just by sequences of constituents but also by the linguistic abilities of the native speakers of any human language. Of course, the sequences and the abilities are not unconnected. If we confine ourselves to sequences, we see that any language has a limited number of basic syntactic constructions but that the number of potential sentences is very large indeed because of the different combinations of lexical items.

The number of sentences is not just large but in principle infinite, as embedding and recursion allow an endlessly vast scaffolding of constructions. In principle, any sentence, no matter how long or complex, can be extended by the addition of *and* together with another clause. (The resulting sentence might not be stylistically perfect or easy to understand, a problem taken up later in the discussion of *competence* and *performance*.)

The connection with the abilities of native speakers lies in the fact that they operate fluently with a set of sentences (not to be confused with their utterances) so vast that for practical purposes it can be regarded as infinite. Although the human memory can store away an amazing amount of information, speakers cannot memorize each individual sentence but use a limited set of rules to produce a limitless set of sentences.

This is not to say that the making up of rules is a process of which speakers are aware nor that they are conscious of the rules. Unless a native speaker of English were a linguist who had made a study of modern English, he would not be immediately able to inform a foreigner of the rules.

Native speakers of a language do more than just produce utterances – they also understand them, that is, they relate them to sentences and make sense of the latter. In many instances speakers can even say whether they find a sentence acceptable, though there are many instances where intuitions are not clear.

It is reasonable to expect the linguist's description to match the speaker's abilities, i.e. to provide a finite set of rules generating an infinite set of sentences and distinguishing correct and incorrect sentences. There is no need to suppose that the linguist's description has anything to do with the way in which speakers store their (unconscious) knowledge. The claim is only that the linguist's description should match the speaker's in capacity, though even this relatively modest claim raises problems, which relate to the topics mentioned earlier of competence and performance.

The formalism of generative grammar comes from a part of mathematical logic dealing with the theory of *abstract automata*. The basic ideas of this theory are quite simple. Let us assume that there is a box B inside which there is a man M with a desk, paper and pencils. On one side of B there are two slots, one marked *input*, the other *output*. If a number is written on a piece of paper that is pushed through thè input slot, M takes it and performs certain computations. If and when he finishes, he writes down the number obtained from the computation on a different piece of paper and pushes that through the output slot.

We also assume that M has a set of explicit instructions as to how the computation is to be done. These instructions can be denoted by P. We also have to assume that B can be enlarged to hold any amount of paper, and that M is inexhaustible and has a constant supply of electric light, etc.; it is not important how long it takes an answer to appear.

The system B-M-P is referred to as R.

Let us suppose that M is applying the function $f_1(x) = 2x$. That is, a numerical replacement for x is written on the piece of paper pushed through the input slot and M multiples the input by 2. In addition, M has explicit instructions about the steps in the computation, very simple in the case of multiplication by 2.

A more complex function is $f_2(x) =$ the xth digit in the decimal expansion of π. Again it is simple to provide instructions, though they are longer than the list for the first function.

Next consider the function [$f_3(x) = 1$ if a run of *exactly* x successive 7s occurs somewhere in the decimal expansion of π; $f_3(x) = 0$ otherwise]. It is not known whether finite instructions exist for computing this function.

The questions investigated in this branch of mathematical logic concern what constitutes admissible instructions P, and how the behaviour of M is to depend on P. These questions lead to others, such as whether a list of instructions exists for every function. Attempts to resolve the first question, about admissible instructions, have all involved a finite alphabet of symbols and precise rules for making arbitrarily long formulae with the symbols, and an admissible P has been taken to be any finite sequence of formulae from the symbols.

The behaviour of M has usually involved operations such as writing down symbols, moving one symbol at a time backward or forward in the computation, moving backwards or forwards in P, and operations for transcribing or ejecting from B a possible answer or output number. M is usually endowed with a finite short-term memory that at any point in the computation preserves symbols written or examined on certain preceding operations.

The finite alphabet of symbols corresponds to the vocabulary of the grammar, e.g. S, NP, $\rightarrow$ and the rules for making arbitrarily long formulae correspond to the rules for rewriting symbols as one or more symbols.

That there should be these correspondences is not surprising. What Chomsky (and Harris and Hockett before him) saw as desirable was that an explicit grammar should specify or generate all the correct sentences of a language and none of the incorrect ones. Just as a function like [$f_1(x) = 2x$] is described by mathematicians as generating a set of numbers, $\{0, 2, 4, 6, 8, \ldots\}$ if x is a non-negative integer, so a grammar can be thought of as a function that generates a set of sentences. The problem is then to develop a set of procedures for computing the function, i.e. for generating the sentences; Chomsky had the inspiration to turn to the field of abstract automata and the ability to modify and extend the available procedures to handle natural language.

Once a set of procedures has been established for generating the correct sentences of a language, they can be used to determine whether a given sequence of surface forms constitutes a correct sentence, i.e. whether it can be generated by the grammar along with a correct structure. Similarly, the procedures for computing functions in mathematics can be used to determine whether a given number can be generated by a given function.

A set of objects, e.g. numbers, that can be enumerated but for which there exists no procedure for determining whether a given object is a member of the set or not is a *recursively enumerable set*. A set of objects for which such a procedure does exist is called a *recursive set*. Functions for which a finite list of computational procedures exists are *recursive functions*. For this reason it is sometimes said that generative grammars draw their formalism from the theory of recursive functions (or from the theory of abstract automata).

What is the significance of the latter name? Sets of procedures P and the behaviour of M are referred to as 'machines on paper'. In fact, one of the earliest sets of procedures, developed by a British mathematician Turing, is known as a Turing machine. ('Automaton' is equivalent to 'machine'.) The automata are abstract because they are confined to paper, and are not instructions for working actual machines.

We have already referred to Chomsky's interest in the linguistic abilities of human beings, in connection with which he introduced the notions of *competence* and *performance*. On the first page of Chomsky's *Aspects of the Theory of Syntax* is this sentence: 'Linguistic theory is concerned primarily with an ideal speaker–listener, in a completely homogeneous speech-community, who knows its language perfectly and is unaffected by such grammatically irrelevant conditions as memory limitations, distractions, shifts of attention and interest, and errors (random or characteristic) in applying his knowledge of the language in actual performance.'

He goes on: 'A grammar of a language purports to be a description of the ideal speaker-hearer's intrinsic competence . . . . A fully adequate grammar must assign to each of an infinite range of sentences a structural description indicating how this sentence is understood by the ideal speaker-hearer.'

The reservation about 'grammatically irrelevant conditions' is already familiar from the discussion of idealization in BM (pages 12–14) but the 'ideal speaker–hearer' is new. One persistent but mistaken view is that such a grammar describes how people set about producing or understanding utterances. This view is wrong, but Chomsky does see a generative grammar as describing the knowledge that the ideal speaker–hearer possesses of his native language.

Generative grammar possesses to a certain extent some of the properties to be found in speakers – the ability to generate or specify an infinite set of sentences and to recognize incorrect sentences – but, as said earlier, there is no need to suppose that speakers store their knowledge in exactly the way information is stored in a generative grammar. Indeed, the concept of the ideal speaker–hearer is not only unnecessary but erroneous.

Over the past fifteen years much work has been done by psycholinguists to find out to what extent a correspondence can be established between generative descriptions of English and the competence of real speakers of the language, insofar as the latter can be inferred from the behaviour of informants during experiments.

It is now recognized that there are no grounds for assuming that, e.g. transformations, are psychologically real. A retreat has been made to the more modest view that it is surface structures that are psychologically real. Unfortunately, no experimental evidence clearly indicates any psychological reality for deep structures.

While it is not surprising that surface constituents like NPs appear to be psychologically real, many linguists hold that there is more to syntax than just sequences of constituents. There are also dependencies between constituents, which are not well handled by Chomskyan grammar. There is the lack of good distributional evidence for VPs, and there is the view that the verb is the central or governing constituent in a sentence.

There is no space here to go into the details of the various arguments. What is important is that there are other conceptions of syntactic structure than that embodied in Chomskyan generative grammar and that it is a good deal premature for a theory that talks only about sequences of constituents to be thought of as describing the ideal speaker–hearer's competence.

These difficulties with competence are not lessened by the various changes within the Chomskyan model, which lead one to ask exactly which version of the model is to be taken as the description of competence. The Chomskyan model has introduced a radical change in the concepts of endocentric and exocentric constructions (BM, pages 253–60). The classical conception is that if a construction has the same distribution as its head, the construction is endocentric. A construction without a head is exocentric. NPs and APs are endocentric; VPs and PPs are exocentric.

Now all constructions are analysed as endocentric, not on the basis of distribution but on the grounds that every construction has a characteristic constituent. On this view the head of a VP is a V and the head of a PP is a P. This change in the treatment of constructions is important, especially as the new approach, taken a step further, shows that the head or central constituent in a sentence is the V, but it is not explicitly discussed. It affects the notion of competence because it is essential to know whether the distinction between endocentric and exocentric constructions has any psychological reality. If it has, Chomsky's notion of competence needs revision. Even if the distinction has no psychological reality, Chomsky's notions need examination, because we then get into the verb-central question.

Another question relating to competence concerns its nature and scope. One of the abilities of the mature native speaker is to produce utterances appropriate to the situation and any theory of competence must be capable of correlating situations and sentences. This is an argument not against Chomsky's work but in support of extending his grammar.

A weightier objection to his notion of competence arises from the observations about the lack of psychological reality for transformations. The relevant concept is that of *adequacy*, which can be explained with respect to *John is easy to please* and *John is eager to please*. A grammar that attains *observational adequacy* merely states that these sequences are correct. A grammar that attains *descriptive adequacy* states that the sequences are correct but it also provides the information that *John* is the direct object of *please* in the first sentence but the subject of *please* in the second sentence.

The grammar that attains *explanatory adequacy* goes beyond the other grammars, because it not only provides the information conveyed by them, it also relates the structures of the two sentences to other structures such as *John's eagerness to please*, **John's easiness to please*, *It is easy to please John*, **It is eager to please John*.

This sort of explanatory adequacy can be called *internal explanatory adequacy*, to distinguish it from another aspect of explanatory adequacy that is even more important for Chomsky. For him, the construction of grammars is far removed from the activity of the linguist describing data and his intuitions about it. Chomsky assumes that the concepts of grammatical structure and significant generalization used in generative grammar are the tools used by the child learning its native language (or, as Chomsky puts it: 'constructing an internal representation of his language . . . on the basis of presented linguistic data').

Chomsky further assumes that the child has a linguistic theory that specifies the layout of possible grammars and a strategy for choosing one grammar rather than another. Looking at grammars from this standpoint and distinguishing between generative grammars as descriptions of data written within the generative framework, Chomsky further stipulates that generative grammar as a general theory attains explanatory adequacy if it constrains the layout of possible grammars so that the child chooses only a grammar that accounts for relations between different constructions. This can be called *external explanatory adequacy*. A particular grammar attains explanatory adequacy if it is preferred to other grammars by the explanatory general theory.

We need not be concerned with what constitutes good grounds for preferring one grammar to another if both relate structures. The problem comes under the heading of *evaluation*, and a term much bandied about in this connection is *simplicity*. It can be given two interpretations. A trivial and literal one takes into account the number of rules in a grammar or the number of symbols in each rule; and a more interesting interpretation equates 'simplicity' and 'generality', i.e. the amount of data covered and the number of generalizations.

This excursus on adequacy has come back to a point where we can cross back to competence. If we take the moderate view that generative grammar is a sophisticated instrument with which the linguist describes language, talk of different levels of adequacy is wholly appropriate. It is the duty of the linguist to reveal as many inner relations as possible and to make the greatest number of interesting general statements consonant with the data. It is desirable to have a general theory of grammar that obliges linguists to write such grammars. For the extreme view held by Chomsky the notions of evaluation and simplicity are less useful, for there is not the slightest ground for supposing that native speakers strive towards the generality and elegance prized by linguists. Studies of children learning their native language have yielded no evidence that these criteria are important and sometimes provide evidence that allows the investigator to infer rules of a rather untidy and particular nature.

It has been remarked that if the analogy of the brain as a computer is pursued, two sorts of economy can be discerned. One is economy of storage, which is the goal of generative linguists, who store lexical items in a highly abstract form and relate one item to several morphs by complex rules. The second economy is in the looking up of lexical items, and it is precisely this task that is made difficult by that type of storage. Economy can be won here by storing lexical items in a fairly concrete form. That is, instead of one abstract item, each address in the dictionary contains as many items as there are related surface morphs (see pages 133–48 on the extended lexicon) together with information about the environment in which each morph occurs.

Such a treatment of lexical items, unacceptable to many linguists within transformational grammar, is very plausible in the light of what is known about the human memory with its capacity for rote learning. This is not to deny that human beings make up rules – there is plenty of evidence for this – but their rules seem to be low-level rules of the sort used in the extended lexicon (for which no psychological reality is claimed) rather than complex rules relating, e.g., *opaque* and *opacity*.

These considerations cast doubt on the notion that a generative grammar describes the competence of an ideal speaker–hearer. The weaker view, that it is a method of description of data, is less exciting but arouses less controversy and avoids many pitfalls. It is probable that if the notion of competence had never appeared generative grammar would have aroused far less hostility inside and outside linguistics, for it is an excellent way of handling embedding and conjoining in natural language.

The final topic in this chapter is the nature of T-rules. T-rules have been talked of as though they carried out operations: moving constituents, deleting constituents, adjoining new constituents. The feeling that operations are performed is reinforced by the term 'generate', which most non-mathematicians interpret as equivalent to 'create', though it is taken by mathematicians in the static sense of 'be associated with or related to'.

When the notion of transformation was introduced into linguistics by Harris it had the static interpretation. How is a static T-rule to be understood? Consider subject–verb inversion. On the static interpretation it says that a phrase marker that can be analysed into an NP, a V and some other constituents is related to a phrase marker in which the order of the NP and V is reversed.

The assumption lying behind this conception of T-rules is that phrase markers are created elsewhere, and T-rules are checking devices that inspect pairs of phrase markers to see if the members of each pair are indeed related. PS rules too can be considered as a checking device. The rule S → NP VP, for instance, can be read as an instruction that the phrase marker that is presented first for checking must contain an S as the topmost node, with two nodes, labelled NP and VP, immediately below it.

Another possibility, compatible with the static interpretation, is that there is an existing stock of syntactic structures (which are not being manufactured elsewhere) and that the rules define various paths through the structures. (Remember that the rules are not supposed to mention specific lexical items.) The PS rules on this view specify what the starting point of a journey can be – any phrase marker not meeting the specifications laid down in the PS rules cannot be a starting point – and the T-rules indicate which phrase markers can be reached from any given phrase marker, without saying how it can be reached.

That it is the static interpretation of T-rules that is the basis of Chomsky's work is indicated by his talk of grammars as specifying or characterizing the sentences of a language and of T-rules as expressing relations between sentences. In the work of other linguists in the generative framework, however, the static vocabulary is replaced by dynamic vocabulary, with T-rules described as carrying out operations and producing derived phrase markers.

The use of dynamic vocabulary has been dismissed by one linguist (Kimball) as merely figurative speech, simply a manner of talking that should not be taken literally. (This applies to any dynamic expressions in this book.) It is true that operations are logically equivalent to relations, since, to borrow an example from Hockett, the binary operation of addition by which $2 + 3 = 5$ can be interpreted as a ternary relation holding between the ordered triad of numbers (2,3,5). Hockett comments further: 'Relations seem static, whereas operations seem dynamic – seem to generate something which we perhaps did not know was there.'

The use of dynamic vocabulary is so widespread that one might suspect that there is indeed a dynamic conception of T-rules even if various linguists had not in the past two or three years stated explicitly that there are two conceptions. The static one has been described above and the dynamic one regards PS rules as creating or building up phrase markers from the initial symbol and T-rules as creating new phrase markers out of the basic ones.

The distinction between static and dynamic conceptions stems from an ambiguity in the status of abstract automata. These are considered by some to be mere machines on paper expressing relationships between, e.g., a function and a set of numbers, without any connection with real-time machines. Another interpretation is that they are closely connected with computing procedures. The author of one paper on Turing machines describes himself as investigating 'operations of the sort performable by digital computers under explicit deterministic programmes of instructions' and another linguist (Sampson, on p. 169 of his book *The Form of Language*) explains 'automaton' as denoting an abstract entity that is related to a computer in the way that, e.g., a mathematical function is related to the line on the graph paper used to represent that function. A computer is a physical realization of the kind of mathematical system called an automaton.

The interpretation of generative grammars as creating structure is parallel to the interpretation of abstract automata as specifying procedures that can be realized as computer procedures.

One problem is that generative grammars of the sort outlined here are not satisfactory as specifications of procedures. When attempts were made to realize sets of rules as computer programs in order to test the grammar for consistency, the rules had to be supplemented by special rules ensuring that, e.g., in relative structures once a particular NP had been generated an identical NP would be generated inside the embedded S. Without such extra rules there is no guarantee that there will be an NP in the embedded S identical with the head NP and a new start, using up expensive computer time, has to be made. If the rules are merely checking already created structures, a phrase marker that fails to meet the SA of the relative clause T-rules is rejected, without cost, and the next pair of phrase markers comes up for inspection.

We have covered a number of very important topics rather briefly to show reasons why generative grammar has attracted a lot of attention over the last twenty years and why it continues to attract attention. To round off the discussion two observations are in order. The first is that, in spite of critical remarks about the alleged psychological reality of transformations, there is a relationship between linguistics and psychology. There is no dispute about the psychological reality of some concepts in phonology nor of certain surface constituent structures. The various analyses of surface syntax by linguists provide hypotheses for psychologists to test, and the relationships that linguists reveal are often such that the linguistically untutored speaker must also be aware of them. The question is how?, which affords more material for the psychologist. Even more interesting is semantics, and here too syntax (and morphology) is important, since not only synchronic syntax and morphology but historical changes in those parts of language systems afford clues to semantic structure and the way speakers perceive the world.

The second point is shorter but perhaps more important. In order to discuss the large issues with any understanding it is essential to persevere with and master the details of generative descriptions of some areas of some language.

Technical terms

abstract automata
competence
descriptive adequacy
evaluation
external explanatory adequacy
internal explanatory adequacy
machine on paper
observational adequacy
performance
recursive function
recursive set
recursively enumerable set
simplicity

12 Extending the lexicon

The purpose of this part of the book is to show how, within the same framework, different analyses can be developed of the same areas of syntax and the function of each component in the grammar can be modified. Chapters 12–14 deal with specific areas of English (though much of what is said about the functions of each component in the grammar is valid with respect to other languages), and chapter 15 provides an overview and critique of the modifications.

Let us begin the review with affix hopping (page 36). The conditions attaching to this rule reveal one source of complexity, namely the involvement of several different categories. Moreover, the operation itself is complex, including not just the permuting of two constituents but the creation of extra structure by Chomsky-adjunction. Whenever a T-rule creates extra structure it is worth asking whether the analysis is adequate. Finally, just what is the status of the boundary symbol – constituent, or symbol that makes a bad rule work? – and exactly where it is to be attached in phrase markers?

Another objection to affix hopping is that it deals with the internal structure of words, the duplication of constituents being caused by the desire to show explicitly that a form like *played* consists of a base and a suffix, and realizes a lexeme and a grammatical morpheme. The rule cuts across the distinction drawn in BM between syntax and morphology: do the complexities of the rule arise from ignoring a distinction that was held to be valid and valuable?

In the face of such objections, we should remind ourselves of the facts that the rule was devised to capture. In English the morph realizing Tense always occurs at the end of the first constituent in the verb sequence. Forms of the progressive BE are always followed by a verb base plus *ing*, and forms of HAVE are always followed (except for irregular verbs) by a verb base plus *ed* (in the written language).

These facts are captured by affix hopping and in a very direct fashion. Tense is a separate constituent that is moved into whatever constituent is immediately to its right. BE and *ing*, HAVE and *pp* start out dominated by a single node, Prog and Perf respectively, with *ing* and *pp* being moved round whatever constituent is to their right. Another analysis might not achieve such directness, but is there any other means in a generative grammar for expressing the facts expressed by affix hopping?

Now there are other aspects of the analysis requiring further consideration. One of the complexities in affix hopping is that the same operation is applied to different pairs of constituents, but this reflects a decision to regard these constituents as different and to give them different labels.

We can begin by examining the labels. Traditional grammar talked of 'auxiliary verbs' – verbs whose particular function in a sentence was to help the main verb. The main verb denotes an action whereas the auxiliary verbs merely convey information as to whether the action is completed (perfective) or still in progress (progressive), whether it is definitely taking place or is only a possibility (DO, MAY, CAN). The syntactic corollary of the semantic facts is that sentences have to contain a main verb, whereas auxiliary verbs are optional constituents.

Generative grammar has taken over the label 'Auxiliary' for the node that holds together the constituents in the verb sequence other than the main verb. The auxiliary constituents do not occur in random order – if there is a modal verb it has to occur first, if there is a form of HAVE it has to occur immediately after the modal verb and before any form of BE – and these are the reasons why these constituents are regarded as different and given different labels. The latter make it simple to write a PS rule that lines up the major auxiliary constituents in the correct order (Aux → T (M) (Perf) (Prog)) and to write a T-rule that shifts the affixes into their correct position.

The interesting thing is that the labels do not contain the term 'VERB'. 'Modal' relates to the meaning of the class of verbs it labels, and 'Perfective' and 'Progressive' relate to the meaning of the construction in which they occur. What is missing is an indication that the constituents concerned are verbs; indeed it is as though we used completely different categories like AnimateConcrete or ConcreteHuman instead of using features like [+Animate] on nouns. Of course, there is no ordering problem with the nouns, but their example does suggest that 'Modal', 'Progressive' and 'Perfective' be relegated to features distinguishing different types of verb, all with the feature [+Aux].

With respect to morphology there is no doubt that the modals, HAVE and BE are verbs, though it is not so clear that they are verbs with respect to their syntactic properties, i.e. with respect to the word classes or sequences of word classes they combine with. Only the modals cause real difficulties, since they do not combine with nouns or adjectives but only with HAVE, BE or a main verb (*He may have written, He should be ready, He can write*). HAVE and BE combine, as the only verb in a sentence, with noun phrases, BE combines with adjectives (compare verbs like SEEM, GROW, BECOME) and both HAVE and BE occur in the progressive (*He has a car, He is an idiot, He is foolish, We are having the annual inspection tomorrow, He is being an idiot.*) Neither typically occur in the passive, but they are not alone in this respect: *His mother was resembled by her two daughters, *An idiot was seemed by him.*

These facts suggest that the auxiliaries be viewed as verbs marked [+Aux] and that their lexical entries contain the appropriate feature [+Modal], [+Progressive] or [+Perfective]. But if CAN, HAVE and BE are all verbs there is no way in which a PS rule can ensure that they occur in the correct order. That is true, but ordering is a co-occurrence relation; for example, in *might have been wrong*, *might* can be described as co-occurring with *have* to its right, *have* as co-occurring with *might* to its left and *been* to its right, and co-occurrence relations are exactly what the strict subcategorization and selectional features express. This being so, there is no reason why the VP should not be regarded as containing a series of verbs, the correct order being achieved by the lexeme-insertion rules.

This solution entails changes in the description of the relationship between lexemes and grammatical morphemes on the one hand and morphs and word forms on the other. According to the proposals of BM lexemes are inserted into phrase markers and combinations of lexeme and grammatical morphemes are spelt out as word forms by the orthographic rules after the T-rules have applied.

Being T-rules, the orthographic rules could spell out sequences of morphemes as single morphs (see pages 55–6). The deep structure contained, e.g., a progressive construction with the morphemes BE and *ing*, which was then moved, but under the new proposal that the VP contain a series of verbs it is not possible to say that one verb is BE and *ing* and another verb is WRITE. We are obliged to list the actual forms of the lexeme in the lexical entry and insert the appropriate form into a given environment. For example, *writing* is the form of WRITE that occurs in the frames [*was* __], [*is* __] etc. and *written* is the form that occurs in the frames [*have* __], [*had* __], etc. *Write* is the form that is inserted in the frames [*can* __], [*should* __], [*they* __], etc.

Some simplification is required if each entry is not to contain a forbiddingly long list of frames. For instance, it appears that all the forms of FRIGHTEN will have inherent, strict subcategorization and selectional features, and similarly for all the forms of HAVE, BE and the modals. (Incidentally, these features, in addition to their role in the statement of co-occurrence restrictions, could also play a role when the description of syntax is associated with a description of meaning, since they could be considered as signals that direct the semantic description to the appropriate semantic structure for a given syntactic structure.)

One important fact of English needs to be described in terms of the new proposal, the marking of Tense on whatever verb is first in the verb sequence. The moveable-Tense analysis is not available, but in any case that was associated with a different view of the verb phrase. If we say 'Tense is marked on the first constituent in the verb phrase' we are led to think of Tense as a separate constituent added to something else, whereas if we say 'verb lexemes have various forms and only those forms occur in first position in the verb phrase that realize a lexeme and Tense' we think of choosing from a set of forms the forms appropriate to a particular environment.

For example, in the lexical entry for RUN are the forms *ran*, *run*, *runs* and *running*. The first three forms have the inherent feature [±Past]; it has a syntactic role, in that it could be used to generate correct combinations of verb and adverb, and also a semantic role, since it could be used as a signpost for the rules that correlate syntactic structure with semantic ones. *Run* occurs twice in the lexical entry, once with the feature [+Past] and once without.

There is also the problem of number. The traditional view, that verbs agree in number with their subject noun, is embodied in the verb number agreement rule (page 53), but this rule cannot be used either, as it presupposes that lexemes are inserted into phrase markers, that features are copied from one lexeme to another and that lexemes and features are spelled out as word forms. The new proposal has word forms inserted directly, which excludes the agreement rule but does allow the use of selectional features.

The relationship between verb and noun with respect to number can be considered parallel to that with respect to animacy. What is at issue is not merely whether a verb co-occurs with an object noun but what type of object and subject nouns it requires, and the notion of 'type' can be extended from the familiar properties of animacy, abstractness, etc. to the property of number. Selectional features already indicate whether a subject noun is animate, human or inanimate, abstract, etc. and can easily indicate whether a subject noun is singular or plural. When a verb form is inserted into a phrase marker its selectional features are transferred to the appropriate N nodes, with the result that only a noun with, e.g., [+Human] in its lexical entry can be attached to an N node that has received that feature from a verb. In the same way, when a verb form *runs* is inserted the feature [+sg] is transferred to the subject N node, which can thereafter be filled only with singular forms like *boy*, *dog*.

As this account of verb number agreement will seem strange to readers thirled to traditional grammars of English, it is worthwhile emphasizing that from a *syntactic* point of view it could be said that the verb determines the number of the noun. From a *semantic* point of view, of course, number is a property of objects, and since nouns denote objects number must be an inherent property of nouns. Such are the assumptions of traditional grammar. Here we are concerned with describing syntax in its own terms. The syntactic facts of English do not decide between the two views of verb–noun agreement, but our framework does permit a decision. The remodelling of the lexicon obliges us to use selectional features to handle number, and since we have decided to transfer features from verbs to nouns the feature [±sg] is also transferred.

Before looking at detailed lexical entries, let us sum up the new proposals.

1 The lexicon contains an entry for each lexeme in the sense that, e.g., RUN is the heading for an entry that contains all the associated orthographic forms.

2   The Aux constituent has been abandoned, along with Modal, Progressive, Perfective and Tense. Instead, the VP contains a sequence of verbs and the strict subcategorisation frames specify the correct order.
3   Number agreement between verb and noun is handled by specifying in the selectional feature for each verb form whether the subject noun is singular or plural.

Although the lexicon is given a bigger role, we avoid the complexity of affix hopping. The lexical entries contain more detail but the devices by which the details are specified are required anyway. This is important with respect to the overall complexity of the grammar because it means that new devices are not invented to bolster the new analysis of VP and two awkward T-rules are dropped. Furthermore, the power of the grammar is not increased and the way is not opened to many different analyses of the same data (page 163).

Note that the verb number agreement rules on page 53 are awkward because they handle an awkward phenomenon. Number agreement does not affect modal verbs nor the past tense forms of any verb except BE, and these facts are now easily captured in the selectional features for verbs.

It was said above that the lexical entry for RUN contained the form *runs* but this statement is misleading. Consider the entry for FRIGHTEN, which should, according to that statement, contain the forms *frightens*, *frighten*, *frightened* and *frightening*. If all these separate forms are listed, and all the corresponding forms of all the other regular verbs in English, not only is the lexicon very bulky but several generalizations are lost. For instance, there is a general rule that *s* is added to the base forms of English verbs in order to derive past-tense forms and *ing* to derive present participles.

These generalizations can be stated if the lexicon contains a set of rules for handling word structure. The forms of FRIGHTEN can be derived thus. The lexical entry contains the base form *frighten* and various sets of features. If the inherent feature [+Past] is in the set chosen, *frighten* is not inserted directly into the phrase marker but is first passed through a rule that adds *-ed*. If [−Past] is chosen, another rule applies to add *-s* (provided the feature [+sg] is present). If the strict subcategorization feature [+[V__]]
[+Prog]
is present, the base form is subjected to a rule that adds *-ing*.

Once the appropriate rule has applied, the derived form is inserted into the phrase marker. The fact that, e.g., *played* consists of two morphs is captured but is not reflected in the phrase marker. Instead the information has to be retrieved from the derivational history of the sentence and the information as to which morphemes are realized by which morphs has to be obtained by inspecting the features in the lexical entries and the morphological rules.

Since one consequence of increasing the work of the lexicon is to make lexical entries more complicated, let us consider how the entries can be kept simple. One way is to distinguish features that apply to every form of a lexeme from features that apply to only one form, and to establish a convention that the first sort of feature is stated immediately under the lexeme, i.e. the general heading of the entry, and is picked up by each form before it is inserted into a phrase marker.

For example, every form of FRIGHTEN has the feature $[-\text{Aux}]$, which therefore need be stated only once. Both forms of CAN occur before a verb, i.e. have the feature $[+ _{VP}[\_\_V\ X]]$, which can be stated once as a feature of the lexeme rather than as a feature of each of the two forms.

Unfortunately the distinction between features of a lexeme and features of a single form is not always easy to apply. For reasons explained in the following chapter, past participles passive like *frightened* are analysed in this revised grammar as adjectives and the Passive T-rule is jettisoned. This means that all forms of FRIGHTEN have the category feature $[+\text{V}]$ except *frightened*, which has $[+\text{A}]$. Moreover, every form of FRIGHTEN has an animate object noun with the exception of *frightened*, which has an animate *subject* noun.

Does the existence of the single maverick form oblige us to state the selectional feature $[+[\_\_\text{Det}\ _N[+\text{Animate}]]]$ several times, once for *frighten*, once for *frightens*, etc.? Or can we retain the idea of stating certain features only once in the whole lexical entry? The latter is possible if a second convention is accepted to the effect that the category feature for a lexeme can be overridden by a category feature attached to one of the forms in the lexical entry with the lexeme as its address. By extending the convention to other kinds of features, the lexeme FRIGHTEN can have the features $[+\text{V}]$ and $[+[\_\_\text{Det}\ _N[+\text{Animate}]]]$ and the form *frightened* can have $[+\text{A}]$ and $[+[\text{Det}\ _N[+\text{Animate}]\_\_]]$.

We have to balance the complexity of the extended lexicon against the simplification of the transformational component. The next chapter will show strong distributional reasons for treating the past participle passive as an adjective, and in any case the extra convention does permit the lexical entry to be kept simple.

Another way to achieve simplicity is to employ redundancy rules (page 42). Let us assume first that the lexicon contains the three morphological rules in **1** that add the appropriate suffix to a base form.

1   Rule 1: $X \Rightarrow X$ *ed*
        Rule 2: $X \Rightarrow X$ *ing*
        Rule 3: $X \Rightarrow X$ *s*

Corresponding to these rules are the features [+Rule 1], etc. and a rule applies only if the lexical entry contains the correct rule feature. In many cases the rule feature does not need to be listed in the lexical entry but can be added by a redundancy rule. For instance, *s* is added to a verb base only if the verb is non-past and singular. This can be expressed by the rule **2i** which says that if the features [−Past] and [+sg] are present, the feature [+Rule 3] can be added. Rule **2ii** says that a form that is to be inserted to the right of the progressive BE has the suffix *-ing*. Rule **2iii** says that *-ed* is added by Rule 1 if the verb is past tense, and rule **2iv** says that *-ed* is also added if the form is to be inserted to the right of the perfect. For all non-auxiliary verbs the feature [+sg] or [−sg] is relevant only if the verb is non-past, which is expressed by rule **2v**.

2   Redundancy rules

i $[-\text{Past}] \ \& \ [+\text{sg}] \Rightarrow [+\text{Rule } 3]$

ii $[+[\begin{smallmatrix} \text{V} \\ +\text{Prog} \end{smallmatrix} \quad \underline{\quad} \ (\text{NP})]] \Rightarrow [+\text{Rule } 2]$

iii $[+\text{Past}] \Rightarrow [+\text{Rule } 1]$

iv $[+[\begin{smallmatrix} \text{V} \\ +\text{Perf} \end{smallmatrix} \quad \underline{\quad} \ (\text{NP})]] \Rightarrow [+\text{Rule } 1]$

v $[-\text{Past}] \ \& \ [-\text{Aux}] \Rightarrow [\pm\text{sg}]$

vi $[+\text{A}] \ \& \ [-\text{Aux}] \Rightarrow [+\text{Rule } 1]$

A saving can also be made with respect to the subcategorization frames. As things stand, FRIGHTEN has the lexical entry in **3**.

3
$$\text{FRIGHTEN}$$
$$[+V]$$
$$[-\text{Aux}]$$
$$[+[\_\_\text{Det }_N[\ +\text{Animate}]]]$$

frighten **a** $[+[\ \ \ \ V\ \ \ \_\_\ \ \ \ NP]]$ **b** $[+\ _{VP}[\_\_\ \ NP]]$
    $[+\text{Modal}]$

  c $[+[\ V\ \_\_\ NP]]$ **d** $[+[\ \ \ \ V\ \ \ \ \_\_\ \ \ \ NP]]$
    $[+\text{Prog}]$ $[+\text{Perf}\_\_]$

  e $[+A]$
    $[+[\text{Det }_N[+\text{Animate}]\_\_\ ]]$

This entry says that the base *frighten* occurs in various environments and the redundancy rules add information about which morphological rules apply in which environment. One difficulty is that all the subcategorization frames **a–d** have to be stated in the entry for each lexeme, which misses the generalization that every regular verb in English has these frames. The generalization can be captured if the features $[+V]$ and $[-\text{Aux}]$ are taken as predicting the subcategorization frames. In the entries for, e.g., RUN and CUT, the irregular past tense and past participle forms are listed separately along with the frames and the redundancy rules will supply these entries only with the remaining frames.

The generalization that tensed forms occur only in first position in VP can be captured by allowing $[+\ _{VP}[\_\_NP]]$ to predict $[\pm\text{Past}]$ for non-auxiliary verbs and by allowing $[+\ _{VP}[\_\_V]]$ to predict $[\pm\text{Past}]$ for auxiliary verbs. Both predicting features indicate that the form occurs in first position in VP and no other frame predicts $[\pm\text{Past}]$. The generalization is not captured so clearly for irregular verbs, in whose entries the above features are listed separately, but at least the tense feature appears only with the subcategorization frame in which the verb is in first position in VP. The extra redundancy rules are given in **4**.

4

i $[+V]$ & $[-Aux] \Rightarrow [+[\quad\quad V\quad\quad \_\_ NP]]$
$\qquad\qquad\qquad\qquad [+Modal]$

$\quad$ & $[+ _{VP}[\quad \_\_ NP]]$ & $[+ _{VP}[\quad V\quad \_\_ NP]]$
$\qquad\qquad\qquad\qquad\qquad\qquad\qquad\quad [+Prog]$

$\quad$ & $[+ _{VP}[\quad V\quad \_\_ NP]]$
$\qquad\qquad\quad [+Perf]$

ii $[-Aux]$ & $[+ _{VP}[\quad \_\_ NP]] \Rightarrow [\pm Past]$

iii $[+Aux]$ & $[+ _{VP}[\quad \_\_ V]] \Rightarrow [\pm Past]$

One more generalization must be made. The vast majority of transitive verbs in English can occur in the passive construction. For these verbs a redundancy rule $[+V]$, $[+[\_\_Det$ $_N[+Animate]]] \rightarrow [+A]$, $[+[Det _N[+Animate]X\_\_]]$ (to take the frame for FRIGHTEN) adds the appropriate category feature (passive participles being treated as adjectives) and selectional feature. The above redundancy rule is called up by $[+Passive]$, while the entries for the verbs that cannot occur in the passive contain $[-Passive]$. This is an arbitrary way to block undesirable passives but with our present knowledge of the passive in English the verbs that cannot occur in the passive seem to have nothing in common semantically or syntactically. As the passive forms of irregular verbs are listed in the lexicon, a convention is needed whereby the redundancy rule does not add $[+A]$ to a lexical entry already containing $[+A]$ but merely fills in the selectional feature.

The lexical entry for FRIGHTEN is now as in **5**.

5 $\qquad\qquad\qquad$ FRIGHTEN
$\qquad\qquad\qquad$ *frighten*
$\qquad\qquad\qquad$ $[+V]$
$\qquad\qquad\qquad$ $[-Aux]$
$\qquad\qquad\qquad$ $[+[\_\_ Det _N[+Animate]]]$

Redundancy rule **4i** adds the subcategorization frames, **4ii** adds the tense feature to give the sets of features in **3**. The rules in **2** then add the remaining necessary features. The passive redundancy rule copies the occurrence of *frighten* and assigns it $[+A]$ and the subcategorization frame.

It was suggested earlier (page 137) that number agreement between noun and verb be handled by a feature being imposed on the subject noun from the verb, which is done by selectional frames that must now be specified. The frames required are $[+[\text{Det}\ _N[+sg]\underline{\quad}]]$ and $[+[\text{Det}\ _N[-sg]\underline{\quad}]]$. They are not listed in lexical entries but are added by the redundancy rules in **6**, which say that the assignment of the frames depends on the presence of $[\pm sg]$, which is itself assigned by rule **2v**.

6

i $[+sg] \Rightarrow [+[\text{Det}\ _N[+sg]\underline{\quad}]]$

ii $[-sg] \Rightarrow [+[\text{Det}\ _N[-sg]\underline{\quad}]]$

As the presence of $[+sg]$ depends on the presence of $[-\text{Past}]$, number agreement only applies to non-past forms. Rule **2vi** applies only to the traditional past passive participles, since it is only adjective forms of verb lexemes that have $[-\text{Aux}]$.

The redundancy rules apply to the regular verbs in the language but the irregular verbs do not lend themselves to such treatment and need more complex entries. For instance, irregular past tense forms like *ran* or *taught* simply have to be listed in the lexical entry, which reflects the view that *ran* cannot be segmented into smaller morphs. *Runs* and *running*, however, can be derived by the morphological rules, though minor adjustment rules are required to handle the double letters in forms like *running* and *cutting*. We will assume that the lexicon has a separate section for irregular verbs in which the redundancy rules do not apply. Entries for CAN, HAVE and BE are given in **7**, **8** and **9**.

7   CAN
$$[+V]$$
$$[+\text{Aux}]$$
$$[+\text{Modal}]$$
$$[+\ _{VP}[\underline{\quad}V\ (X)]]$$

can   *could*

$[-\text{Past}]$ $[+\text{Past}]$

The strict subcategorization frame indicates that the forms of CAN occur first in the VP, followed by another V and possibly some other constituent(s): *He could have come* (X = V), *He could swim that river* (X = NP), *He could have swum that river* (X = V NP). Note that the conventions about features of lexemes and features of forms apply in this part of the lexicon although the redundancy rules do not.

8
$$\text{HAVE}$$
$$[+\text{V}]$$

have

a $[+\text{Aux}]$

  $[+\text{Perf}]$

  $[+[_{\text{VP}}[\underline{}\text{V}\quad(\text{X})]]]$

  $[-\text{Past}]$

  $[+[\text{Det}\ _{\text{N}}[-\text{sg}]_{\text{N}}\underline{}]]$

b $[+[_{\text{VP}}[\quad\text{V}\underline{}\text{NP}]]]$

  $[+\text{Prog}]$

  $[+\text{Rule 2}]$

  $[+[\text{Det}\ _{\text{N}}[-\text{sg}]\underline{}]]$

c $[+[_{\text{VP}}[\quad\text{V}\underline{}\text{X}]]]$

  $[+\text{Modal}]$

d $[+_{\text{VP}}[(\quad\text{V}\quad)\underline{}\text{NP}]]$

  $[+\text{Modal}]$

  $[+[\text{Det}\ _{\text{N}}[-\text{sg}]\underline{}]]$

has

a $[+\text{Aux}]$

  $[+\text{Perf}]$

  $[+[_{\text{VP}}[\underline{}\text{V}\quad(\text{X})]]]$

  $[-\text{Past}]$

  $[+[\text{Det}\ _{\text{N}}[+\text{sg}]\underline{}]]$

b $[-\text{Aux}]$

  $[+[_{\text{VP}}[\underline{}\text{NP}]]]$

  $[-\text{Past}]$

  $[+[\text{Det}\ _{\text{N}}[+\text{sg}]\underline{}]]$

had

a $[+\text{Aux}]$

  $[+\text{Perf}]$

  $[+[_{\text{VP}}[\underline{}\text{V}\ (\text{X})]]]$

  $[+\text{Past}]$

b $[-\text{Aux}]$

  $[+[_{\text{VP}}[\underline{}\text{NP}]]]$

  $[+\text{Past}]$

c $[+[_{\text{VP}}[\quad\text{V}\underline{}\text{NP}]]]$

  $[+\text{Perf}]$

Set **a** of features for *have* allows for *They have bought a house* and *They have been buying a house*, while set **b** allows for *They are having breakfast*. Set **c** allows for *They might have a dog* or *They*

might have found it or *They might have been inspecting the site.*
Set **d** enables the grammar to handle *They have a large house.*
Similar remarks apply to the sets of features for *has* and *had*, the
only extra comment being that set **c** for *had* allows for *He had had
breakfast.*

9

$$
\text{BE} \\
[+V] \\
[+_{VP}[\underline{\quad} \left\{ \begin{array}{c} V \\ A \\ NP \end{array} \right\} \quad \left\{ \begin{array}{c} A \\ NP \end{array} \right\}]]
$$

be

a $[+ _{VP}[\ V \underline{\quad}]]$ **b** $[+ _{VP}[\ V \underline{\quad} \left\{ \begin{array}{c} A \\ NP \end{array} \right\}]]$
  $[+Modal]$ $[+Prog]$
                       $[+Rule\ 2]$

been   *is*
$[+ _{VP}[\ V \underline{\quad}]]$ $[-Past]$
  $[+Perf]$ $[+[Det\ _N[+sg]\underline{\quad}]]$

are   *was*
$[-Past]$ $[+Past]$
$[+[Det\ _N[-sg]\underline{\quad}]]$ $[+[Det\ _N[+sg]\underline{\quad}]]$

were
$[+Past]$
$[+[Det\ _N[-sg]\underline{\quad}]]$

In the entry for BE the subcategorization frame attached to the
lexeme indicates the environment in which all BE forms occur,
namely a V with or without a following NP (*He is sleeping*), and
adjective (*He is clever*) or an NP (*He is an engineer*). The various
left-hand environments are listed separately.

The diagrams in **10** and the following paragraphs explain how
the strict subcategorization rules determine the order of constituents. The PS rule that expands VP generates the structures in
10 – intransitive verbs are left out of account for the moment.

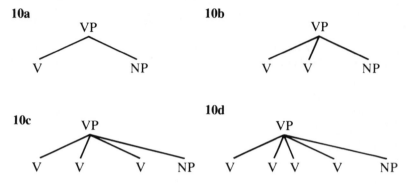

10a presents no problems. The subcategorization frame for CAN and other modal verbs prevents any modal form from being inserted into this tree, and the frames for other lexical items allow phrases like *is a student*, *has a car* and *writes poetry*.

In **10b** the frames allow phrases like *could write poetry, could be an idiot, has written poetry, is writing poetry, is being a fool, has been a fool*. The crucial convention is that the first V node is filled first, then the second and so on across the tree.

In **10c** the first V can be a CAN form or a HAVE form, since the subcategorization frames prevent a BE form or a main verb form from being attached to the first V in a sequence of three V nodes. If a HAVE form is inserted, the frames prevent a main verb from being attached to the next V node, only *been* having the appropriate frame.

If a modal verb is inserted into the first V node, the frames allow either *have* or *be* to be attached to the second V node, and thereafter the same constraints apply as with **10b**.

With respect to **10d**, the frames allow only a modal verb to be attached to the first V node and thereafter the same constraints apply as with **10c**.

The lexicon can also handle agreement inside NPs. On page 54 there is a T-rule specifying the occurrence of *a* and *some*, depending on whether the noun is singular or plural. Number, like Tense, was treated as a separate constituent and, like Tense, is to be demoted to the status of an inherent feature on nouns, [+Count] being rewritten as [±sg]. The association of [+Count] and [±sg] captures the fact that in English only nouns denoting individual countable objects can be made plural. Only [±sg] needs to be specified in lexical entries, as a redundancy rule can fill in [+Count].

Like regular verb forms, regular noun forms are subjected to a rule that adds the appropriate plural affix to the base, the grammar thereby conveying the information that *boys* and *churches*, etc. consist of two morphs, one of which realizes [−sg].

Just as selectional features ensure correct combinations of subject noun and verb, so they can specify correct combinations of determiner and noun. For instance *boys* takes into a phrase marker the selectional frame $[+ _{NP}[\text{ Det } \_\_]]$, which ensures that the
$[-sg]$
Det, if there is one, will receive [−sg]. This copied feature will in turn ensure that *some*, *these* or *those* occurs but not *a*, *this* or *that*.

The morphological rules for nouns are shown in **11**, followed by some lexical entries in **12**.

11 Rule 4: $X \Rightarrow X\ s$
   Rule 5: $X \Rightarrow X\ es$

12

BOY
[+N]
[+[Det ___]]

OX
[+N]
[+[Det ___]]

boy
[+ [Det ___]] ;   [+[Det ___]]
   [+sg]   [−sg]

ox   *oxen*
[+[Det ___]]   [+[Det ___]]
   [+sg]   [−sg]

[−sg]
[+Rule 4]

THE
[+Det]
[+[___ N]]
[+sg]

THIS
[+Det]

this
[+[___ N]]
   [+sg]

these
[+[___ N]]
      [−sg]

A
[+Det]

a
[+[__N]]
   [+sg]

some
[+[__N]]
   [−sg]

[±sg] in the entry for *the* indicates that this form occurs with both singular and plural nouns. Most of the inherent features have been omitted from the entries for convenience but the full entries contain [±Human], etc. The order in which forms are inserted into phrase markers suggests a chain of dependencies: verbs are inserted first, controlling the type of noun, and then nouns are inserted, controlling the form of the determiner.

Exercises

See page 161.

13   The passive

As mentioned on page 139, an alternative description of the passive construction is to be proposed. This change is not prompted by the extension of the lexicon, but by distributional facts not accounted for by the Passive T-rule, though it is more easily incorporated in a grammar without affix hopping.

Like affix hopping, Passive is one of the classic T-rules, and like affix hopping it is complex, not simply permuting constituents but creating new structure with the addition of a prepositional phrase. Moreover, in most transformational descriptions of English this is the only prepositional phrase that is not introduced by the PS rules. Why should there be this exceptional PP? There may be a peculiarity in English or a peculiarity in the description, and the latter possibility must be explored first.

In any case, the extended lexicon precludes the usual transformational account, which is possible only if lexemes are inserted into deep structures, have affixes attached to them and are realized as word forms. Now it is proposed that word forms be inserted directly into deep structures and the Passive T-rule can be retained only if word forms are replaced by other word forms: e.g. *wrote* by *was written*. This is a strange operation for rules that are supposed to handle general syntactic structures.

A more serious defect is that the Passive T-rule ignores the distribution of forms like *written*, which are described in traditional grammar as participles. This label expresses the view that these forms are like both verbs and adjectives, but the transformational account says that these are verbs to which an affix is added.

In what respects are the passive participles similar to adjectives? Many adjectives and participles are identical in form – *the locked door/The door was locked by Bill, the broken vase/The vase was broken by Tom*. The passive construction would not be alone in consisting of BE A PP, a sequence that occurs in sentences like *The boss was enthusiastic about my plan, The idea was unintel-*

ligible to Mary. Note also phrases like *the vase broken by Tom* (*cost £50*) which seems parallel to *the idea unintelligible to Mary* (*is in fact the best one*).

The distribution of adjectives proper and passive participles do not coincide completely. Some participles occur after SEEM but not all: *He seemed hurt, The vase seems broken* but not **The boy seems helped*. Not all passive participles can occur between the determiner and the noun in an NP: **the helped boy*. Some phrases, such as *the dug garden*, are not easily judged correct or incorrect.

On the other hand, not all adjectives occur in attributive position – **the afraid man* – and some do not occur in predicative position – **The accident is major*, **The reason is main*. A second problem is that verbs like MELT have separate adjective and passive participle forms. In **1a** *melted* is a participle and in **1b** *molten* is an adjective. Note the incorrectness of **2a** and the unclear status of **2b**.

1a   The lead on the roofs was melted by the heat of the fire
1b   The molten lava poured down the mountainside
2a   *The lead on the roofs was molten by the heat of the fire
2b   ?The melted lava poured down the mountainside

As mentioned on page 296 of BM, *molten* denotes a state resulting from a process and *melted* relates to the process itself. **1a** describes a process, which is one semantic reason why *molten* cannot occur in it, but *melted* too is coming to denote the resultant state, as in *The melted wax clung to the candle*. *Molten*, originally a passive participle, came to occupy only frames available to adjectives denoting states, and this close connection between participles and adjectives in the historical development can be taken as corroborative evidence of this analysis.

One objection to the analysis comes from the English construction shown in **3**.

3a   The nobles were taught a lesson by Canute
3b   The barons were promised gold by the king

While there are NP BE A PP constructions other than the passive, there are no constructions NP BE A NP PP except the type of passive in **3**. There is no difficulty in ensuring that only some of the forms we want to call adjectives actually occur in this construction, since only adjectives from three-place verbs will be provided with the subcategorization feature [+[BE__NP PP]].

Since **3a**, **3b** represent a type of passive that is possible for only a small number of verb lexemes in English, the best course is to let the typical passive decide the issue and assign *taught* and *promised* to the class of adjectives on the ground that outside the construction in **3** they occur only in adjective positions.

It should be mentioned, as a counter to the above objection, that some passive participles can be preceded by *very* or *more/most*, as in **4**.

4a She was very surprised by the news
4b He was more dismayed than I was by the team's defeat

The deep structure proposed for *The house was being built by this firm* is shown in Figure 93.

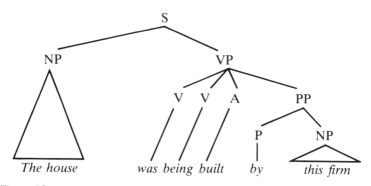

Figure 93

This structure is generated by adding an optional PP to the sequence on the right of the arrow in a PS rule (cf. page 135). The rule will read: $VP \rightarrow (V)\ (V)\ (V)\ V \begin{Bmatrix} A \\ NP \end{Bmatrix} (NP)\ (PP)$. This generates structures like *The house has been built by this firm* (NP V V A PP), *The house might have been being built by this firm* (NP V V V V A PP), and *He had been taught a lesson by his opponent* (NP V V A NP PP).

These rules do not relate passive sentences to their active counterparts. This can be done by a rule of implication that makes use of the notions of Agent and Patient (pages 171ff.). The rule states that the structure $\underset{[+Ag]}{NP_1}\ X\ V\ \underset{[+Pat]}{NP_2}$ implies the structure

NP_2 X A P NP_1, where V and A are taken from the same
[+Pat]   [+Ag]
lexical entry, and ensures that whatever semantic interpretation is
assigned to an active sentence is also assigned to the corresponding
passive.

When the lexicon was extended, emphasis was placed on the fact
that no new devices were introduced but that an existing device
was being given a larger role. Although implication rules have not
been mentioned in this introduction, they are not being invented
only to handle the relation between active and passive sentences
but are needed to express the relation between, e.g. *The church is
to the left of the town hall* and *The town hall is to the right of the
church.*

We began this chapter by saying that the abandonment of the
Passive T-rule was not a consequence of the changes made to the
lexicon and the deep structure, but these changes do entail modifications to some T-rules. Neg placement (page 96) is changed to
the rule in **5** below, Neg attraction (page 97) to the rule in **6**, and
tage formation (page 104) to the rule in **7**.

5 Neg placement

SA: X $_{VP}$[Neg   V   Y]$_{VP}$ Z

1   2   3   4   5

SC: 1 ∅ 3 − 2 − 4 5

Condition: V ≠ x *ing*

6 Neg attraction

SA: X $_{VP}$[V   Neg   Y]$_{VP}$ Z
                [+Aux]

1   2   3   4   5

SC: 1 2/3 4 5

7 Tag formation

SA: X   NP V_1 ⟨∅⟩$_1$ Y
                [+Aux]   ⟨Neg⟩$_2$

1   2   3   4   5

SC: 1 2 3 4 5 V_1 ⟨Neg⟩$_1$ Pron
                        ⟨∅⟩$_2$

The major relative clause and interrogative T-rules remain the same but the description or complements, for reasons connected with distribution and the extended lexicon, is to be revised. This is the topic of the next chapter.

Exercises

See page 161.

14 Complement structures revisited

The account of complements presented in chapter 8 is the standard transformational one. For all that, the rules creak in several places, and the extended lexicon provides an opportunity to revise the account.

Generative grammar allows analyses to be assessed in a much more detailed fashion than is possible with traditional grammar. For example, we can ask whether all the rules make general statements about syntactic structure or whether some of them are overly particular. With respect to complements, there are indeed general rules, such as equi-NP-deletion, extraposition and raising, but there are also 'tidying up' rules like POSS movement, TO movement and T/M deletion. In the light of the remarks on keeping syntax and morphology apart POSS movement in particular begins to look suspicious, as it handles the internal structure of nouns.

Even raising and equi-NP-deletion are open to criticism. With respect to raising, we can ask why sentences like *The lion seems to be happy* and *It seems that the lion is happy* are derived from the same deep structure. The infinitive phrase and the noun clause are both complements of *seems*, but this is identity of function, not distribution. They do describe the same situation, and this has been the most important consideration, supported by the view that complementizers are minor grammatical items of no semantic import. If sentences are equivalent in meaning, so the argument went, derive them from the same deep structure so that they can be correlated with the same semantic structure with the minimum of fuss.

The semantic point is gained but the syntax is complicated by the need to have subject to subject raising sometimes optional and sometimes obligatory, depending on the verb in the matrix sentence. Another possibility is that the sentences are equivalent in meaning because they describe the 'same' situation from different angles; so they should be derived from *different* deep structures but related via implication rules, as proposed for active and passive sentences (pages 151–2). The sentence *It seems that . . .* enables the speaker to talk about the whole situation, whereas *The lion seems . . .* enables the speaker to talk about a property of the lion. Simplicity in the correlation of syntax and semantics is not sufficient reason for a single deep syntactic structure if it causes severe problems for mappings within the syntactic component.

In addition to rules that are morphological rather than syntactic and doubts about the semantic equivalence of sentences, there is distributional evidence not explained by the analysis on pages 74–93. Consider first of all the structure of gerunds. Is a construction like *his breaking off the engagement* to be regarded as parallel to *his broken engagement*? In spoken English utterances are to be heard that can be related to sentences such as *All this not practising the piano and forgetting to do your homework will have to stop.* In this sentence the gerund *not practising . . . homework* is preceded by *all this*, a sequence that usually precedes nouns, which arouses the suspicion that the gerund should be analysed as a noun and that forms like *his* should be excluded from the gerund and analysed instead as a determiner, like *all this*.

If *his* in *his breaking off the engagement* is treated as a determiner, and if the remainder, *breaking off the engagement*, is treated as noun-like (as a *nominal*), the motivation for deriving gerunds from underlying sentences is greatly reduced. On this alternative view, gerundial phrases no longer contain a subject noun, a verb and an object noun but only a verb and an object noun. It is interesting that the deep sentence analysis is not unequivocally supported by the distributional evidence even if *his* is not regarded as a determiner. Gerunds cannot contain tensed verb forms or modals, which makes them very unlike sentences, but this evidence is often ignored, as it is a simple matter to devise a T-rule to remove the unwanted constituents. However, as soon as we see the parallel between *He broke off the engagement* and *his breaking off the engagement* as a matter for the semantic component and pay attention to the distribution of *his*, etc., the fact that gerunds lack tense and modal verbs assumes greater significance.

If gerunds are not to be derived from deep sentences, how is the grammar to capture the fact that *Writing a novel is easy* is interpreted as having an indefinite subject? The solution proposed on page 86 was that the deep subject be ONE, though *One's writing a novel is easy* is at best stilted and calls for a special rule of ONE deletion. Another solution regards the information that the person doing the writing is unspecified as being inferred from the surface structure (see the remarks on pages 165–8); this accords better with the fact that there are sentences with subjectless gerunds for which an analysis with ONE is not appropriate: *Calculating the volume generated by a curve was not possible before Newton and Leibniz* and *I believe that burning heretics was common in medieval Europe.*

As a final piece of syntactic evidence, note that gerunds like *his breaking off the engagement* and NPs like *his books* share an important syntactic property. In a structure like $_S$[*I think* $_{NP}$[*his books*] *are magnificent*] the whole NP can be moved to the front to derive *His books I think are magnificent*, but the determiner *his* cannot be moved on its own, as this would derive **His I think books are magnificent*. Similarly, in $_S$[*I find* [*his breaking off the engagement*] *quite incomprehensible*] the whole phrase *his breaking off the engagement* can be moved to the front of the sentence to yield *His breaking off the engagement I find quite incomprehensible*. The *his* on its own, however, cannot be moved, and if *his* in both sentences is treated as a determiner a general constraint can be stated forbidding the determiner alone to be moved out of an NP.

The revised analysis of *his breaking off the engagement* is shown in Figure 94.

Where does the form *breaking* come from? In the standard

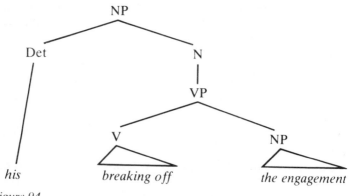

Figure 94

transformational analysis ING is generated under the COMP node and moved to the right of the first constituent in VP once Tense and Modal have been deleted. On the revised analysis *breaking* is stored in the lexicon with the appropriate subcategorization features; i.e., one of the subcategorization frames associated with *break* is [+ $_N$[$_{VP}$[—(NP)]]], which calls up [+Rule 2] on page 140.

The determiner in structures like that of Figure 94 is typically a demonstrative like *that* or a possessive like *his*, *Bill's*, etc., but not often *the* or *a*. If we decide to exclude the latter two, their lexical entries will include the feature [− $_{NP}$[—$_N$[VP]]], which prevents them from occurring to the left of a noun containing a VP.

Note that treating *his* or *Bill's* as a determiner and *breaking* as the form that occurs in a VP dominated by N does not prevent us from regarding the *'s* and the *ing* as signalling a complement. The standard analysis is faulty in concentrating on the signalling role of these constituents without fitting them into the patterns of constituent structure.

The conventional transformational description of infinitives can also be challenged. To begin with a minor point, not all occurrences of *for* ... *to* go together as a complementizer. In *For the best student to fail the exam would be humiliating*, *for the best student* can be regarded as a prepositional phrase separate from the infinitive phrase *to fail the exam*. The correctness of this analysis is borne out by the possibility of the prepositional phrase occurring at the end of the sentence, as in *To fail the exam would be humiliating for the best student*.

As always, there are complications, because the *for* ... *to* could function as a complementizer, as is made clear by the addition of a second *for* phrase: *For the best student to fail the exam would be humiliating for the Department*. The alert reader will observe potential differences in intonation and rhythm (in planned reading aloud): there can be a pause after *student* if *for the best student* is a prepositional phrase but not if *for* and *to* are mere markers of a complement. These differences in the signal are not taken into account by the standard transformational description of complements.

What is a major point is the status of *to*, since there are sentences in which *to* could be taken as a preposition, especially after verbs of movement. The examples in **1** are from newspapers and recent novels.

1a   . . . has led to 4000 being led off
1b   . . . and we never came close to finding out what it was
1c   Audley swung round to find Faith staring in the barn doorway
1d   He did not know what had moved him to love Susie
1e   He set off to face the terror of the labyrinth
1f   He has grown to be quite different

If *to* could be treated as a preposition in the above constructions, this would shed light on a difficulty that arose in earlier work. There is in English a pseudo-cleft construction with the general schema WHAT NP V BE NP: *What my wife likes is a novel by Emma Lathen*. This construction used to be regarded as a test for NPs, it being supposed that only NPs could occur after BE. If sentences like *What he is is very brave* are acceptable, the construction is not in fact a test for NPs (unless *very brave* can be analysed as an NP), but a more serious drawback for the linguist who wishes to treat infinitives as NPs is that not all infinitives occur in the pseudo-cleft construction anyway:

2ia   The vet condescended to examine the budgie
2ib   *What the vet condescended was to examine the budgie

2iia   The boss tends to be suspicious of new secretaries
2iib   *What the boss tends is to be suspicious of new secretaries

2iiia   The editor was tempted to accept the story as true
2iiib   *What the editor was tempted was to accept the story as true

The unacceptability of the **b** examples in **2** can be explained if *to* is a preposition: if CONDESCEND and TEMPT are taken as verbs of movement and analysed by analogy with, e.g., *The discovery of gold tempted hordes of people to the Yukon*. The structure now being proposed for the examples in **1** and **2** has a verb followed by a prepositional phrase, except for **1d**, which has a verb followed by a noun phrase and then by a prepositional phrase. That is, **1d** is taken as parallel in structure to *They moved him to London*. The structure of **1f** is shown in Figure 95.

Note the parallel between the structures assigned to infinitives and gerunds: both are VPs dominated by N. The above examples with verbs of movement lend themselves to the V PP analysis but the analysis does not always apply so easily. Verbs such as TEACH

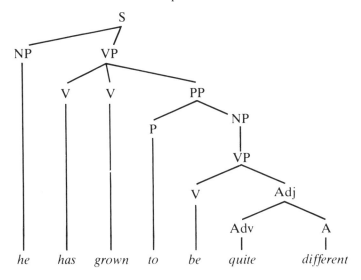

Figure 95

and PERSUADE can be construed as followed by a PP – *I taught him to swim* ('My teaching brought him to the state of being able to swim') and *I persuaded him to listen to our arguments* (*We persuaded him into the pub*) – but there are sentences like *To learn up all these irregular verbs is a right slog* where *to* does not seem to be a preposition. With respect to the latter example we will continue to apply the standard analysis of *to* as a complementizer, but we will revise the standard analysis so that *to* is not derived from *for to* and so that the infinitive phrase is a VP dominated by an NP (Figure 96).

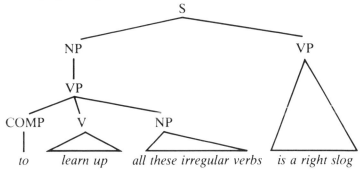

Figure 96

Under this analysis VPs as well as S have a COMP node and the complementizer *to* would be attached to this node.

Sentences like *I want him to do linguistics*, *I consider him to be incompetent* and *The plan was stated to be foolproof* are analysed as containing a V followed by an NP in object position which is in turn followed by a PP. In these instances the syntactic evidence is not strong but WANT can be followed by the sequence NP PP, as in *I want him in Glasgow by tomorrow*, *I want the papers on my desk, not in your office*. CONSIDER is occasionally followed by NP PP: *I consider him among the greatest scientists of this century*, though a case could be made for deriving such examples by deleting *to be*. STATE is not usually followed by NP PP but it does make semantic sense to regard *to* as a preposition since the plan is moved, by the statement, into the class of foolproof plans. There is no syntactic evidence against this analysis, which means that *to* can be interpreted as denoting movement after forms of STATE and after verbs of movement.

Like *to*, *for to* can sometimes be seen as a complementizer and sometimes as a preposition. Where the preposition test mentioned earlier fails, the structure to be assigned is that in Figure 97, which shows the deep structure of *For the boat to be wrecked would be a disaster for the company*.

On the other hand, a sentence like *The police appealed for volunteers to come forward* can be seen as parallel to *The police appealed for help in the murder case* or *The police appealed for*

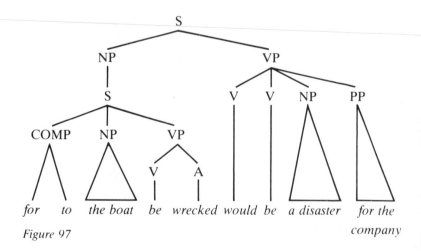

Figure 97

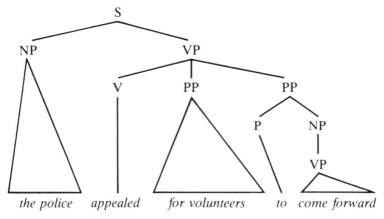

Figure 98

volunteers for the special constabulary, which permits the PP
analysis (Figure 98).

The upshot of the discussion is as follows. In a number of constructions *for to* can be treated as a complementizer but in other
constructions *for* can be treated as a preposition, and in infinitives
with *to* alone the *to* can sometimes be analysed as a preposition
too. Historically, *for* and *to* began as prepositions – indeed many
occurrences of these forms are still indisputably prepositions, as in
for John, *to London* – but some occurrences acquired the function
of complementizers. Historical development has left an untidy
situation in modern English which is not well handled by the
monolithic treatment of these forms as complementizers, it calls
for a more fragmented analysis in terms of complementizers and
prepositions.

Exercises to chapters 12, 13 and 14

1

The lexical entry for CAN on page 143 reflects some features of
modal verbs in literary English: they have no form in -*s*; they have
no infinitive (**to can*), no participles (**canning*, **canned* – the
latter form exists but realizes a different lexeme); they are not
followed by infinitives (**can to read*); and do not co-occur with
other modals (**can should*).

Which of the following verbs are like CAN? Work out the

distribution of all the verbs and write lexical entries for them on the revised model. Do not confine yourself to literary English.

WILL   KNOW   NEED   NEED   OUGHT   LIKE   SEE
TASTE   RESEMBLE

(For a résumé of all the formal properties of modal verbs, see, e.g., Palmer's *Modality and the English Verb*, Longman 1979, pages 8–10.)

2

Write lexical entries that handle the revised analysis of complements and the co-occurrence restrictions shown in question **3i–iii** on page 92. (The existence of general restrictions – if there are any – can be captured by redundancy rules using the features [+factive] or [+emotive] – see the first note on page 93.)

3

English does not provide scope for rules handling inflectional morphology but languages like Latin do. Write lexical entries and morphological rules for the nouns and verbs in the Latin sentences below. NB Since there are few nouns and verbs in the sentences, the rules you devise will seem like the proverbial sledgehammer to crack a nut. Remember that your rules apply to many more nouns and verbs and assume a basic subject noun – object noun – verb order.

puer puellam monet	'(the) boy – advises – (the) girl'
puella puerum monet	'(the) girl – advises – (the) boy'
puer puellae invidet	'(the) boy – envies – (the) girl'
puella puero invidet	'(the girl – envies – (the) boy'
puero invideo	'I envy – (the) boy'
puellam moneo	'I advise – (the) girl'

4

Collect examples of past participles passive from written and spoken language.
(a) How many of them occur with *very*, etc.?
(b) How many can occur in the comparative constructions (*as big as*, *bigger than/more difficult than*)?
(c) How many can occur in the frame Det__N?

15 Conclusions

In this section we have seen how the standard model of transformational grammar can be modified. If we consider the changes purely with respect to syntax and morphology it is clear that they are beneficial. Not only has the boundary between syntax and morphology been firmly drawn but a number of T-rules have gone: passive, affix hopping, verb number agreement, equi-NP-deletion, raising, T/M deletion, POSS movement and ING movement.

Some of these rules, especially equi-NP-deletion and subject to subject raising, are complex and involve large structural changes; their elimination significantly reduces the amount of structural manipulation permitted to T-rules. Other rules, in particular passive and affix hopping, caused more trouble than they were worth. Many discussions of rule ordering centre on one or other, or both, of these rules; their disappearance makes it possible to abandon the principle of extrinsic ordering. The disappearance of the four rules mentioned in this paragraph, along with verb number agreement and T/M deletion, make another simplification possible: all T-rules can be made optional. (Possible exceptions to this statement, such as the Neg movement rules and *to* movement can be dealt with in a different way (page 165).)

The abandonment of extrinsic ordering and making T-rules optional place severe limitations on the sort of deep structures that linguists can postulate. Rule ordering especially made it possible for linguists to save even the wildest deep structure by devising rules that applied in a particular order. Without ordering, much more care has to be taken over the deep structures and the room for manoeuvre is cut down still further by all rules being optional.

There are two routes to the limited model presented in this section. One way is to examine the system of rules *qua* system and to decide, on general criteria pertaining to rule systems, that the rules really are too unconstrained and powerful and that, no mat-

ter what the rules are describing, constraints have to be placed on
them. The other way is to pay more attention to the distribution of
constituents. For example, instead of setting up complete sentences and reducing them to small surface constituents we looked
at the surface distribution of infinitives and gerunds and decided
that the data was more compatible with an analysis in terms of a
simple VP, which can be preceded by a preposition. Attention to
distribution led us also to re-analyse the passive construction.

Unfortunately, the imposition of the constraints has to be paid
for. A complete description of a language is a repository of all the
information about its phonology, morphology, syntax and semantics; moreover, not just a set of pigeon-holes separated by barriers
but a series of interconnected pigeon-holes. The general problem of
how to capture the interconnections can at least be stated clearly
if we think of three series of connections with respect to syntax
and semantics: connections between syntactic constructions,
connections between syntactic and semantic constructions, and
connections between semantic structures.

A connection of the first sort is expressed by the T-rule of
subject–verb Inversion; a connection of the second sort is involved
in the mapping of any syntactic construction on to its corresponding
semantic structure (see pages 201ff. for a discussion of semantic
structures); and an example of a connection of the third sort is the
rule that says *X is to the left of Y* implies *Y is to the right of X*, and
vice versa. The semantic component seems the appropriate place
for such an implication relation.

A central part in transformational grammar has been played by
the need to express relations between syntactic constructions and
relations between syntax and semantics. As we saw on pages 49–50
and 79–80, the description of syntax has been influenced by the
desire to ease the mapping of syntax on to semantics; hence structures like [Jack wanted [Jack to see the film]] which are collapsed
into *Jack wanted to see the film*. The information, essential to the
semantic component, that the same person has the desire and is to
see the film is set out explicitly in the deep structure. It is for
semantic reasons, to capture the implication relation between them,
that *It seems that the lions are happy* is derived from the same deep
structure as *The lions seem to be happy* – in spite of the fact that
subject to subject raising deletes Tense and Modal and is obligatory
when FOR . . . TO is present.

Deep structures, that is to say, have been influenced not just by the facts of distribution but by the wish to prepare the way for the link-up between syntax and semantics, but some deep structures that were required, or were thought to be required, for a smooth link-up did not reflect the facts of surface distribution and could be mapped into surface structures only by massive structural changes. The attitude reflected in the preceding chapters is to regard massive structural changes with suspicion and to take as the primary criterion the distribution of constituents. This recommendation to focus on surface syntax does not mean that syntax is turning its back on semantics: as will be made clear in the next section, distribution provides a number of insights into semantic structures and close attention to it benefits the study of semantics just as much as the study of syntax.

How are only correct surface structures to be generated with the limited T-rules? How are syntactic constructions to be mapped on to semantic structures? The first problem is perhaps phrased infelicitously, since it propels one into thinking that all sources of unacceptability should be cut out before the final derived structure is specified by the grammar. This view, however, does not follow necessarily from the classic definition of a grammar as a device that generates all and only the correct sentences of a language – but it is closely associated with it.

A different approach is to say that a grammar specifies that certain sentences are correct and that others are not. Possible incorrect structures are rejected by the PS rules, which ensure a basic correct order, e.g. determiner preceding noun; by the lexicon, which ensures, e.g., that nouns requiring a determiner do indeed occur with a determiner; and by the T-rules, which ensure, e.g., that correct relative clause structures are generated, etc.

A grammar, considered as a checking device (pages 129–31), can specify correct and incorrect structures at any level, including that of surface structure. If T-rules are to apply unordered and optionally, incorrect surface structures may be derived. Since T-rules cannot check surface structures, their role being to map one phrase marker on to another, an extra set of rules is needed to reject incorrect surface structures. These rules are *surface filters*. Suppose that Neg movement has not applied. A surface filter – *Neg NP VP – marks the structure wrong. It was observed above that when a system of rules is modified, simplification in one part of the system usually complicates another part. And the limitations placed on T-rules do have to be compensated for (though the hope is that the cost will not be excessive), since a set of simple T-rules and a set of simple filters outweigh the disadvantages of a single set of complex T-rules.

As an instance of the sort of advantage offered by surface filters, consider the combination of verb and particle in *I called up my friend*. The particle *up* can occur either immediately after the verb or at the end of the sentence, as in *I called my friend up*. The particle has to occur at the end of the sentence if the object NP is a pronoun: *I called up him* versus *I called him up*. In the standard model the rule that moves the particle to the end of the sentence applies optionally if the object NP contains a full noun but obligatorily if it contains a pronoun. To capture all possibilities the rule either has two SAs or it has a condition attached to it. With a surface filter, however, a very simple rule can be stated, applying to the sequence V Particle NP, and the surface sequence* [V Particle   N   ] is rejected by the filter.
   [+Pronoun]

Surface filters can also be employed in the description of interrogative sentences. Since DO forms are optionally inserted into phrase markers, and since subject–verb inversion moves to the front of the sentence whatever constituent is in first position in VP, sentences like *Came the knight to the castle?* are generated. These sentences can be marked either by a surface filter as archaic or as incorrect. The filter required is of the form *$_S$[V   X] –
                                         [−Aux]
though this filter would need to be more carefully formulated if it is not to block imperative sentences. The rule of DO deletion, preventing the formation of sentences like *He does be polite* and *He does have written his essay*, can either be retained and made optional or, the simpler course, it can be abandoned and these incorrect structures can be caught at the surface by a filter.

The problem of linking up syntax and semantics is not so tractable. Consider interpreting sentences like *John wants to see Naples*. In the revised model there is no overt NP *John* in subject position before *see* and the task for the semantic link-up is to construe *John* as the subject of *see*. In general, given a structure NP_1 V_1 *to* V_2 NP_2, NP_1 is interpreted as the subject of both V_1 and V_2, provided V_1 is a form of WANT, HOPE, PROMISE, LONG, PRAY, EXPECT, LEARN, TRY, etc.

Another infinitive construction is exemplified by *John persuaded*

Bill to see Naples. This has the structure NP_1 V_1 NP_2 $_{PP}[to$ $_{NP}[V_2$ $NP_3]]$, and NP_2 is construed as the subject of V_2, provided that V_1 is a form of PERSUADE, EXPECT, FORCE, COMPEL, ENTREAT, TEACH, etc. If V_1 is a form of PROMISE, NP_1 is construed as the subject of V_2.

In passive sentences with the adjective form of PERSUADE, e.g. *Bill was persuaded (by John) to see Naples*, the NP that is the subject of the BE form is construed as the subject of the infinitive form. Such sentences have the structure NP_1 V A (PP) *to* V NP_2, and if the optional PP is excluded there is a parallel between them and sentences like *Bill was keen to see Naples* with respect both to syntax and interpretation, *Bill* being the subject of *was* (*keen*) and of *see*. The rules that construe NPs as the subjects of Vs are known as *rules of construal*.

The general problem illustrated by the above examples is that of *control*, what is controlled being the 'understood' subject of infinitives. V_1 controls which NP is the 'understood' subject, the choice of NP varying with the type of verb and construction. Although the mapping of syntactic constructions on to semantic structures is not our concern here, with the revised account of complements the rules of construal might mark V_1 and V_2 with the same index, which would ensure that the correct semantic structure is selected with a noun for each of the subjects, overt or understood, in the syntactic structure. That is, the semantic structure corresponding to *John forced Bill to see Naples* resembles the standard deep syntactic structure $_S[$JOHN FORCE BILL INTO $_S[$BILL SEE NAPLES$]]$ in having two occurrences of BILL. In other respects it differs, since, e.g., it contains INTO, which is not a complementizer.

Another problem with the semantic link-up relates to the interpretation of reflexives. In *John fancies himself* the reflexive is construed as identical in reference with *John*. As with infinitives, the standard model has deep structures like $_S[$JOHN FANCY JOHN$]$ with two identical NPs, one of which is replaced by the appropriate reflexive pronoun. Even this deep structure, however, does not specify that both occurrences of JOHN denote the same object and this information has to be supplied by indices assigned to the NPs.

The need for indices, coupled with the extra checking device of filters, suggests a different treatment of reflexive pronouns, one in which they are generated in the base. There is no difficulty with sentences like *The boys admired themselves (in the mirror)* provided that number agreement between subject noun and reflexive pronoun is handled by a filter which rejects *The boys admired himself* but not *The boys admired themselves*. The statement of the filter is not quite straightforward, however, as reflexives can occur not just to the right of the main verb but inside infinitives, and noun clauses: *Towser tried to scratch himself, Bill claimed that the car had been bought for himself, not his wife.*

Special rules mark ordinary nouns and reflexive pronouns as *co-referential* (referring to the same person or thing), and they apply to the same structures as the filters mentioned above. Indices also have to be assigned to ordinary pronouns to indicate which NP they are co-referential with. In *Bill gave him the book Bill* and *him* cannot be co-referential but in *As soon as he arrived, Bill began working*, *he* and *Bill* might or might not be co-referential.

In the standard model pronouns, like reflexives, were substituted by T-rules for full nouns and the last example above derived from a deep structure [[AS SOON AS BILL ARRIVE] BILL BEGIN WORK], the first occurrence of BILL being replaced by *he*. The rules that substituted pronouns were subject to various conditions. For example, in the deep structure [BILL RESIGN [AFTER BILL BE DEMOTE]] the second occurrence of BILL can be replaced by *he* but not the first. The difficulty is that the sentence *He resigned after Bill was demoted* is not syntactically incorrect: it is just that *he* is not co-referential with *Bill*. The revised account concentrates on developing a simple syntactic structure, and from a syntactic point of view there is no restriction on the occurrence of pronouns (excluding reflexives). What is restricted is the reference of pronouns, a matter for the rules of construal.

Since *He resigned after Bill was demoted* is syntactically impeccable, the standard model would in any case have to generate some pronouns in the base, since there is no full NP that could be regarded as replaced by *he*. Instead of generating some pronouns in the base and some by T-rule, the revised account generates all pronouns in the base. Unacceptable structures like **When himself left the firm, it collapsed* are intercepted by the rules of construal. Every reflexive pronoun has to be assigned the same index as another full NP in the sentence, which must precede it, and if there is no full NP for a reflexive to be co-referential with the rules of construal mark the sentence as incorrect.

One question left unasked is where the link-up of syntax and semantics takes place. For various reasons, some mentioned on pages 49–50, linguists working with the standard model assumed that deep syntactic structures were mapped into semantic structures. One revision of the standard model envisages the link-up at the level of surface structure, though one difficulty is that relative clause and interrogative T-rules have applied to move constituents to the front of the sentence. To facilitate the link-up it is supposed that *traces* are left behind by the moved constituents so that the semantic rules can determine, e.g., whether a relative pronoun is the direct or indirect object of a verb. With the revised model presented here, the link-up could take place at the level of deep structure, which would remove the need for traces, but it must be emphasized that linguists have only just begun to explore ways of linking syntax and semantics.

To conclude this section on the revised model, attention must be drawn to the fact that for some linguists the restrictions placed on T-rules are not motivated solely, or even principally, by the desirability of a highly constrained system of rules *per se*. We saw (page 125) that Chomsky posits a very close link between generative grammar and the competence of native speakers of any language. Working on the assumption that native speakers of a language acquire approximately the same grammar, Chomsky and others argue that only if the grammar is highly constrained can it be explained why native speakers acquire the same grammar. The grammar is so constrained that there is only one solution for the speakers to find.

The attitude that informs this volume is that while there is a link between the linguist's work and the psycholinguist's, transformational grammar does not necessarily possess any degree of psychological reality. What is important with respect to psychological reality is the surface structure, both in its organization and as a clue to semantic structure (see following chapters). The limitations placed on the T-rules reflect a wish to make the rules as simple as possible, and the view that surface distribution is of central importance, with allegedly 'minor' constituents like prepositions and complementizers just as important as full nouns and verbs. By itself close attention to surface distribution leads to simpler T-rules, and further simplification follows from observing the distinction between syntax and morphology.

Whatever the motives, recent trends in transformational grammar have been towards a tighter description of syntax, though it may be asked whether traces make a positive contribution to that goal. The description offered here avoids the worst excesses of 'wild' transformations, avoids traces, and represents a moderate position *vis-à-vis* current developments.

Technical terms

co-referential (pronouns/nouns)
rules of construal
surface filters
trace

16 Introduction to case grammar

The preceding chapters cover only one part of traditional syntax. Nothing has been said about the concepts of subject, object, indirect object, agent, patient, and so on, although they are prominent in descriptions of languages from every region of the world. Chapters 18 and 19 of BM were devoted to these topics, and we continue that discussion here by asking how these concepts are to be incorporated in a generative grammar.

This question opens a Pandora's box of problems, perhaps the most vexing being the relationship between syntax and semantics. Although the topic cannot be investigated in detail, the major points should be outlined. It is usually assumed that the cognitive meaning of a sentence can be represented as a labelled bracketed string or a tree diagram but the nature of the constituents is controversial: some linguists employ the familiar categories of noun and verb, and others borrow predicates and arguments from logic. Relating to this difference is the important question of how representations of semantic structure can be judged. What criteria determine the constituents of the semantic structure and their arrangement into trees? This question deserves a whole book to itself; we merely touch on it in the discussion of the roles that the participants in a process (compare chapter 18 of BM) can be regarded as playing.

The general principle of the following chapters is that syntax and morphology are a signpost to semantic structures (see the remarks on pages 131–2). The transformational analysis of certain areas of English syntax paid attention to the distribution of constituents, an attention which should not be relaxed when meaning is under investigation. The value of this principle is demonstrated by the difficulty of deciding what the most general roles are and how many need to be postulated, and with respect to the appropriate arrangements of constituents in trees representing semantic structure.

Another major question is the relation between representations of semantic structure and representations of syntactic structure. It is essential to associate, e.g. *Who did the party choose as its leader?* with the tree showing its semantic structure, but trees show deep and surface syntactic structures, not to mention intermediate structures; is the association to affect the deep, or the surface structure, or both?

In the past ten years all the possibilities have been tried, and for present purposes it is not necessary to make a decision (though our inclination is towards the surface structure). We can discuss the number and type of roles required and the constituents needed for representations of semantic structure without being caught up in the problems of mapping syntax into semantics. It is possible to consider in general whether information on roles should be put in the lexicon or deep syntactic structure or in the semantic structure, though an apparently attractive and simple solution may be excluded by difficulties in the formulation of rules. No attempt will be made to write a set of rules, a decision which reflects the current state of investigations. This should not obscure the fact that the whole discussion of participants, processes and grammatical relations has been greatly sharpened by being set within the framework of a transformational grammar.

Of the terms mentioned in the first paragraph of this chapter, 'subject', 'object' and 'indirect object' refer to grammatical functions, 'agent', 'patient', etc. refer to roles. We can clear some ground by first disposing of functions. It was remarked (pages 330–9 of BM) that it is not easy to assess the importance of functional concepts like 'subject'; in modern linguistics these terms are used as labels for structural positions. A further comment was that the functions of subject, object and complement seem to have an important role in syntax and semantics.

There is evidence that roles are very important for semantic analysis and descriptions of case inflections and prepositions, but 'subject', etc. are best regarded as convenient labels for positions in surface constructions. The typical subject in English – typical in the sense of most frequent and taken as the starting point in descriptions – is a noun denoting an animate being peforming an action, but the data of pages 288–318 of BM demonstrate that the role of Agent is far from being the only one associated with subject position in English sentences. This fact is not diminished in importance by the suggestion that a noun in subject position can in certain circumstances be given a more 'active' interpretation than it receives in other positions. For example, *John* in *John loves Mary* seems to be connected with a more active role than *John* in *Mary pleases John/is dear to John*. This difference of interpretation can be attributed to the occurrence of *John* in subject position and the influence of the typical subject noun on our interpretation.

We will see (pages 215–17) that the interpretation of the typical object noun affects our interpretation of nouns in object position, but these influences need not affect the premise that 'subject', etc. are best taken as labels for structural positions, since what is crucial is not the position itself but its typical occupant and the typical occupant of the preceding verb position.

It has been suggested that the distinction between a noun in direct object position and a noun preceded by a preposition is paralleled by a difference in meaning. While there are differences in meaning, they are not as great as has been suggested and do not support the view that the notion of direct object rather than patient is important for semantic interpretation. The argument that direct object is important for semantics starts with sentences like **1a**, **1b**, where a verb is followed by an NP and a PP.

1a The vandals smeared the new wall with paint
1b The vandals smeared paint on the new wall

In **1b** the NP *the new wall*, occurring after a preposition, may or may not be construed as 'the whole new wall' (witness the acceptable sentence *The vandals smeared paint on the new wall but fortunately less than half the bricks were marked*). On the other hand, in **1a**, in which *the new wall* is in direct object position, the only interpretation is 'the whole wall', as is borne out by the peculiarity of **The vandals smeared the new wall with paint but fortunately less than half the bricks were marked*. These examples are discussed further on pages 215–17.

The interpretation associated with **1a** has been called 'holistic'; it has been asserted that it always correlates with a direct object noun, whereas nouns preceded by a preposition are assigned a non-holistic interpretation. Other examples that allegedly illustrate the distinction are in **2–4**.

2a John climbed the mountain
2b John climbed up the mountain

3a   John leapt the chasm
3b   John leapt over the chasm

4a   A yellow sports car travelled this road last night
4b   A yellow sports car travelled on this road last night

The suggestion is that **2a** describes a situation in which John climbed the whole mountain, right to the top, but that **2b** describes a situation in which John only climbed part of the mountain, failing to reach the top. **4a** supposedly describes a situation in which the car travelled the whole length of the road, whereas **4b** describes a situation in which the car travelled over a part of the road. Similarly, **3a** supposedly describes a successful leap right to the other side but **3b** describes an unsuccessful leap.

Note first that some speakers of English do not interpret **2a** and **2b** differently. Over the past three years groups of students at Edinburgh have been asked to specify the situation described by **2a–4a** and that described by **2b–4b**, and so far no student has felt that the sentences in each pair described different situations. (The students were not told beforehand what theoretical issues were involved.)

Although in isolation the sentences in each of the pairs **2–4** were not judged to be different in meaning, a difference could be brought out by the addition of clauses, as in **5**.

5a   John climbed up the mountain but ran out of food halfway up and had to come down
5b   John leapt over the chasm but caught his foot on a
branch and fell to his death

One explanation for the reactions of the students to **2–5** is that the NP V P NP structure leaves it open whether the action was completed. With a suitable continuation the action is taken as uncompleted but with no continuation some speakers interpret the action as completed. That is, it is not true that nouns preceded by a preposition never receive a holistic interpretation. Rather, direct objects are marked, in that they usually receive a holistic interpretation, and nouns preceded by a preposition are unmarked, in that they receive either a holistic or a non-holistic interpretation. The word 'usually' in the preceding sentence is important, because both the **a** and **b** sentences describe uncompleted actions if the verb is in the progressive (**6** and **7**).

6a John was climbing the mountain when the avalanche hit him

6b John was climbing up the mountain when he fell into a a crevasse

7a John was leaping the chasm when his foot caught on a branch and he plunged into the abyss

7b John was leaping over the chasm when he caught his foot on a branch and plunged into the abyss

If the verb is in the progressive there seems to be no difference in meaning between the **a** and **b** sentences, but if the verb is in its simple form the NP V NP structure is marked for completed action (definitely describes a completed action), whereas the NP V Prep NP structure is unmarked in this respect, i.e. it may or may not describe a completed action depending on the rest of the text and the situation.

A distinction between holistic and non-holistic interpretation has been attributed to other pairs of examples, e.g. *chew a steak/ chew on a steak, vote a strike/vote for a strike, read a speech/read from a speech, punch someone/punch at someone.* The students found it difficult to decide on some of the pairs. It was commented that *chew on a steak* was not a construction they used and that *read/read from a speech* described the same situation. The sentence *Mr Brezhnev read from a prepared speech* would not be given the interpretation that he only read certain passages from the speech.

Vote/vote for a strike presented difficulties; most of the students claimed they did not use or like *vote a strike*, and even those who did use both felt that the difference was one of markedness, *vote a strike* being marked for completion, *vote for a strike* being unmarked, the context determining the interpretation.

There is certainly a difference between *punch someone* and *punch at someone* but it seems possible that the difference resides in *at*, which expresses movement/location in the vicinity of an object without there necessarily being contact. In contrast, *The rocket punched into the wall of the barracks* or *The karate expert punched through a plank* describe the connection of a missile with its target, in spite of the NP V P NP structure.

The only conclusion is that for some speakers of English there is no evidence of a holistic/non-holistic distinction correlating with the structures V NP and V P NP, though there is evidence for a markedness relationship.

While traditional descriptions of languages employ very similar definitions of subject and object, various definitions of 'indirect object' are to be found and they are not satisfactory. Sometimes indirect objects are defined with respect to verbs like TELL, SAY, SHOW, GIVE, which occur in the construction NP V *to* NP. The indirect object is the NP preceded by *to* and the class of verbs is specified in order to avoid *to* NP sequences being classed as indirect objects in sentences like *He went to Dundee*.

Another definition talks of the indirect object noun being indirectly linked to the verb by a preposition (as opposed to being directly linked without a preposition), and the indirect object noun is said to denote the person or thing towards which the action is directed. This definition allows a much larger range of NPs to be classed as indirect objects, since it encompasses, in Indo-European languages, nouns in cases other than the dative, whereas the former definition takes in only nouns in the dative. With respect to a language like French it broadens the range of indirect object prepositions. The typical such preposition in French is 'à', but in his *Le Bon Usage* Grévisse says that the prepositional phrases in the following sentences are indirect objects: *La paresse nuit à la santé*, *Cet enfant obéit à ses parents*, *On doute de sa sincérité*.

Linguists concerned with roles rather than grammatical functions have proposed the role of *benefactive*, associated with e.g. *that student* in *I gave the book to that student*. In relation to this example the notion of benefactive is clear: it is the role attached to the noun denoting the person that benefits from the action. Unfortunately, the notion is applicable to sentences like *I did it for Celia*, which describes the performing of an action for the benefit of Celia, and this means that 'benefactive' is a broader notion than indirect object, certainly as the latter is understood in grammars of English.

An examination of what are traditionally called indirect objects in English reveals that the nouns denote animate beings, whereas the nouns in 'adverbs of direction' denote countries, towns and other inanimate objects. It has been proposed, as a result of these facts, that indirect objects and adverbs of direction be distinguished in descriptions of syntax on the ground that indirect objects can occur immediately to the right of the verb, with no preposition, but adverbs of direction cannot. Relevant examples are given in **8** and **9**.

8a John sent £10 to his cousin
8b John sent his cousin £10

9a The Prime Minister sent an envoy to China
9b The Prime Minister sent China an envoy

It has been alleged that sentences like **9b** are unacceptable, but a moment's reflection reveals that the peculiarity is not in the syntax but in the fact that *China* has to be construed not just as denoting a geographical area but as denoting a benefactive, its people and government. The benefactive interpretation is more plausible in **10**.

10a China sent Britain some of its jade treasures
10b China sent Britain her best physicists to help in the experiment

The corollary of the above examples is that an indirect object noun cannot always occur immediately to the right of the verb. The examples in **11** have been rejected by various classes of students.

11a *The experts attributed Raphael this picture
11b *I forwarded Winifred the letter
11c *The management presented the foreman a gold watch
11d *Kick John the ball
11e *Julie hit Virginia the ball
11f *The critics ascribe Shakespeare this play

There are syntactic patterns common to indirect objects and adverbs of direction. Both can occur in *wh* interrogative sentences with the preposition *to* at the end or the beginning of the sentence, as in **12** and **13**.

12a Who did John send a book to?
12b To whom did John send a book?

13a What place did you travel to?
13b To what place did you travel?

Another property in common is that both occur in active *wh* interrogatives with *to* omitted, but not in passive *wh* interrogatives (**14** and **15**).

14a Who did John send the book?
14b What place did John send the book?

15a   *Who was the book sent by John?

15b   *What place was the book sent by John?

In sentences with an indirect object or adverb of direction in second position preceded by *only*, *to* cannot be omitted, and the same applies in cleft sentences.

16a   Only to the best students would he give this book

16b   *Only the best students would he give this book

17a   Only to Glasgow would he travel by train, because the service is fast

17b   *Only Glasgow would he travel by train

18a   It is to the best students that he gives this book

18b   *It is the best students he gives this book

19a   It is to Lesmahagow that he is flitting

19b   *It is Lesmahagow that he is flitting

12–19 illustrate the syntactic patterns shared by indirect objects and adverbs of direction. One difference, concealed by the use of *what place* in **13–15**, is that indirect objects are questioned by *who . . . to* or *to whom* but adverbs of direction are questioned by *where*. However, this is only one difference to be set against the similarities, and it could be associated with a difference in the sorts of objects that are the end point of the movement, *where* being reserved for inanimate objects, *who* for human beings. Even for a sentence like *He will go to someone for help*, in which *to someone* is an adverb of direction rather than an indirect object, the appropriate interrogative is *Who will he go to for help?* rather than *Where will he go for help?*

The conclusion to be drawn is that there are no syntactic reasons for distinguishing indirect objects from adverbs of direction. The notion of a benefactive is important in semantics; the crucial difference between **9a** and **9b** is that in **9a** *China* is optionally interpreted as a benefactive, and **9b** obligatorily. The benefactive role is examined in more detail on pages 198–200, where the analysis proposed correlates with the syntactic analysis of indirect objects as adverbs of direction. In the syntax it is sufficient to have only the term adverb of direction, with 'benefactive' as a useful label for one type of adverb of direction. (NB. 'Indirect object' is used in a different sense in chapter 19 of BM: it applies to certain nouns immediately following a three-place verb.)

Technical terms

adverb of direction
agent
benefactive
grammatical function
holistic/non-holistic interpretation
indirect object
marked
object
participant
patient
process
subject
unmarked

17   Agents and instruments

Although grammatical relations have been demoted from the central position they occupy in traditional grammar, the roles played by participants in a situation are essential to a description of meaning and to an account of prepositions and case endings. Chapter 18 of BM concluded by asking how many propositional roles should be recognized; is a small number of general roles sufficient or should the 'locative' and 'dative' roles be kept distinct? There might be redundancy in a description that uses both process types and rule features in classifying verbs, but it was observed that rule features could not always be predicted from process types and vice versa.

This chapter argues that there is a place in linguistic descriptions for a small number of general roles (the question of where in a grammar the general roles are to be put is reserved for chapter 21). To argue that a small number of general roles is required does not imply that fine distinctions are not required as well. Consider the agent role. On page 314 fn. of BM it was suggested that it could be stranded out into the initiator of an action, the performer of an action and the cause of an action. Syntactic reasons support this stranding out and indicate a fourth one.

For instance, the pseudo-cleft construction (**1**) allows more than 'basic' agent nouns in the first NP after *what*.

1a   What the wind did was blow down a tree on top of my car
1b   What the computer is doing is play six simultaneous games of three-dimensional chess
1c   What this column does is support the weight of the pediment

The nouns in the first NP after *what* denote a natural force **1a**, a machine **1b** and a lump of stone **1c**, and the final definition of 'agent' must embrace all these examples.

One criterion proposed for agents is whether the noun can occur in the same sentence as a phrase introduced by *in order to*. A corollary of this is that in sentences with such a phrase the main verb denotes an action, but various verbs occur, as shown by **2**.

2a This guerrilla died in order to save his comrades
2b The fugitive lay motionless in order to avoid being hit
2c Their comrade suffered a great deal of pain in silence to be allowed to stay with the expedition

2a and **2c** describe situations in which the guerrilla and the comrade are patients; **2b** describes a situation in which the fugitive, if not a patient, cannot be said to perform an action.

The understood subject in imperative sentences is asserted to denote an agent, with the verb denoting an action, but this is not correct either, as demonstrated by the sentences *Stay absolutely still or the snake will strike, Die a glorious death for your motherland*.

The examples in **2** indicate a *volitive* strand in the agent role, by which is meant that an object brings something about by exerting its will-power. Although the verbs in **2** do not denote actions, the guerrilla, the fugitive and the comrade all exercise their will-power and are therefore regarded as agents. The imperative, while not a test for verbs denoting actions, does seem to be a test for the volitive strand. A sentence like *Kick the defender accidentally* looks like a contradiction; it would probably be given a sensible interpretation by being taken as an instruction to kick the defender but make it look accidental.

2a raises the problem that the guerrilla undergoes the process of dying. In this respect he is a patient; but at the same time he exerts his volition and is an agent. How can one participant play two roles, and how can this be expressed in a linguistic description? Anticipating the discussion on pages 209–12, we can say that the situation described by **2a** can be decomposed into smaller components, one of which is the guerrilla dying, the other his causing the process to happen. Although the surface structure contains only one occurrence of *this guerrilla*, the semantic structure has to contain more than one occurrence of the corresponding semantic unit, one with the agent part of the interpretation, the other with the patient part.

The second strand in the agent role is the *effective* one, so called because it relates to the production of an effect. **1c** illustrates the effective strand best: the column produces an effect simply by its position. Another example is *The falling tree crushed my car*, which describes the effect produced by the tree as a result of the movement transmitted to it without any exercise of volition on its part.

The third strand is the *initiative* one, so called because the person denoted by the agent noun initiates an action by giving a command but without necessarily doing anything else. An illustrative sentence is: *The guard marched the prisoners round the yard*.

The *agentive* strand is exemplified by **1a**, **1b** and also by sentences like *The machine crushed the car flat* and *The flood swept away whole villages*. These sentences describe objects that can be thought of as using their own energy, the object being a living thing, a machine or a natural force. The 'cause' component mentioned on page 314 of BM does not appear above but is incorporated in the agentive strand.

These four components or strands make up the broad notion of agent indicated by the surface syntax (and also by prepositions, as will be seen shortly). The traditional notion of agent is a combination of the volitional and agentive strands, but the important point is that this narrower notion derives no support from the surface syntax.

This is not to deny that the agentive + volitional combination is very frequent, perhaps even typical, nor that some surface structures impose this interpretation. The construction BE AT IT, as in *He was chopping logs when I left and was still at it when I returned* imposes that interpretation, and so do adverbs like *masterfully* and *enthusiastically*.

There is no claim that only verbs denoting actions occur with these adverbs or in the BE AT IT construction. The agentive + volitional interpretation may be most natural with such verbs, but if a verb occurs that does not denote an action the hearer has to assume either that the speaker cannot control his language or that he is expressing himself figuratively.

A distinction is usually drawn between animate agents and inanimate instruments. The above discussion has shown that although the typical agent is an animate being the role is not confined to animate beings and in a similar fashion it can be shown that instruments are not always inanimate.

No complex demonstration in needed. Quite apart from the unusual but perfectly possible situation described by the sentence

Bond seized the would-be assassin and smashed the plateglass window with him, it is possible to regard one person as the instrument by means of which something is accomplished. An unusual example of a sentence expressing such a conception is engraved on a headstone in Dunino kirkyard near St Andrews. The stone is to the memory of one Cleghorn, ' . . . the agent by whose instrumentality the island of Ceylon was annexed to the British Empire'. Of course, *agent* here is not used in the linguistic sense but it does denote a person who acts on behalf of someone else.

Rather than draw a distinction between the types of object that can function as agent and those that can function as instrument, it is better to distinguish between primary causes and secondary causes. In the sentence *The burglar broke the window with the hammer*, *burglar* can be regarded as denoting the object that is the primary cause of the breaking and *hammer* as denoting the secondary cause.

This distinction is signalled in the structure of passive sentences in English. The sentence *The window was broken with this hammer* allows the hearer to infer an agent in the situation though no agent is mentioned. In dialects where *by* and *with* are different in meaning, *by* signals primary causes, and *with* signals secondary causes. If the above sentence were *The window was broken by that hammer*, *hammer* would denote the primary cause and the hearer would not be entitled to make inferences about animate agents wielding the hammer. The hammer might simply have fallen from a shelf, in which case we have an agent in the broad sense, the effective strand being the relevant one.

Just as the description has to accommodate the general notion of agent and the various strands, so a way has to be found of handling the distinction between animate agents and inanimate instruments which also captures the similarity between agents and instruments reflected in the proposal on primary and secondary causes (and in the prepositions/case inflexions by which the roles are expressed). These problems are taken up in chapter 21.

Technical terms

agentive	initiative	primary cause
dative	instrument	role
effective	locative	seconday cause

18 Roles, cases, prepositions: agents and instruments reinterpreted

The examination of agency in the previous chapter was not based merely on intuitions but was anchored in the syntax of English, since the study of meaning requires the same attention to data as the study of syntax. We do not regard two forms as making a larger constituent unless the forms combine in different constructions, and we do not decide whether a particular verb takes an agent role without applying tests, such as whether the verb occurs in the pseudo-cleft construction (see **1** on page 180).

Another test for roles rests on the occurrence of prepositions or case-inflections. Labels like 'agent, 'patient', etc. relate to meaning: we start from the clearest examples which allow of no dispute as to whether a participant is an agent or patient or in some other role. From the clear cases we proceed to the unclear cases, taking account of syntactic constructions, prepositions and case affixes, following the principle that every occurrence of the same preposition or case affix expresses the same role. This principle is stated as strongly as possible so that it either constitutes a firm guideline or can be seen to break down. Weaker statements obscure failures.

This method might lead into an impasse, since *by* expresses agency in *This house was designed by Mackintosh* but not in *We travelled to Inverness by Stirling*. This difficulty is tackled in this chapter. It is proposed that a small number of basic roles can be postulated having to do with location and movement, the argument turning on prepositions and case affixes not just in English but in a number of languages.

The advantage of being guided by prepositions is illustrated by the sentences in **1**.

1a The shelf with the encyclopaedias on it is about to crack
1b The hooligans smeared the door with paint
1c The keys are with your wallet

1d   My brother left with your sister
1e   We ate the meal with chopsticks

It has been suggested that the five occurrences of *with* in **1a–1e** correlate with five different roles: 'possessive' in **1a**, 'objective' in **1b**, 'proximity' in **1c**, 'comitative' in **1d** and 'tool' in **1e**. Accepting this classification leads to as many different cases as there are subsets of lexical items, which goes against the principle that general statements can be made only if minor differences are ignored. For example, attention to the fine detail of distributional patterns reveals many subsets of nouns; only the decision to put the fine detail in the lexicon makes it possible to formulate generalizations in the syntax.

This reliance on prepositions and case affixes runs counter to the usual view of these as minor grammatical items with no meaning of their own, in contrast with major lexical items like nouns, verbs and adjectives. The usual argument in support of this distinction is that a sequence of items like *stormy tall pine bend creak gale dark street weary villager sleep* can easily be interpreted as *It was stormy. The tall pine(s) bent and creaked in the gale. Dark were the streets and the weary villager(s) slept.* The interpretation is not unduly hindered by the absence of articles, verb endings and prepositions, but all it demonstrates is that the bulk of the information expressed by a sentence is carried by nouns, verbs and adjectives. (Note that the time reference in the interpreting sentence is only one possibility: *It is stormy*, *It will be stormy*, *It had been stormy.*)

But it is not demonstrated that the distinction between *the book on the table* and *the book under the table* is any less important for correct understanding than that between *the book on the table* and *the book on the chair.* It turns out that prepositions and case affixes have a valuable part to play in establishing semantic structures.

The main problem is to decide where statements about general semantic structure are to go in a semantic description and where to put information about the semantic properties of individual lexical items. First, however, as we have to catch our general structures, let us return to **1**. All the examples describe situations in which two objects are located next to each other. The encyclopaedias and the paint are actually in contact with the shelf and the door, and the objects in each of the other situations are evidently close to each other.

There are examples in which the noun in the NP preceded by *with* does not denote a concrete object (2).

2a   The speaker with the greatest confidence is not always the one with the best ideas

2b   The boxer with the most skill cannot participate in the competition

2c   Who is that man with the arrogant air?

Confidence, skill and an arrogant air are not like chopsticks or smears of paint, which can be readily observed and located. But the surface syntax and morphology of a language can be regarded as a window on perception and conception. In this case the speakers of English talk of properties such as skill, etc. as abstract objects that are located in or at people and can have people located at them; these constructions provide hypotheses for the psycholinguist to explore.

While it is difficult to place these abstract objects in space as one can concrete objects like chairs, the boundaries of their existence can be located in time. One can determine the length of time that a person has had a skill or confidence or an arrogant air just as one can determine how long someone has had a car or a house; and skill, etc. can cease to exist just as a car can cease to exist.

We could regard the occurrence of *with* in the different sentences as accidental, but this would imply that the surface structure can be ignored or scrutinized as the whim takes us. This view has never been promoted by linguists working on syntax, and its adoption in semantics would be tantamount to recommending that linguists flounder in their intuitions.

The analysis of *with* as expressing location is adopted not just because it is arrived at via an apparently sound working principle but also because data from other languages provides corroborative evidence. It should not be thought that comparing English with other languages is simply a matter of collecting translations of English sentences. The crucial part of the operation is studying the correlations of form and meaning within each language and then comparing the correlations across languages.

Cross-language comparison reveals interesting facts. Just as *with* expresses a possessive relation, a tool relation, and a proximity relation, so these relations are expressed by the same preposition in other languages, 'avec' in French, 'mit' in German, for instance. These prepositions express, *inter alia*, a relation of simple location.

In other languages these relations are expressed by the same set of case affixes but different prepositions. In Russian, for example, the tool and objective relations are expressed by the instrumental case inflections alone, the comitative relation by the preposition *s* and the instrumental case inflections. Again, the instrumental inflections also express a purely locational relation and it is this that is significant, not the presence or absence of a preposition.

If location is chosen as the basic meaning we can explain why, in different languages, the prepositions and case affixes that express the comitative, tool and possessive relations also express location. By 'explain' is meant that a component of meaning has been found that is common to all the relations.

We can predict that in languages not yet studied there are means for describing the sorts of situation described by the sentences in 1 – making allowances for cultural differences – and that the morphs expressing the relations will also express location or will have expressed location at an earlier stage in the history of the languages. (The latter condition is necessary because in some languages prepositions or case affixes have lost their direct correlation with location.)

Examples are not hard to find. In Homeric Greek the dative case on its own expresses location but in Classical Greek, some 300 years later, the dative case could not express location without the help of a preposition. If we consider the expression of location and the tool relation in Homeric Greek, our evidence is that both are expressed by the dative case; but the evidence from Classical Greek is not so straightforward, though the same case is involved.

In Classical Greek the correlation between the dative case affixes and location is not seriously disturbed, because the same prepositions occur with both accusative and dative affixes, the former expressing movement, the latter location. Instances of more serious interruptions of correlation are to be found. In earlier stages of English, *of* expressed 'movement from' as in *He is of Galilee* but has been replaced in this usage by *from*. Although it no longer usually expresses 'concrete' movements, *of* still expresses 'abstract' movement in phrases like *some of this group*, whose meaning can be thought of in terms of some members of a set being moved out of that set (though note phrases like *a man of the people*). One can also say *some from this group*, using the preposition that does express 'concrete' movement from.

One last remark is needed on the cross-language comparisons. It so happens that where English uses the same preposition in **1**, Russian, for instance, uses the same case affixes, with or without a preposition. The correspondence between languages does not need to be so precise. Indeed, it would not matter if a language used five prepositions or case affixes where English uses *with* provided they also expressed concrete location.

This hypothetical situation is partially realized in Finnish. **1b** describes one object being covered by another. In Finnish sentences describing someone's eyes being full of tears or a lake being covered with ice, the nouns corresponding to *tears* and *ice* take a suffix that elsewhere expresses 'location inside'. **1e** describes a relation between a human being and an instrument. In the Finnish equivalent of the sentences *The girl is sweeping with a broom* the noun corresponding to *broom* takes a suffix that also expresses 'location on'. The comitative relation in **1d** is expressed in Finnish by a postposition *kanssa*, which patently consists of a noun base with the suffix *'ssa'* that expresses 'location inside'. The preposition is equivalent to the English phrase *in the vicinity of*.

The central thesis is that general statements about semantic structure refer to location and movement but not to the comitative, tool and possessive relations. Obviously the situations described by **1** vary. **1a** describes one object on top of another; **1d** describes an object near another; **1e** describes an object in the hands of a human. These differences are handled in another part of the description in which information about the type of action is combined with information about the objects associated with the action. This question is pursued in chapter 21; here we distinguish between general semantic relations and other information about meaning.

It is possible to have relations of movement as well as location. In some languages the agent noun is preceded by a preposition that also expresses 'movement from', e.g. *von* in German, *a/ab* in Latin, *hupo* in Classical Greek. To say that movement from is the basic relation underlying agency in these languages does not remove all problems of semantic analysis. For example, the German sentence *Der Wolf wurde von dem Jäger erschossen* ('The – wolf – became – from – the – hunter – shot') can be given two semantic interpretations: 'Shooting went from the hunter to the wolf', or 'The event of the wolf being shot came from the hunter.' Both analyses include a relation of movement from.

Agents are not described in terms of movement from in every

language. In French, for instance, agency is expressed by *par*, which expresses movement up to, through and away from an object, as in *Nous sommes passés par Paris* ('We – are – passed – by – Paris'). This relation is known as prolative, and is the basic meaning of *through*, *by*, and *along*; agency in English is based on the prolative relation, not the ablative one ('movement through' and not 'movement from').

In Classical Greek agency can also be described in terms of location, for in one construction the agent noun appears in the dative case. In some Australian aboriginal languages the suffix attached to the agent noun is identical with the suffix expressing location. In Telugu, a Dravidian language of South India, the agent noun is followed by the phrase *ceti-lo*, *ceti* being translated as 'hand' and *lo* being a morph that expresses location: e.g. *Ali defeated Frazier* is translated as *Frazier Ali ceti-lo odipoyinadu* ('Frazier – Ali – hand at – be defeated he').

Our analysis – known as 'localism' because local or spatial meanings are taken as basic – distinguishes various categories of objects. The sentences in **1** have nouns denoting concrete objects like wallets and walls and paint that can be located in space and time, and there are also the abstract objects like truth or virtue that cannot (so easily, at any rate) be located in space and time. An intermediate category is that of situations, which are easily located in time but not in space. *With* expresses relations between situations as well as between other sorts of object (**3**).

3a With all this fog hanging about it is impossible to land
3b With the workers having decided to stay on strike, the factory will have to close down

Let us go back to agents and instruments to see how these are handled in the localist analysis. The previous chapter concluded that the syntax of English supports a broad notion of agent, and that the distinction between agent and instrument can usefully be replaced by one between primary and secondary causes.

The conclusions based on English data are reinforced by morphological evidence from a number of languages, the essential point being that the same case affix expresses agency and instrumentality. Think of the Russian sentences in **4**, in which the agent and instrument nouns have the affix *-om*.

4a Soldat byl ranen Petrom 'Solder – was – wounded – by – Peter'

4b   Soldat byl ranen mečom 'Soldier – was – wounded – by – sword'

A recent survey of sixty Australian aboriginal languages with systems of case affixes has shown that nouns denoting animate performers and nouns denoting agents generally take the same affix. Where the two classes take different affixes, nouns denoting agents and nouns denoting natural forces like wind and rain take one affix, and nouns denoting tools take another.

The position can be summed up thus. In English the existence of *with* and *by* led to the view that *with* occurred with agent nouns, *by* with instrument nouns. The fact that nouns denoting instruments can be preceded by *with* or *by* prompted a more basic distinction between primary and secondary causes, and the idea that it is misleading to link agency exclusively to nouns denoting animate beings and instrumentality exclusively to nouns denoting inanimate instruments. Both animate beings and inanimate tools can be primary and secondary causes. The morphological evidence fills in the gap between the traditional agent and instrument by showing that in many languages the distinction is not reflected in syntax or morphology.

Of course animate beings are not identical with inanimate instruments or natural forces in all respects, as shown by the peculiarity of the sentences in **5**.

5a   The flood masterfully swept away whole villages
5b   The saw bit enthusiastically into the wood
5c   The policeman and the sledgehammer opened the door inside ten seconds

These examples take us back to the problem of selectional restrictions (pages 42–3). One view is that the sentences in **5** should be regarded as syntactically incorrect because a selectional restriction is broken between the adverbs and the type of noun with which they can co-occur. Adopting another view (page 43), we consider these sentences as syntactically correct but requiring the hearer to make adjustments in his interpretation. When such sentences, or the corresponding utterances, occur in conversation or literature the audience is not outraged at grammatical solecisms but interprets the event described in a different fashion, making the conceptual jumps that lie behind the use of figurative language. The breaking of selectional restrictions is merely a signal to the semantic component that literal interpretation is not appropriate, not a signal for an asterisk to be attached to the sentence.

In connection with primary and secondary causes let us consider the sentences in **6**, which express causal relations.

6a The climbers perished with the intense cold
6b Eventually the fugitives died from starvation
6c He suffers from a severe liver complaint
6d His teeth chattered with fear

The final noun phrase in these examples contains a noun, *cold*, *starvation*, *complaint* and *fear*, denoting a primary cause in the situation described by each sentence. With each of these nouns the broad notion of agent can also be associated:

7a The climbers were killed by the intense cold
7b The fugitives were eventually killed by starvation
7c He was made to suffer greatly by a liver complaint
7d His teeth were set chattering by fear

In English there is a special construction, exemplified in **6**, that is typically reserved for nouns denoting objects that are natural phenomena like heat, cold and disease or mental phenomena like fear, joy or shame. In the general part of the semantic description the different types of objects can be ignored but somewhere, probably the lexicon, nouns denoting natural phenomena are labelled differently from nouns denoting mental phenomena. The labels have a role to play in any account of why *He suffers from an overbearing mother* and *He died from a friendly bear* are curious.

The general part of the semantic description concentrates on the fact that in **6a** and **6d** there is a locative relation between the event of the climbers perishing and the cold, between the event of his teeth chattering and the fear, while in **6b** and **6c** there is an ablative relation between the fugitives dying and the starvation, the suffering and the liver complaint. A major problem for a generative grammar is to bring together the information about general relations and information about particular lexemes; a proposal as to how this can be accomplished is made on pages 201–19.

Technical terms

ablative	dative case	locational relation	prolative
comitative	localism	primary/secondary cause	

19 Patients and experiencers, possession and location

Like the agent role in English, the patient role can be interpreted in terms of movement, since the object undergoing an action can be thought of as the point to which an action moves from the agent. This conception is supported by two pieces of evidence.

In most descriptions of Indo-European languages, and of non-Indo-European languages, the object noun is defined as the noun denoting the thing in the real world to which the action passes from the agent. This view lies behind the use of the term 'transitive' for verbs that denote actions involving agents and patients. This term, deriving from the Latin *trans* ('across') and *ire* ('go'), reflects the notion of something passing from one person to another person or thing. The notion is so appealing intuitively that no linguist has protested against it. (Many have protested against defining the object in purely semantic terms, but that is another matter.)

The second piece of evidence comes from surface structure. In Indo-European languages with case inflexions the object noun is in the accusative case. The accusative case inflexion is also added to nouns denoting the end point of a movement. The object noun, however, is not preceded by a preposition in modern Indo-European languages or in Latin, but movement into a place is expressed by a preposition and a case affix. Consider the Latin *in urbem ire* ('into – the city – to go'), in which *urbem* is the accusative of *urbs*, and *Romam videre* ('Rome – to see'), in which *Romam* is the accusative form of *Roma*.

Although there is no preposition in verb-object noun constructions, the occurrence of accusative case inflexions is suggestive. Evidence even more suggestive comes from one of the oldest dialects of Indo-European. In Homeric Greek constructions describing the movement of an object from one point in space to another, the noun denoting the end point or the movement is in the accusative but not necessarily preceded by a preposition. The sequence Det N V Det N Accusative affix corresponds either to a sentence like *Odysseus hurled the discus* or *We came to Circe's house*, in which the Homeric Greek nouns corresponding to *discus* and *house* are both in the accusative case with no preposition corresponding to *to*.

Another interesting construction occurs in vulgar Latin. In Classical Latin the object noun is in the accusative not preceded by a preposition, whereas nouns denoting the end point of a movement are in the accusative preceded by a preposition (except the names of towns and cities). In vulgar Latin the converse of the Homeric Greek situation is found in that object nouns and nouns denoting the end point of a movement both occurred with a preposition as in **1**.

1a . . . et si unus ad alium cum pugno percuserit '. . . and – if – one – to – other – with – fist – strikes', i.e. 'if one strikes the other with his fist'

1b si unus occiderit ad alium 'if – one – will have killed – to – other', i.e. 'if one has killed the other'

The interesting feature of **1a** and **1b** is the occurrence of the preposition *ad*, which in Classical Latin occurs only in sentences like *Ad insulam navigaverunt* ('To – island – they sailed'). *Ad* occurs in **1a** and **1b**, though they are not usually *explicitly* analysed as describing movement. If *ad* is taken as a clue to semantic structure, however, the object noun *alium* has to be treated as denoting the end point of a movement. What moves is a blow with the fist or killing.

Except in darkness, a fist can be seen as it moves towards a person; even today killing is typically done by the movement of an object towards a person, whether the object is a hand, foot, arrow or bullet. **1b** represents an abstraction from these concrete situations since it describes not the movement of a particular missile but of killing. In spite of the abstraction, **1b** is rooted in observable events, which is what makes it interpretable.

Modern Spanish reflects the vulgar Latin construction in the occurrence of *a* before object nouns denoting human beings: e.g. *visito a Alfonso* ('I am visiting – to – Alfonso'). A similar but separate development took place in Romanian. The Latin preposition *per* ('through') became *pre* and *pe* in Romanian, and probably during the sixteenth centry *pe* began to occur before object nouns. This happened first of all with verbs of conquering or overcoming and then spread to other verbs. The essential fact is that *pe* still expressed movement. Noting this, Spitzer, one of the leading Romance scholars of the earlier part of this century, declared that the local expression *pe* + NP was more concrete than the abstract expression with the accusative case alone. Another Romance scholar, Bourciez, discussing the Spanish construction, says: *'On l'a [le complément] donc considéré comme intéressé à l'action, comme étant le point où elle aboutit'* ('It (the complement) has therefore been regarded as affected by the action, as being its end-point').

These references show that the analysis of patients proposed here is not startlingly new but merely the adoption and extension of ideas that have been stated, even if *en passant*, by other scholars.

Let us turn to the experiencer role. In English this role is closely connected with stative verbs and adjectives like KNOW, BE ASHAMED (pages 238–9 in BM), which are covert in that, their accompanying nouns not having any peculiar affixes, they are revealed only by their syntax. In earlier stages some at least of the stative verbs were overt in that the nouns denoting experiencers occurred in the dative case. Traces of this construction are to be observed in the archaic *methinks* and the even more archaic *Him like oysters*.

In Indo-European languages with cases more examples are to be found, not archaic or peculiar but regular constructions (usually listed in grammars under the heading 'impersonal verbs'). Classical Latin affords the examples in 2 and modern Bulgarian the examples in 3.

2a   Mihi libet 'To me – pleases', i.e. 'I like'
2b   Me paenitet 'Me – sorrows', i.e. 'I am sorry'
2c   Me pudet 'Me shames', i.e. 'I am ashamed'
2d   Me taedet 'Me wearies', i.e. 'I am weary'

3a   Na nego mu e lošo 'On – him – to him – is – bad', i.e. 'He feels ill'
3b   Nego go trese 'Him – him – fevers', i.e. 'He has a fever'
3c   Jad me e 'Fury – me – is', i.e. 'I am furious'
3d   Sram me e 'Shame – me – is', i.e. 'I am ashamed'

In these sentences the noun denoting the experiencer occurs either in the dative case (as in 2a and 3a, though the Slavic case system survives in Bulgarian only in the pronouns), or in the accusative case. In Latin and Bulgarian dative case forms occur with verbs of giving, showing, etc.; like the accusative case forms, they can be regarded as expressing the end point of a movement. The accusative and dative forms never express agency and the role associated with the verbs and adjectives in **2** and **3** is clearly passive. The general relation is that of being the end point of a movement but in the lexicon both the labels 'patient' and experiencer' are required for the conveying of information about individual lexemes.

Relevant to the distinction between patient and experiencer is the fact that some languages, e.g. Russian, assign dative case inflexions to most of the nouns denoting experiencers but reserve the accusative case inflexions mainly for patients.

The general semantic structure for **3d**, for instance, can be glossed as 'Shame come to me', and the structure of **2a** can be glossed as 'Pleasure comes to me'. If these structures seem bizarre, it should be recalled that idioms in English and other languages regularly talk of shame or pleasure or other abstract objects coming to people or of people being in them: e.g. *Sleep did not come easily, Only shame came to the club from the actions of its supporters, In his shame and confusion he could only stutter a few words*.

It is interesting to study the way in which possession is expressed in different languages. The English sentence *John has a book* is identical in form with *John plays chess*, but there are parallels between *John has a book* and *John knows the answer*; witness the peculiarity of *John is having a book* and *What John is doing is having a book*. Nouns denoting possessors have to be associated with a role that is not the agent one. The role is not the patient one either, judging by the fact that in Indo-European languages possessor nouns do not occur in the accusative.

Classical Latin has the construction exemplified by *Johanni est liber* ('To John – is – book'), *Johanni* being the dative case of *Johannus*: the same case affixes are added to nouns denoting possessors and nouns denoting recipients. Unfortunately no decisive synchronic evidence from Classical Latin enables us to choose between a description in terms of location and one in terms of movement.

English offers some evidence in support of a locational analysis. The evidence comes from sentences like *The documents are with my boss at the moment*, *The ball is with Leeds* (taken from a football commentary), *The car is with the dealer just now*. The interesting feature is the occurrence of *with*, which expresses location and it is this which indicates a semantic structure 'A book is at/with John' as appropriate for *John has a book*.

The plausibility of this analysis is demonstrated by possessive constructions in other languages in which possession can only be expressed by a construction identical in form with a locational construction. See the Finnish sentences in **4**.

4a Kirja on pöydallä   'Book – is – table on'
4b Minulla on kirja   'Me on – is – book'
4c Hänellä oli kauniit hampaat 'Her on – are – beautiful – teeth'

The suffix *-lla/-llä* expresses 'location on the surface of' – the technical term in grammars of Finnish is the adessive case. This suffix occurs in **4a**, which corresponds to *The book is on the table*, and in **4b** and **4c**, which correspond to *I have a book* and *She has beautiful teeth*. (Compare *I haven't got any money on me* and *Have you got a match on you?*, with the prepositional phrase *on* + NP.)

Finnish does not have a verb corresponding to HAVE. Indeed, HAVE constructions developed relatively late in Indo-European, and very few, if any, languages outside Indo-European have this construction, expressing instead possession by means of locational constructions.

Before leaving the topic of location we should look at two more constructions that lend themselves to a locational interpretation. The first one is exemplified by *My brother is an engineer*. There is no evidence in the surface structure of English to support the interpretation of *engineer* as a locative in the semantic structure, though the gloss 'My brother is in the class of engineers' is intuitively appealing. There are languages, in contra-distinction to English, with locational constructions corresponding to the English one. For instance, the Russian equivalent is *Brat v inženerax* ('Brother – in – engineers'). *V* is a preposition that elsewhere expresses 'location in' and *inženerax* is the locative plural form of *inžener*. The sequence N *v* N-locative affix is exactly the one that expresses concrete location, as in *Vašington v Soedinennyx Štatax* ('Washington – (is) in – United – States'). *Štatax* is the locative plural of *štat*.

This construction in Russian is limited to nouns denoting trades and professions but it does constitute a small, steady signpost to a semantic structure based on location. Moreover, it is not confined to Russian but is found in Celtic and Finno-Ugric languages.

The second construction is exemplified in *This room is warm* and *Edinburgh is windy*. As with the HAVE construction, there are languages into which these sentences can only be translated by a locational structure. In French the only possibility is *Il fait chaud dans cette pièce* ('It – makes – warm – in – this – room') and *Il fait du vent à Édimbourg* ('It – makes – of – wind – at – Edinburgh'). In Russian the only possibility is *V komnate teplo* ('In – room – warm'). In English it is also possible to say *It is warm in this room* and *It is windy in Edinburgh*. The appropriate semantic structure can be glossed 'Warmth is in this room' and 'Wind is in Edinburgh'.

Although *My brother is an engineer* and *This room is warm* are assigned the same general semantic structure with a locational relation, the properties of individual lexical items will enable the grammar to specify whether a sentence describes the membership of a profession or the temperature of a room, or indeed possession of an object.

Technical terms

accusative case
adessive case
experiencer
impersonal verb
locational construction
stative verb

20   Indirect objects reanalysed

Parallels between indirect objects and goals were mentioned in chapter 19 and chapter 16 described the syntactic similarities between indirect objects and adverbs of direction. The similarities increase if case affixes and prepositions are taken into account. Consider the Russian sentences in 1.

1a   Ivan dal Maše knigu 'Ivan – gave – to Maša – a book'
1b   Ivan narubil Maše drova 'Ivan – chopped – to Maša – wood'
1c   Ivan ubral Maše posudu so stola 'Ivan – took away – to Maša – dishes – from – table'

All the sentences in 1 contain *Maše*, the dative form of *Maša*, a girl's name. The English translations are *Ivan gave a book to Maša, Ivan chopped wood for Maša, Ivan cleared the dishes off the table for Maša*. In Russian the dative case inflexions express a basic meaning of 'movement towards', and this interpretation can easily be extended to 1a. The giving of something to someone is typically not held to take place unless an object has passed from one person to another, and *Maša* can be regarded as denoting the end point of the movement of the book.

This analysis of giving in terms of movement is not necessarily appropriate for every language. For instance, the dative case inflexions in Classical Greek have to be analysed as expressing location and a sentence like *Ho strategos edoke himation to stratiote* ('The – general – gave – cloak – to the – soldier') is associated with a semantic structure glossed as 'The general caused the cloak to be at the soldier'. This analysis is perfectly compatible with the above one in terms of movement, as it is possible to concentrate on the movement itself or the end point of the movement. The relationship between, e.g. *John went to London* and *John was in London* (at some time after his going there) can be handled by a rule of implication that applies to all sentences containing a verb of movement.

It is not obvious at first sight whether a movement analysis is possible for **1b** and **1c**, for the simple reason that it is difficult to decide exactly what object does the moving. It could be argued that it is the wood that moves in the situation described by **1b**, though *narubit'* ('chop') does not belong to the same semantic class as *dat'* ('give'), but **1c** is even less amenable.

On the other hand there is evidence of movement – if we keep to the principle that surface syntax and morphology are not accidental. In Russian itself the dative form *Maše* in **1b** and **1c** can be replaced by *za Mašu*. *Mašu* is the accusative singular form of *Maša* and the sequence *za* + N + accusative inflexion expresses 'movement to behind something', in contrast with *za* – N – locative inflexion, which expresses 'location behind something'. In Bulgarian, another Slav language, *za* is the preposition that expresses 'movement towards' and the Bulgarian sentences corresponding to **1b** and **1c** contain *za Maša* (Bulgarian has lost its case inflexions).

In the Finnish sentences corresponding to **1** the noun corresponding to *Maša* is in the allative case, the allative suffixes expressing 'movement on to'. In French the noun denoting the person who benefits from the actions described by **1b** and **1c** is preceded by *pour*, which also expresses movement towards, as *Il est parti pour Paris*.

The question, then, is: what moves? One plausible answer is that a whole event moves to the person concerned. On this interpretation **1c** has a semantic structure 'Ivan caused an event (Ivan cleared the dishes off the table) to move to Maša'; **1b** is a halfway house between **1a** and **1c** in having a semantic structure 'Ivan caused an event (Ivan chopped wood) to move to Maša' but also describing a situation in which Maša is left in possession of something concrete, the wood.

Talk of events moving to people is not as implausible as it may seem at first. There are common constructions in various Indo-European languages that patently describe the movement of events (2).

2a It fell to the chairman to cast the deciding vote
2b Il m'arrive souvent de voyager en Europe
2c Es fiel ihm zu, dem Erlkönig zu begegnen
2d Emu dovelos' služit' na zapadnom fronte

Literal translations are: **2b** 'It – to me – happens – often – to – travel – in – Europe'; **2c** 'It – fell – to him – to – the – Erlkönig – to – meet'; **2d** 'To him – led itself – to serve – on – Western – front.'

All these sentences have as one of their constituents an infinitive phrase describing an event: the casting of a vote, travelling in Europe, meeting the Erlkönig, serving on the Western front. The person to whom the event happens is denoted by a noun either in an oblique case or preceded by a preposition. The significant feature is that all four sentences contain verbs that elsewhere express concrete movement. The English has *fell*, the French *arrive*, the German *fiel . . . zu* ('fell – to', elsewhere used of a door slamming shut) and the Russian *dovelos'*, *s'* being a reflexive suffix, *do* a form that also occurs as a preposition with the meaning 'as far as', and *velo* being the neuter past tense singular form of *vesti* ('lead').

A similar analysis is offered by Helbig and Buscha in their *Deutsche Grammatik*.

Finally, one further advantage of the movement analysis is that it can be explained why experiencers and benefactives are realized by the same case inflexion in some languages, e.g. Russian: both are the endpoint of a movement, and this is what is captured in the general part of a semantic description.

21 Roles and relations in generative grammar

The preceding remarks about case inflections and prepositions are based on the localist hypothesis, the hypothesis that all relations are spatial, i.e. based on location and movement. We are concerned here only with localist analyses of roles such as agent, patient, etc. but localist analyses have been proposed for various areas of language, especially tense and aspect. In view of earlier comments on the relationship between linguistics and psychology, it is worth mentioning that the localist hypothesis accords with the generally held view that the location of objects in space and the movement of objects through space are fundamental to the development of our cognitive faculties.

It is important to understand the arguments used in support of the localist hypothesis. A major one, employed throughout the previous chapters, turns on cross-language data: in a large number of languages of different families, the morphs expressing relations between nouns and verbs/other nouns typically express location or movement as well as agency, etc. This can be accounted for only if location and movement are taken as basic.

A second argument relates to the ways in which languages change through time; in particular, when a case inflection or preposition loses its connection with concrete location or movement it is typically replaced by a morph that does have such a connection. Consider the substitution of *in front of* for *before* (in, e.g., *before the house*), the replacement in North American English of *behind* by *in back of,* and the present competition between *until* and *up to* in, e.g., *I'll be here until/up to three o'clock.*

A third argument is based on figurative language, which typically involves the description of something abstract by means of expressions that are closely connected with concrete location or movement: e.g. *He's far from stupid, The scheme came to fruition.* Consider also the example quoted on page 158, *The vet condes-*

cended to examine the budgie and the colloquial *The vet didn't lower himself to examine the budgie*.

In this chapter the discussion of how roles can be captured in a generative grammar makes crucial use of the localist hypothesis. The relations that turn up are *prolative* ('movement through'), *ablative* ('movement from'), *locative* ('location in, on, etc.'), *absolutive* ('the object that moves or is located'), and *allative* ('movement to').

How can the analyses offered in the preceding chapters and in chapter 18 of BM be captured in a generative grammar? Chapter 18 of BM hints at two ways in which a grammar can be modified, both involving the recognition of a propositional structure separate from the deep and surface syntactic structures. The propositional structure represents the types of processes or states and the roles connected with each type, information about mood, tense, aspect and negation being stripped off and placed in a modality component whose internal organization has not been specified. In the propositional component verbs and nouns are in principle unordered, though the usual representations put the verb first.

The proposals differ in their treatment of role information. One suggestion is that [+agent], [+patient] etc. be made features imposed on nouns in a propositional structure when a verb is inserted into it from the lexicon. The other suggestion was that the propositional structure contain a new category of items called 'cases' (not to be confused with case affixes in surface structure). Descriptions of language that include a category of cases are known as case grammars and the general approach, known as case grammar, is associated with Charles Fillmore. Fillmore himself says that he was not attempting to abolish the standard model, merely to point out an interesting and central area of language previously ignored by generative grammar and to suggest a way of talking about it within the standard model. Contrary to Fillmore's own intention, his writings have been regarded by many as introducing a radically new model, which makes it necessary to comment on the adequacy of a description with a propositional component employing cases.

Figure 99 shows the propositional structure for *The thief opened the box with a jemmy* as proposed by Fillmore. In the diagram A stands for 'agent', O for 'objective' and I for 'instrument'. K stands for 'Kasus', an item that is realized by a preposition and/or a case affix. The language being English, each K domi-

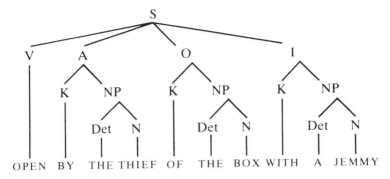

Figure 99

nates a preposition. The choice of OF as the objective preposition is based on nominalizations like *the opening of the box by the thief with a jemmy*, though this analysis might prove difficult to defend.

Fillmore uses the above sort of structure to express a number of ideas about syntax and semantics. He wants to state explicitly that with respect to propositional structure – or role structure – no one noun is more important than the others, though traditional grammar and Chomsky's generative grammar give prominence to the subject noun. This prominence is most obvious in the latter, since even in representations of deep structure the subject NP is out on its own while the other NPs are in the VP.

Fillmore attacked the traditional distinction between 'pure' and 'labelled' relations. In English pure relations were supposedly expressed by the position of the noun relative to the verb, without the help of a preposition, whereas labelled relations were expressed by prepositions. Having demonstrated that all the relations signalled by position alone could be signalled by prepositions, Fillmore adopted the view that all relations were labelled, i.e. that in the propositional structure all relations had a label and a Kasus element. The label carried information for the semantic component to operate on.

A third notion reflected in Figure 99 is that prepositions and case affixes have the same functions in surface syntax – expressing roles and linking nouns to verbs. This similarity is captured by deriving both prepositions and case affixes from the K constituent, but it is not clear how the linking function is expressed.

Finally, Fillmore showed that the notions of subject and object, whether in traditional or generative grammar, were of little or no relevance to semantic interpretation, but that roles were of crucial importance. This followed, he argued, from the fact that nouns in subject and object position could be associated with a variety of roles. This point is of no consequence for a grammar that confines itself to specifying syntactic structures in syntactic terms, but it does affect a grammar that tries to bring together syntax and semantics.

Chapters 18 and 19 of BM and chapters 16–22 in this volume make it obvious that we accept Fillmore's general ideas on the importance of roles, but there remain problems relating to the propositional structures. The roles themselves can be criticized, but there is as little point in this as in complaining that Newton's theory of gravity does not mention relativity. The lack of rules can be criticized, but this fault is shared by all attempts to describe semantic structure and to integrate descriptions of syntax and semantics into a single grammar. The lack of rules may be regrettable in view of the advances made in the description of syntax but unformalized ideas are not necessarily unformed and void of interest. It is worth pointing out that to date, systems of rules that allegedly integrate syntax and semantics achieve – or seem to achieve – their goal by handling a very small amount of data and working with limited notions of syntax and semantics.

In any case, there are more important questions to discuss, such as the status of the cases, the constituents, A, O and I in Figure 99. These cases are a new type of constituent – or should we say that there are as many different case constituents as there are different cases or roles; since there is no indication that all these items are instances of the same constituent. A similar problem arises in descriptions that do not employ features as well as constituents. Instead of animate nouns or abstract nouns being shown as nouns that happen to be abstract or animate, independent categories of Nanimate and Nabstract have to be set up (pages 134–5).

The difficulty with Nanimate, etc. was circumvented by features, which is all the more interesting in that the major part of the discussion in chapter 18 of BM makes use of features such as [+agent]. This attractive solution avoids introducing a new type of constituent – one for which there is no distributional evidence – and enables us to say that an agent noun is a noun that happens to have a particular property associated with it. The parallel with animacy and abstractness can be extended, because just as a particular verb may require an animate noun to its left, so it may require an agent noun to its left and patient noun to its right; the noun on the left is interpreted as denoting an agent, the noun on the right as denoting a patient. This information can be handled by adding [+agent] and [+patient] to the appropriate noun nodes when the verb is inserted into a phrase marker.

We leave on one side for the moment the question whether features like [+agent] are necessary in a description of syntax, but it should be clearly stated that features are already needed for the encoding of various sorts of information. Not only does the description employ a device already in use but it does away with the need to introduce a new type of constituent. This accords with the general principle that a grammar should use a small number of different categories and devices.

Despite their advantages, features do not get rid of one problem that intrigued Fillmore: how to show that case affixes and prepositions signal the same semantic information as well as having the same linking function in surface syntax. The latter problem, which takes us into a different view of syntactic structure, is too broad in scope for this textbook but the first is of immediate concern, being connected with another inadequacy in Fillmore's suggestions.

Fillmore, and he is not alone, uses the terms 'role' and 'relation' interchangeably. In one passage he speaks of the different roles expressed by case endings/prepositions and of the roles associated with subject or object position, and in another passage he talks of case endings/prepositions expressing relations between nouns and verbs. But are roles equivalent to relations? This is best answered with reference to the discussion of Fillmore's roles of agent and instrument and their reinterpretation in terms of location and movement.

Consider *John is with Bill* and *John hit the nail with a hammer*. From a localist point of view *with* expresses location in both sentences; there is a *relation* of location between John and Bill and between John and the hammer. John is located in the proximity of Bill and of the hammer. At the same time the roles played by John are different: in the situation described by the first sentence his role is called 'neutral' – he is simply in a location without playing any of the other roles – whereas in the situation described by the second sentence his role is one of agent. Similarly, Bill plays a comitative role in one situation but the hammer plays an instrument role in the other.

These examples show that a description of language has to include both roles and relations. The view that the semantic skeleton represents objects in a relation of movement or location is supported by the cross-language data but the skeleton has to be fleshed out with information about roles. One way of handling roles and relations is to include information about roles in the syntactic component of the grammar, as proposed in chapter 18 of BM, and to keep information about relations for the semantic component, to which we return shortly.

Chapter 18 in BM refers to propositional structures consisting of a verb and one or more nouns. These structures or frames are a good way of classifying constructions with respect to roles, semantic type of verb and corresponding syntactic structures; **1** shows a propositional structure and two syntactic structures corresponding to it.

1a   *agent*   *action*   *neutral*   *goal*
         source *directed*
                   causative   *patient*
                   possessive

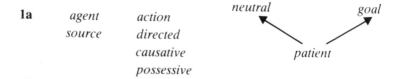

1b   Mary gave the book to John / Mary gave John the book

The propositional structure shows that the same type of verb (indeed, the same verb in these examples) occurs in both sentences. The noun to the left of the verb is marked as both agent and source: Mary causes the book to move to John, and is also the point from which the book moves. The book plays only a neutral role, but can be presented as the patient (*gave the book . . .*) or simply as neutral (*gave John the book*). John is the point to which the book moves, but can also be presented as the patient (*gave John the book*).

These propositional structures show nouns as being associated with two roles simultaneously, but they load a large number of features on to the verb and they do not fit easily into the extended standard model. Leaving on one side the number of roles associated simultaneously with one noun, we can begin by asking what the purpose of the verb features is. It was observed (pages 293–4 of BM) that the feature [action] at least has syntactic correlates: action verbs occur in passive structures, in pseudo-cleft constructions and in the answers to questions like *What did X do?* If the pseudo-cleft construction (*What X did was . . .*) is derived by T-rule from the deep structure underlying an ordinary declarative sentence, presumably the SA of the rule mentions the feature, so the rule only applies to structures with an [action] verb. The other syntactic correlates, however, cannot be found an interesting function in the grammar. [action] is not needed to describe the passive because the restriction on which verbs have past participle passive forms is handled in the lexicon by strict subcategorization frames; since no grammar is capable of handling pairs of question and answer systematically, the relevance of [action] in that respect is only potential.

The features [directed], [causative], and [possessive] have no syntactic correlates but are a convenient encapsulation of different bits of meaning. [directed] indicates that the action is directed at something, [causative] that a state of affairs is brought about, and [possessive] that the state of affairs involves something moving into someone's possession. If in a description of syntax alone, these three features can be dispensed with; in linking descriptions of syntax and semantics, the features can be seen as triggers that help the grammar to correlate a given syntactic structure with the appropriate semantic one. Given such a linking of syntax and semantics, the objections against traditional grammar do not apply. Many descriptions of languages prepared in that framework not only failed to keep syntax and semantics apart but classified syntactic categories with semantic criteria. In the description here, syntactic structures are analysed on their own terms first and then put into correspondence with semantic structure; far from semantics being the point of departure, the guiding principles are that semantics cannot be tackled properly without an adequate description of syntax and that syntax and morphology afford insights into semantics.

If [causative], [possessive] and [directed] have no role in an account of syntax alone, it is equally doubtful whether [patient], [agent], [source] etc. have a role either, except in the mapping of syntax into semantics. It might seem that they could be used in the selectional frames for prepositions, *by* being the English preposition that co-occurs with agent nouns. However, *by* also co-occurs with nouns denoting places (*by Stirling*), with time expressions (*by four o'clock*), with abstract nouns (*He succeeded by sheer determination*) and with gerunds (*We alerted the coastguards by firing a distress rocket*). Time expressions with *by* co-occur with any kind of verb but the other *by* phrases co-occur with action verbs only – the exception being expressions like *sat by the fire*, in which there is a [state] verb and a noun denoting an object with reference to which the location of other objects can be specified. Perhaps [+Concrete] is sufficient for the latter property, but the feature has nothing to do with roles and in most of the above examples it is the verb type that is important, not the noun in the prepositional phrase.

Even if the role information were applicable in a description of syntax, the propositional structures proposed by Fillmore raise problems for T-rules. Since all the nouns are to the right of the verb, they have to be moved into appropriate positions for the surface syntax. For example, the structure of Figure 99 can be realized as **2a** and **2b**.

>**2a**   The thief opened the box with a jemmy
>**2b**   The box was opened by the thief with a jemmy

If the agent constituent is not present, **3a** and **3b** are possible realizations, and if the I and A are not present **4** is possible.

>**3a**   The jemmy opened the box (after the other tools had proved unsuccessful
>**3b**   The box was opened with the jemmy/by the jemmy
>**4**   The box was opened.

The T-rules that move the nouns have to be extremely detailed and complex. There are various candidates for subject position, depending on what cases are present in the propositional structure and the T-rules have the task of deleting the K element where necessary. (In **2–4** the O noun is never preceded by a preposition but the other nouns occur with and without prepositions.)

A second objection is that the T-rule that maps the propositional structure into passive sentences still falls foul of the objections based on distributional criteria (see pages 149–51), namely that the past participle is an adjective on distributional criteria. There have been proposals that surface adjectives and verbs be derived from a single deep category, called 'verb' or 'predicator', but the arguments for the proposal have either not stood up to close scrutiny or have rested on the controversial claim that BE forms do not occur in deep structure.

Of course the relationships between **2**, **3** and **4** have to be expressed somewhere in the grammar, but there is an alternative to deriving them all from a very abstract deep propositional structure and that is to handle them by implication relations. As described on pages 164–5, the syntactic component of the grammar generates structures that are mapped into semantic structures and in addition a set of implication rules states relations of implication either between syntactic structures (deep or surface?) or between semantic structures. These rules state that **2b** implies **2a**, that **3b** implies **3a**, that **3c** implies *Someone opened the box with the jemmy*, and that **4** implies *Someone opened the box*.

The statement of implications is not necessarily straightforward but their inclusion in the grammar allows us to maintain a relatively simple set of T-rules generating a respectable number of constructions and sentences. A balance must be struck between not throwing away an imperfect but workable formal system before another equally general system is available and refusing to consider any views on syntax and semantics that are expressed in a different formal system or in no formal system.

Some problems require intricate solutions, and if the syntax is kept simple other parts of the grammar grow more complex. If the syntax cannot accommodate Fillmore's views that all nouns can be regarded as modifiers of the verb, that prepositions and case inflexions have the same semantic function, and that all relations can be regarded as labelled, then a place must be found for them in the semantic component. This is also the home for the localist analyses proposed in the previous chapters.

We look at several sentences of the sort discussed on pages 288–315 of BM in order to illustrate the relationship between the classification of verbs offered there and the localist semantic structures. The semantic structure of *The student read a book* is

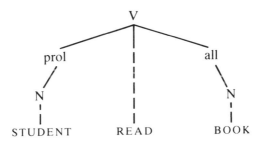

Figure 100

shown in Figure 100. It is not intended as the last word on semantic structures but merely as an example of the constituents and their arrangements.

Figure 100 is not to be interpreted as saying that the nouns are constituents of the verb but rather that the nouns are modifiers of the verb, which is taken to be the central constituent. The items *prol* (for 'prolative') and *all* (for 'allative') are not a new kind of constituent but labels for the branches joining the verb and the nouns. The labelled branches reflect the relations between verbs and nouns, and between two nouns, though this possibility is not illustrated here. They correspond to prepositions and case affixes in representations of surface syntax. 'Allative' reflects the view that an action is directed towards some object (compare the feature directed on pages 291–2 of BM), and 'prolative' reflects the view than an action moves by way of someone.

Figure 100 offers nothing corresponding to the articles in the English sentence, nor is there any mention of tense. These items do not relate directly to this discussion of roles and relations, but in any case a semantic analysis of tense is undoubtedly more complex than its treatment in the syntactic component. Although in many languages the morphs signalling time reference are attached to the verb in a sentence, it is the whole sentence and not just the verb that is modified. This suggests a description of whole events – process or state and participants – as being located in time.

Figure 101 shows the semantic structure corresponding to *John broke the lock with a jemmy. Loc*, for 'locative', captures the localist view that *with* expresses location.

Putting syntactic structures in correspondence with semantic

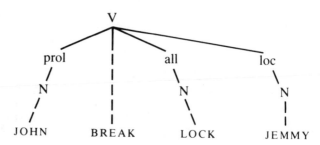

Figure 101

ones enables us to escape from various dilemmas, the major one being the confusion of roles and relations. *John is working with Bill* and *John is working with a hammer* have similar semantic structures in that both BILL and HAMMER are connected to the verb by a branch labelled 'loc'. In the syntactic component, however, the verb assigns either [+comitative] or [+instrument] to the noun following it. BILL is marked in its lexical entry as typically associated with the role of agent or patient or comitative, and HAMMER with the role of instrument or patient. If *Bill* is attached to a [+comitative] noun node and *hammer* to a [+instrument] noun node, no difficulties are raised for semantic interpretation, but if *hammer* is attached to a [+comitative] noun node, the clash between the features [+comitative] and [+instrument] warns the semantic component that a literal interpretation is not possible.

Another dilemma that vanishes is whether to have both 'dative' and 'locative' roles (see page 327 of BM). Chapter 16 showed that a clear distinction could not be drawn between indirect objects and adverbs of place. The one difference lay in the construction NP V NP NP (e.g. *We gave him a present*), in which the second NP was held to be an indirect object and not an adverb of place. However, sentences like *China sent Britain her best nuclear physicist* demonstrated that the crux of the matter was whether the NP immediately to the right of V could be easily interpreted as a benefactive, since whatever occurred in that NP would have a benefactive interpretation put upon it. This is handled by optionally assigning [+benefactive] to NP_3 in the construction NP_1 V NP_2 *to* NP_3. The assignment of the feature is optional because sentences like *We sent a book to Bill* and *We sent engineers to France*, *Bill* and *France* can denote merely the point to which the book and the engineers travelled or they can denote the people intended to benefit from the book/engineers. In this a role feature has a syntactic function, since nouns marked [+benefactive] can be moved to the position immediately to the right of the verb. The semantic structure for *We sent a book to Bill* is in Figure 102.

The structure dominated by V_2 is glossed 'The book moved from us to Bill'. The structure dominated by V_1 is glossed 'By (way of) us came V_2', i.e. the event of the book moving from us to Bill' and is the semantic structure corresponding to the verb CAUSE (page 305 in BM). In localist terms, 'X causing an event' is represented as 'An event coming from or by way of X'.

The structure in Figure 102 sheds light on the assignment of

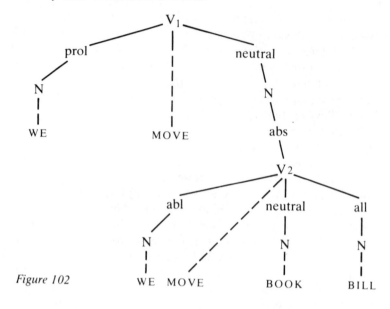

Figure 102

two role features to nouns in the propositional structures (pages 305–6 in BM). The event described by *We sent a book to Bill* is analysed as two sub-events, one of causation – 'We brought it about that' – and one of an object moving – 'a book moved from us to Bill'. In the first sub-event the speakers are agents and in the second one they are the point from which the book moved: hence the features [+agent] and [+source] attached to the initial noun in propositional structure **78** on page 305 of BM.

The localist approach analyses possession as location, *Bill has a car* being assigned the semantic structure CAR BE LOC BILL. Giving and sending are analysed in terms of movement; the implication between *John gave Bill a car* (*at time t*) and *Bill had a car* (*at time $t + 1$*) has to be captured in a component of the grammar given over to the listing of implications. One consequence of this analysis is that whereas the above features [+agent] and [+source] correspond to different relations in the semantic structure, the feature [+possession] in propositional frame **78** on page 305 of BM corresponds not to an item in the semantic structure in Figure 102 but to the semantic structure of location implied by Figure 102.

On pages 311–12 of BM there are examples, described as 're-flexive', such as *John hurt himself, John killed himself, John sat down*. They are reflexive in that John performs an action on him-

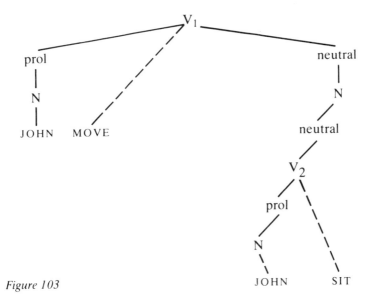

Figure 103

self, which is reflected, at least for *John sat down*, in the assignment of two features to the N in the propositional structure. As in Figure 102, these features correspond to different roles in a complex semantic structure (Figure 103).

The structure of Figure 103 is glossed 'John caused John to sit'. Other intransitive verbs in English lend themselves to this analysis and even the simple verb GO can be associated with a reflexive structure, as indicated by the archaic expression *betake oneself*. Note that the paraphrase relation between *The soldier went to the guardroom* and *The soldier betook himself to the guardroom* is not being used as an argument with respect to the syntactic description of these examples. They derive from different syntactic deep structures but correspond to the same semantic structure.

Where English has simple intransitive verbs GO AWAY and STAND, French has expressions with a reflexive pronoun, *s'en aller* and *se tenir debout* or *se lever*. Either the *se* is dismissed as an accidental property of these expressions that has no bearing on their interpretation or it can be taken as parallel to the *se* in *se blesser*. The working principle that syntax and morphology are a guide to semantic structure obliges us to adopt the latter view, which fits with the reflexive structure in Figure 102. The same structure is appropriate for *John jumped the horse over the fence* (page 314 of BM), except that the prolative noun under V_1 is JOHN, and the prolative noun under V_2 is HORSE.

As a final example of how the propositional frames of chapter 20 of BM are incorporated in a generative grammar consider sentences with result participants, e.g. *Velasquez painted the Rokeby Venus*, and *John burnt a hole in the carpet*. On page 291 of BM the object NP in these sentences is given the features [neutral] and [result]. The latter corresponds not to a relation in the semantic structure but to an embedded S containing the noun EXISTENCE, as in Figure 104.

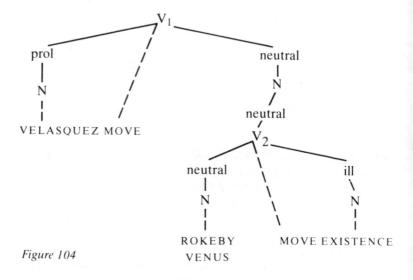

Figure 104

Ill stands for 'illative' (= 'into (interior)') and the entire structure is glossed 'It came by way of Velasquez that the Rokeby Venus came into existence'. This is not the whole story, because CAUSE COME INTO EXISTENCE corresponds to a number of verbs, e.g. BURN (*He burned a hole in the rug*), DIG (*They dug a hole in the lawn*), LIGHT (*They lit a fire*), BORE (*They bored a tunnel through the hill*). One way of handling these resultative verbs is to put information about how the bringing into existence is achieved into the dictionary entries for the various lexemes. All the resultative verbs have the features [+causative] and [+existence], which guide the grammar to the appropriate semantic structure, but not all semantic information is stored in the semantic structure. The more particular bits of information are included in the lexical entries, leaving the semantic component to account for the most general relations. For a full semantic description it may be necessary to allow the semantic component to refer back to the lexicon.

The sentences examined so far have posed few difficulties for semantic analysis but some examples are not so straightforward, for instance **80** and **83a** (page 306), **85–6** (page 307) and **102a** and **102b** (page 309) in chapter 18 of BM, reproduced here as **5–7**.

> **5a** John robbed Mary of £10
> **5b** John stole £10 from Mary
> **6a** The Chinese supplied arms to the Vietcong
> **6b** The Chinese supplied the Vietcong with arms
> **7a** John planted roses in the garden
> **7b** John planted the garden with roses

Although they differ in syntax, **6** and **7** are classified in terms of the propositional frame in **8**, except that **7** has L goal and agent.

8

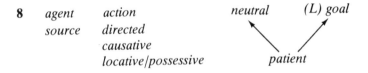

agent	*action*	*neutral*	*(L) goal*
source	*directed*		
	causative		
	locative/possessive	*patient*	

Apart from the verb being labelled [possessive] with respect to **5** and **6** but [locative] with respect to **7**, the difference lies in the role to which [patient] is added. *John planted roses in the garden* has the propositional frame with $\begin{bmatrix} \text{neutral} \\ \text{patient} \end{bmatrix}$ whereas *John planted the garden with roses* has the frame with $\begin{bmatrix} \text{L goal} \\ \text{patient} \end{bmatrix}$. In **7a** *roses* has the neutral role and is in direct object position, but in **7b** the direct object is *garden*, which has the locative role. On this analysis **7a** is regarded as describing the same situation as **7b**, there being a minor difference in the order of constituents in the surface syntax.

In spite of its appeal, this analysis does not sit easily with the criteria for determining whether in the syntactic component two sentences should be derived from a single deep structure by different transformations. There is a difference in the order of constituents accompanied by a difference of preposition, though this might be of no import given the accepted transformational relationships between *John gave a book to Bill* and *John gave Bill a book*. What makes the difference more serious is that there is not just a change in constituent order with the deletion of a preposition but also the addition of a preposition. When *the garden* is moved into direct object position *in* is deleted and *with* inserted before roses. NP movement and preposition deletion can be accommodated but the addition of a preposition should make us pause.

7a and **7b** are parallel in syntax to **1a** and **1b** on page 173, which turned out to be different in meaning. **7a** and **7b** also differ in meaning, since **7b** implies *There were roses all over the garden* but **7a** does not. Perhaps this difference is due to 'focusing', the positioning of a constituent next to the verb instead of at the end of a sentence, but this does not seem plausible. The difficulty is that 'focusing', as normally understood, is a superficial pheno-menon such as the NP movement that converts *I just can't stand these new-fangled ideas* into *These new-fangled ideas I just can't stand*. The movement of the NP does not affect the sort of situation that can be described by the sentence but merely puts the NP into prominence, a quite different relationship from that between **7a** and **7b**, which describe different situations.

There are other reasons for rejecting focusing. The NP move-ment mentioned in the previous paragraph takes place late on in a syntactic derivation but there are constructions, exemplified in **9** and **10**, which show that the movement proposed for **7b** would have to take place at an early stage in the derivation.

9a Roses are certain to be planted in the garden by John
9b The garden is certain to be planted with roses by John

10a It is roses that John planted in the garden
10b It is the garden that John planted with roses

The significance of these examples is that sentences like **9a** and **9b** are derived by subject raising (pages 81–4). If *roses* or *garden* is to be raised, it has to be in subject position when sub-ject raising applies, which means that it is in subject position at an early stage in the derivation. Similar remarks apply to **10a** and **10b** with respect to the T-rule that generates the cleft construction. (Within grammars that do not employ subject raising or clefting T-rules the argument would rest on the large discrepancy between **7a** and **7b** in syntax and the significant difference in meaning.)

The evidence supports a solution in which **7a** and **7b** are generated separately in the syntactic component and correlated

with different semantic structures. In the semantic structure for
7a *roses* is in the patient role and *garden* in the locative: an appropriate gloss is 'John cause: roses be in the garden'. In the semantic
structure for **7b** *garden* is patient and *roses* – locative: an appropriate gloss is 'John cause: the garden be with roses'. If there is a
semantic relation it is one of implication, since **7b** implies **7a**,
though not vice versa.

5a and **5b** pose the same problem with the prepositions as **7a**
and **7b** but there is the extra difficulty that they contain forms of
different verb lexemes, R O B and S T E A L. These differences alone
preclude a transformational relation between them in the syntactic
component and indicate different semantic structures. The structure for **5a** is glossed 'John caused: Mary move from £10', i.e.
Mary is parted from her money, and the structure for **5b** is 'John
caused: £10 move from Mary', i.e. the money is parted from Mary.
5a and **5b** are closely related in meaning – it can be argued that the
'same' situation is viewed from different angles – though it does
not follow that the sentences should be put in correspondence with
the same semantic structure. Another possibility, which accords
with the syntactic/morphological guidelines, is that the structures
are in a relation of bilateral implication: **5a** implies and is implied
by **5b**.

A further point to be made in connection with **7a** and **7b** is that
the garden has a holistic interpretation (page 173) when it is in
direct object position but not when it occurs after a preposition.
The relevance of the direct object position is that nouns here typically denote the patient, the object affected by the action, and the
patient is usually taken to be completely affected by the action
unless there is information to the contrary, e.g. if there is an
adverb like *partly: The garden is partly planted with roses, John
planted the garden partly with roses and partly with Michaelmas
Daisies*. This interpretation applies to **5** and **7** and also to **6, 6a**
describing a situation in which what happened to the arms was
that they moved to the Vietcong and **6b** describing a situation in
which what happened to the Vietcong was they came to be with
weapons. As with **5a** and **5b**, a relation of bilateral implication can
be established.

Evidently the investigation of roles and relations has gained
greatly by being set in a definite framework of description with
clearly delimited components. Instead of simply classifying verbs
by various propositional frames we can ask questions about what

sorts of information are concerned and which component is best for which sort. To this is added the advantage of having a reliable, sophisticated description of syntax and morphology to guide us in deciding what semantic structures are required.

It may seem that some information is not presented in this scheme as attractively as in the classificatory scheme of chapter 18 of BM. There it was possible to say that **5a** and **5b** describe the same situation and have the same propositional frame, different nouns being moved into subject and object position depending on which participants the speaker wants to make prominent, the choice of ROB or STEAL being governed by the choice of subject or object. Now there is no longer a single propositional frame but two semantic structures and two different syntactic derivations; in fact, four if the passive sentences are taken into account. But the two semantic structures are still shown to be equivalent by an implicational rule, and the description of thematic relations (page 361 in BM) specifies that the passive is a device for allowing a patient noun to occur in subject position and be given a certain prominence as the starting point of the message. It also specifies that the NP in direct object position is more prominent than the NP in a prepositional phrase (note the omissibility of *£10* in **5a** but not **5b**). No information is lost, and spreading it out over the components enables us to preserve a relatively simple set of rules for the syntax, compared with the complicated rules required to map a single propositional structure into different surface syntactic structures with different verbs and prepositions.

Nobody has yet written rules that map surface syntactic structures into adequate semantic structures. It is simpler to correlate a whole syntactic structure with a whole semantic structure rather than to go through a series of intermediate structures each of which differs in one detail only from the preceding one (which is how the description of the syntax is organized), but even this modest goal has not been attained. The disparity in treatment is due to the vast amount of work on syntax over the last twenty years and the greater complexity of semantic structures, but it should not obscure the advances that have been made.

Technical terms

absolutive
case grammar
case grammars
localist hypothesis
pure/labelled relations

22 Patients and benefactives

The previous chapter mentioned the sentence *John sat down*, whose syntactic structure contains an intransitive verb but whose semantic structure required both an agent noun and a patient noun, the agent and patient nouns denoting the same person. The sentences in **1** also contain intransitive verbs and also require a patient noun in their semantic structure, though the agent and patient nouns denote different objects.

1a The men are out hunting
1b I'm reading
1c She's been painting all morning

Verbs like HUNT are treated in transformational grammars as 'pseudo intransitives', in that they are inserted into a deep structure with an object NP that is subsequently deleted (*I'm hunting something ⇒ I'm hunting*). Verbs like GO cannot be inserted into a structure with an object NP because they never occur with an object NP in surface structure (*I'm hunting something, I'm hunting tiger*).

A third type of sentence with an intransitive verb but requiring both agent and patient nouns in its semantic structure is exemplified in **2**.

2a My brother is shaving
2b Margaret is busy washing
2c The dog is scratching again

2a–2c, like **1**, could be derived by deleting an object NP. The person referred to by *my brother* could be a barber shaving his customers, Margaret could be washing clothes, and the dog could be scratching the door. Another interpretation is that the agent and patient are identical. Although in other Indo-European languages reflexive pronouns signal identity of agent and patient, they rarely occur in **2**, at least in standard written English.

When they do occur with such verbs, the interpretation is ambiguous. *The head barber never shaves himself* can be interpreted 'As for the head barber, he never does any shaving to others' (= *The head barber himself never shaves*) but it can be interpreted 'The head barber never gives himself a shave'.

The sentences in **3** exemplify another English construction whose semantic structure is more complex than appears from the syntax.

3a These books sell very quickly
3b This cloth cuts very easily
3c The new material washes beautifully
3d This wool knits up without any trouble

These sentences are identical in structure with other sentences containing intransitive verbs, e.g. *John ran very fast*, but they are interpreted differently. *John* in the last example denotes an agent but the nouns in **3** denote patients. There is some implication that the quick selling of the books or the easy cutting of the cloth was due to the skill of the unmentioned agent, but the speed or ease of the process is primarily determined by some quality of the books, cloth, etc.

This construction is not confined to habitual processes cf. **4**.

4a These books sold very quickly last week
4b The cloth was cutting beautifully this morning
4c She found that the wool knitted up without any trouble yesterday

Sentences like **3** and **4** have been called 'process-oriented', but a more appropriate term is 'patient-process oriented'. In contrast, the sentences in **5** are 'agent-process oriented' because not only is there an agent noun but the quality of the process is understood to reflect the skill of the agent.

5a Our new assistant sold these cars very quickly last week
5b The apprentice cut the cloth beautifully this morning
5c Being very skilful, she knitted up the wool without any trouble

Passive sentences in which there is no agent noun are in a no man's land between the patient-process and the agent-process oriented constructions, as they are capable of both interpretations. *These cars were sold very quickly* attracts the agent-process interpretation, whereas *These cars are sold very quickly* attracts the patient-process interpretation more readily.

It is not clear which verbs can occur in the patient-process oriented construction. In his *Modern English Grammar*, Jespersen lists about thirty verbs, with examples from Defoe and Goldsmith to Shaw and Barrie, including *The middle storeys do not let, Four babies, none of whom photographed well, The story told well.* Other examples are *She doesn't scare/frighten easily, Mr Howard amuses easy* and *The course rides well* (from a television programme on equestrian competitions).

According to Jespersen, *His novels sell very well* presents the books as active, as 'selling themselves', and this interpretation gains plausibility if we accept that some semantic correlate should be provided for the reflexive pronoun in, e.g., *Les livres se vendent bien*. The obvious correlate is a structure 'The books cause: The books move to someone'.

The drift of the above paragraphs is that even a sentence without an object noun may require a patient noun in its semantic structure, and similar arguments can be made for sentences like those in **6**, without a benefactive expression in their surface syntax.

6a   My brother is going to buy a bike
6b   My brother is going to buy a bike for his girlfriend
6c   My brother is going to buy himself a bike

In utterances corresponding to **6c**, *himself* may or may not be given prominence via the pitch and rhythm pattern. On the other hand, in utterances corresponding to sentences like *My brother is going to buy a bike for himself* the pronoun is typically prominent.

Note that **6c** differs from **6b** with respect to the intended owner of the bike and that **6a** leaves the ownership vague. The interpretation that comes to mind first is that the speaker's brother is going to buy a bike for himself, but this is not the only interpretation, as the following exchange shows: *My brother is going to buy a bike. Yes, I know he's got one already. It's not for himself, it's for his girlfriend*.

One way of capturing the similarities and the differences between **6a**, and **6b** is to postulate the same general semantic structure for all three, the essential element being a benefactive noun. In the structure **6a** the benefactive is either empty or dominates SOME ONE but it dominates full lexemes in the structures for **6b** and **6c**. There is no need to generate a reflexive pronoun in the deep syntactic structure of **6a** and then delete it, as the relationship between **6a** and **6c** is adequately captured via the semantic structure.

Sentences with forms of BUY, SEND, etc. are obvious candidates for the benefactive treatment but there are other sentences for which it is appropriate, in view of the reanalysis of indirect objects in terms of concrete objects and events moving to people (pages 198–200). One candidate is **7a**.

7a   The general destroyed the city
7b   The general destroyed the city for his allies
7c   The general destroyed the city for himself

7a leaves it open for whom the general destroyed the city, though the first interpretation is probably that he did it for himself. **7b** and **7c** contain a benefactive expression, and **7a–7c** can be handled in the same way as **6a–6c**. The parallel between **6c** and **7c** is not complete with respect to syntax, as *The general destroyed himself the city* is odd for written British English. It would not sound odd coming from a character in a Western, and this construction may enter some dialect or dialects of British English.

There is a connection between benefactives and sentences with forms of SHAVE, WASH and SCRATCH. Grammars of English usually cite the sort of sentence in **2**, but **8** and **9** exemplify other constructions, equivalent in meaning, that are typical of spoken English.

8a   My brother is having a shave
8b   Margaret is having a wash
8c   The dog is having a scratch

9a   My brother is giving himself a shave
9b   Margaret is giving herself a wash
9c   The dog is giving itself a scratch

(Perhaps the most frequent construction is *My brother is getting shaved* and *Margaret is getting washed*, but these, while compatible with the analysis to be proposed, are not as interesting with respect to semantics.) One can also *have a swim/walk/run/jog/ a kick/swing at someone/a nibble at an apple/a sleep*. Some speakers of English talk about *having read of a book* or instruct children to *have a play* before bedtime. Similarly, one can *give a dog (or person) a walk/run/kick/blow/bath/a look at the paper/ a loan of a book/a bite of an apple*.

The significance of these examples is that GIVE has been analysed in terms of causing an object to move to someone, and HAVE in terms of an object being located at someone. Of course, sentences like *My brother has red hair* and *My brother is having a shave* are not fully parallel in syntax, since sentences describing the possession of concrete objects do not normally contain the progressive construction. This however can be attributed to the fact that *have a shave* describes a more dynamic situation that *have red hair*. If we are to be consistent and follow the principle that syntax and morphology are a guide to semantic structure, then GIVE and HAVE in **8** and **9** should also be analysed in terms of movement and location. In **8** and **9** and sentences like them, SHAVE, WASH, SCRATCH, NIBBLE, etc. are nouns syntactically, like TABLE, CHAIR, LOG. The latter three denote objects in the world, and to be consistent we should take the similar syntactic behaviour of SHAVE and LOG as indicating that SHAVE, etc. also denote objects, albeit abstract ones. This approach is legitimate if we remember that our semantic structures do not represent the world as it is represented in theoretical physics but as it is perceived and conceived by human beings.

Granted the validity of this position, **9a** has the semantic structure MY BROTHER CAUSE: A SHAVE MOVE TO MY BROTHER. It follows from this analysis that the object noun in *My brother shave himself* is [+patient] and corresponds to an allative noun in the semantic structure, as in Figure 100. The difference is that *shaved* corresponds not to a single verb but to a more complex semantic structure containing the noun SHAVE. *My brother gave himself a shave* has a noun [+agent] – *brother*, a noun [+neutral] – *shave*, and a noun [+benefactive] – *himself*, but corresponds to the same semantic structure as *My brother shaved himself*.

There is not space here to go into the question of whether this analysis can be extended to every verb, but it is worth pointing out that it explains certain aspects of the syntax and morphology of the verb in Classical Greek. In grammars of Classical Greek three sets of verb paradigms are distinguished: active, middle and passive. The passive, like the English passive, can be viewed as a device for putting the patient first in a sentence. As in the English, the agent noun is preceded by a preposition and can be omitted **10**.

10a   Hoi politai kōluousi tous stratiōtas ('The – citizens – are hindering – the – soldiers')

10b Hoi stratiōtai kōluontai (hupo tōn politōn) ('The –
soldiers – are being hindered (by – the – citizens)')

Hoi is the nominative plural form of the definite article, *tous* –
the accusative plural form and *tōn* – the genitive plural form. The
noun following the article is of the same case and number. *Hupo*
is a preposition that elsewhere is translated as 'down from'.
Kōluousi is third person plural, present tense, active and *kōluontai*
is third person plural, present tense, passive.

The middle and passive forms are identical except for the
future and aorist, and middle forms do not occur with a *hupo*
phrase.

The various meanings expressed by the middle forms are not
easy to state and what follows is a selection of highlights. One
elementary grammar says: 'The Middle Voice has various
meanings, the prevailing idea being *self-advantage*, that is, the
Subject of the Verb is also the Recipient or Remoter Object'
(Abbott and Mansfield *A Primer of Greek Grammar*, p. 65). This
statement can applied with least difficulty to **11**.

11a Ho dēmos tithetai nomous ('The – people – place –
laws', i.e. 'The people make laws for themselves')
11b Apepempeto autous ('He – sent away – them')

In **11a** *tithetai* is the third person singular, present tense, middle
voice form of *tithenai* ('to place'). It could be translated simply as
'The people make laws', but the prepositional phrase *for themselves* is necessary to convey the full force of the middle form in
Greek. The middle is obligatory in Greek as the sentence *tithēsi
nomous* ('They place – laws'), in which *tithēsi* is third person
singular, present tense, active, can only describe the laying down
of laws by a lawmaker for someone else.

In **11b** *apepempeto* is middle, though the corresponding active
form, *apepempe*, could have been used instead. **11a** can be given a
straightforward semantic structure describing laws as located at
the people (the Greek dative expresses location; page 198) but
11b requires the sort of semantic structure indicated by **8** and **9**,
one describing an event as located at a person and glossed as '(A
sending them away) was at him'.

While self-advantage is patently part of the meaning expressed
by **11**, it is not so obviously appropriate to the semantic analysis of
12.

12a   Louo ton hippon ('I am washing – the – horse')
12b   Louomai ('I am washing (myself)')

12a and **12b** illustrate beautifully the distinction between active and middle forms but it is not immediately evident what a suitable analysis is. One possibility is that **12b** corresponds to a semantic structure in which there is an agent and a patient, both nouns denoting the speaker. This analysis has the disadvantage that it provides a semantic correlate for middle forms different from that proposed for the middle forms in **11**. We have seen that transitivity can be interpreted as the movement of an action from one object to another, which is suitable for Classical Greek as the patient noun in the NP active V NP structure takes a case inflexion that also expresses movement.

In contrast, the semantic structure proposed for **11** describes the location of an event at a person, and a similar structure is proposed for **12b**: 'A washing is located at me'.

In this semantic structure there is no agent. Since a benefactive has to be postulated in relation to sentences in which there is no benefactive phrase, like *My brother is going to buy a bike*, it may be that an agent has to be postulated, yielding a structure 'I cause a washing to be located at me'.

If Classical Greek had only active and middle constructions, a sentence like **12b** would be vague as to who caused the washing to be located at the speaker. It would be clear, of course, that the speaker is affected by the washing. If the source of the event is someone other than the person at whom the action is located, this can be signalled by a prepositional phrase, e.g. *hupo tōn amphi-polōn* ('by – the – handmaidens'), to invoke a typical scene from *The Odyssey*. It is generally held that the passive construction in Classical Greek developed from the middle construction in just this way, and that the creation of separate future and aorist passive paradigms occurred relatively late in Greek.

The assumed historical development of the passive explains the identity of middle and passive forms, and the semantic analysis proposed here makes it clear why such a development was possible. The passive and middle constructions are both concerned with the person at whom an action is located or, as the traditional grammars put it, with the person affected by the action.

Just as *My brother is going to buy a bike* is vague with respect to the benefactive, so **12b** is vague with respect to the source of the washing. There is, however, no vagueness attaching to a verb form that is clearly middle. The aorist middle corresponding to *louomai* is *elousamēn* and this can only be interpreted as describing a situation in which the speaker washed himself. The aorist passive, *elouthēn*, can only be construed as describing the washing of the speaker by someone else.

The passive in Classical Greek has now been associated with a semantic structure involving the location of an action at someone, although the active is analysed in terms of an action moving to someone. The different analyses do not impede an understanding of why active and passive sentences are felt to be related, because the relationship can be explained by implication rules. The sentence *He has come to Edinburgh* implies *He is in Edinburgh*, i.e. sentences describing movement to a place P imply sentences describing location at P, and this implication holds even if the objects that move or are located are abstract.

There are further facts that deserve a comment. Grammars of Greek recognise a third use of middle forms in sentences describing someone acting on an object belonging to himself, as in **13**.

> **13**   Luomai ton hippon ('I – am loosing – the – horse', i.e. 'I am untying my horse')

Luomai is the first person singular, present tense middle form *luein*. The idiomatic translation of **13** should not be allowed to conceal the structure of the Greek sentence. Putting together the analysis of patients as the end point of a movement and the analysis of middle forms as expressing the location of an action at someone, one semantic structure for **13** is: '(A loosing moves to the horse) is located at me'. That is, an action is located at the speaker and the action is the loosing of the horse.

This information is to be stated in the general semantic structure. **13** is confined to the description of situations in which the horse belongs to the speaker, but it is not clear whether it should be stated as an additional specification of the whole construction or as idiosyncratic information about the interpretation of the definite article. This use of the definite article in Classical Greek is reminiscent of the use of *the* in English: e.g. *The wife's going off on holiday tomorrow*. The important point is that there is no possessive pronoun in the Greek sentence, just a definite article, and the syntax of the Greek is different from that of the English.

Consider **12b** again. In practice, it is only single verb forms that occasion difficulties of interpretation and the context often eliminates unsuitable interpretations. If middle and passive forms occur with agent or patient nouns there is no problem, since middle forms occur with a noun in the nominative case and a noun in the accusative case and passive forms occur with a noun in the nominative case and a prepositional phrase introduced by *hupo*.

The fact that middle verb forms specify that a person X undergoes an action performed on X by his or her self sheds light on the meaning of deponent verbs, which denote the carrying out, not the undergoing, of an action but have only middle forms: e.g. *poreuomai* ('I march'), *maxomai* ('I fight'). It also helps to explain why some verbs have active forms in all tenses except the future, the future forms being middle: e.g. *feugō* ('I flee') – *feuksomai* ('I will flee'), *diōkō* ('I pursue') – *diōksomai* ('I will pursue').

The essential point is that the middle form does not signal a radical change of meaning but merely the close involvement of the agent in the action. Experiencer nouns, too, can occur with middle verb forms, the future of *akouō* ('I hear') being *akousomai*. Whether a middle form is regarded as expressing self-advantage, as is traditionally said, is a pragmatic matter determined by the lexemes in the semantic structure and by context. The Athenian commander who announces that he, in his single ship, will pursue twenty Persian ships could not be deemed to be deriving any advantage from his action, even if he did use *diōksomai*. There is always close involvement, however, and this is captured by the semantic structure 'be located at X'.

23 Prepositions and case affixes in surface syntax

In traditional grammars of Indo-European languages a distinction is drawn between *grammatical* and *local* case affixes and prepositions. (*Local* means 'expressing location or movement in space or time'.) We have assumed that all prepositions and case affixes (except the nominative) correlate with local meanings. The nominative case affixes can express any role, their main function being to signal which noun is the subject of the sentence. One old view is that nominative case affixes express agency, but this is too general. It applies to the typical NP V NP structure in which the first noun denotes an animate performer and the V denotes an action, but not to other structures or to untypical sentences like *Caesar videt insulam* ('Caesar – sees – island'), *Caesar* being a nominative form.

The traditional distinction between grammatical and local cases can be invoked in relation to the nominative in Indo-European and in Finnish; Finnish has sixteen cases, each consisting of two suffixes whose occurrence is phonologically conditioned. Three cases – the nominative, accusative and genitive – have no local function in the modern language, and their occurrence can be adequately described in terms of surface syntax. Perhaps a thorough study would reveal idioms that would permit the accusative case suffixes to be treated as expressing the end point of a movement, but the core syntax alone does not support this analysis.

In Indo-European languages with case systems the accusative case also has the local function of signalling movement, which justifies the directional analysis of patients. With the exception of the nominative, all the case inflections in Indo-European have both grammatical and local functions, a fact that speaks against inflections being classed as either local or grammatical. Even on the weaker hypothesis that case endings have both types of function but that the functions are not connected, it is difficult to explain why both functions attach to prepositions and case affixes in

Indo-European and in non-Indo-European languages, and why prepositions and case affixes that originally had a local function (e.g. *of* in English) lose their association with concrete location or movement. The localist says they come to express only abstract movement or location and from that stage progress to lose all connection with semantics and serve only as relational items in the surface syntax.

The sort of problem posed for the localist by this change of function is illustrated by the Russian sentences in **1**.

> **1a** Ivanu ponjatna eta teorija ('To Ivan – understandable – this – theory')
>
> **1b** Ivan ponimaet etu teoriju ('Ivan – understands – this – theory')

On page 195 it was stated that in Russian dative case inflections are associated with the experiencer role. This statement applies to **1a** with the dative case form *Ivanu* but **1b**, although equivalent in meaning to **1a**, has the structure of the typical sentence describing an agent acting on an inanimate patient, e.g. *Ivan krasit etu komnatu* ('Ivan – is painting – this – room'). *Ponimaet* is a verb form and *teoriju* is an accusative singular form. In spite of the structure, the suggestion that Ivan is doing something to the theory is not plausible. If the question is asked, in Russian or English, *What is Ivan doing to this theory?* the answer cannot be *He understands it*. There is not even any evidence that **1b** presents Ivan as playing a more active role. The most we can say is that **1b** is one of the favourite sentence types of Russian and is used whenever possible.

Sometimes the NP V NP structure does present someone as playing a more active role. It has been alleged that the English sentences *The picture pleased the connoisseur* and *The connoisseur liked the picture* differ in syntax but have the same semantic structure. Neither describes an action and the occurrence of *pleased* or *liked* is taken to be determined by which noun occurs first.

> **2a** Marija ljuba/nravitsja Ivanu ('Marija – dear/pleases – to Ivan')
>
> **2b** Ivan ljubit Mariju ('Ivan – loves – Marija')

In **2a** *ljuba* is an adjective agreeing in number and gender with *Marija* and *nravitsja* is a reflexive verb agreeing in number with *Marija*. *Ivanu* is the dative case form of *Ivan*, and **2a** can be analysed as describing the movement of some object – call it pleasure – from Marija to Ivan. Mary has an effect on Ivan.

In **2b** *ljubit* is a verb form agreeing in number with *Ivan* and *Mariju* is the accusative form of *Marija*. While it is correct that Ivan cannot be said to be doing anything to Marija, the nominalization corresponding to **2b** reveals an interesting fact. The nominalization is *ljubov' Ivana k Marii* ('love – of Ivan – to – Mary') and the significant fact is the occurrence of *k* ('towards') and the dative case form *Marii*. These indicate that **2b** can be regarded as describing the movement of love from Ivan to Marija. This does not mean that Ivan is actually doing anything, but it seems that **2a** and **2b** present the same situation from different angles and are best handled by an implication rule.

The moral is that in NP V NP structures where the V is a stative verb the noun in the accusative case sometimes denotes the end point of a movement and sometimes does not. The amount of evidence available for each stative verb varies, there being none for PONIMA ('understand') and just enough for LJUBI ('love').

The final topic in this section is the case affixes added to subject nouns in Indo-European and other languages. The constituents do not always occur in the NP V NP order of English, as will be evident from the Latin sentences in **3**.

3a	Puella agricolam monet	('Girl – farmer – advises') i.e. 'The girl advises the farmer'
3b	Agricola puellam monet	('Farmer – girl – advises')
3c	Puella laborat	('Girl – works')
3d	Agricola laborat	('Farmer – works')

3a and **3b** have transitive verbs, **3c** and **3d** have intransitive verbs. The first noun in each sentence has the same case inflection, whereas the nouns after the transitive verb have a different case inflection. In terms of subjects and objects, the subject nouns of transitive and intransitive verbs take the same inflection, the nominative, and there is a different case inflection, the accusative, for the object noun of transitive verbs.

Consider now the Basque sentences in **4**.

4a	Gizonak ogia jan du	('The man – some bread – eaten – has')
4b	Gizona ethorri da	('The man – has come')
4c	Ogia ona da	('The bread – good – is')

4a, which describes an animate agent acting on an inanimate object, has a transitive verb; the subject noun of this transitive verb has a case affix *k* that does not appear with any other noun in **4a–4c**. The noun form *ogia* occurs in **4a** and **4c**; in **4a** it denotes the patient, whereas in **4c** it denotes the object possessing the property of being good.

Also, *gizona*, which has the same affix (or lack of affix) denotes an agent, though not one acting on another object. In terms of subjects and objects we can say that in Basque the object nouns of transitive verbs and the subject nouns of intransitive verbs take the same case affix, but that there is a special affix for the subject noun of a transitive verb.

To explain the case marking in Latin and Basque it is necessary to recall that in the typical NP V NP structure in English and other languages the V denotes an action, one NP denotes an animate agent and the other NP denotes an inanimate patient. Other NP V NP structures are considered parasitic on this one. The category of animacy is particularly important; the typical NP V NP structure carries no risk of misinterpretation in literal language, but if both agent and patient are animate it has to be made clear which NP denotes the agent and which the patient. There is no risk of confusion in the interpretation of sentences with intransitive verbs.

Latin and Basque look different with respect to the NP V NP construction, but the different morphologies are merely different ways of avoiding the same potential confusion. Latin has a special inflection for patient nouns in the NP V NP structure, and Basque has a special suffix for the agent noun in that structure.

That suffixes like *k* acquire the function of marking the subject noun of any transitive verb whether the verb denotes an action, is evident from the following Eskimo data adapted from Jespersen's *Philosophy of Grammar*.

5a	Pe lip Nano (q) takuva	('Pele – the bear – saw') i.e.
		('Pele saw the bear')
5b	Nanup Pele takuva	('The bear saw Pele')
5c	Pele omavoq	('Pele lives')
5d	Nano (q) omavoq	('The bear lives')

The subject nouns of the intransitive verb (let us call *o mavoq* a verb) in **5c** and **5d** have the same suffixes as the object nouns of the transitive verb *takuva* in **5a** and **5b**. There is a special suffix for the subject nouns of the transitive verb in **5a** and **5b** – *Pelip* and *nanup*, the difference between *ip* and *up* probably being phonologically conditioned – although the verb does not denote an action. Although the nominative case inflections in Indo-European can now only be analysed as marking the topic of a sentence there is evidence that the nominative case inflection *s* that occurs with 'third dimension' Latin nouns derives historically from a morph marking agent nouns.

The occurrence of the same suffix on the object nouns of transitive verbs and the subject nouns of intransitive verbs may have semantic justification. The subject noun of some intransitive verbs denotes a patient, as shown by the fact that the questions *What happened to Angus?* can be answered by *Angus fell*, *Angus died*, *Angus slept*. Recall also the discussion of *John sat down* (pages 212–13).

It is possible to imagine an ideal language in which there is one suffix for the subject noun of a transitive verb, say *X*; another suffix, *Y*, for the agent noun with an intransitive verb; a third one, *Z*, for all patient nouns, whether with transitive or intransitive verbs. If English possessed these suffixes the sentences in **6** would occur.

6a   Angus-X trampled the flowers-Z
6b   Angus-X ran down the hill
6c   Angus-Z died
6d   The flowers-Z faded

Languages like Latin are 'nominative-accusative' and languages like Basque are 'ergative'. It would be more accurate to talk of nominative-accusative and ergative constructions, for many allegedly ergative languages have an ergative system of case affixes in some constructions but not all. For instance, Georgian has an ergative suffix only in sentences with an aorist verb form, i.e. one denoting completed action. Conversely, nominative-accusative languages may have constructions in which there is a special marker for the agent noun, e.g. the passive in English and Latin, in which the agent is marked by the prepositions *by* and *a/ab*.

Technical terms

ergative language/construction
nominative-accusative language/construction

Notes on sources

Chapters 1–11

The source of these chapters is Chomsky (1965), but more accessible to students are Akmajian and Heny (1975) and Huddleston (1976). Burt (1971) concentrates on the cycle and rule ordering. The best shortest account of phrase structure rules, the restrictions on them and the need for transformations is Postal (1964). His comments on other models can be omitted. Arguments that transformations are unnecessary are offered by Reich (1969), Hudson (1976) and Schachter (1976).

The proposal that verbs and adjectives assign selectional features to nouns derives from suggestions in Kuroda (1969); and the COMP node, suggested by Bresnan (1970), is in general use, though the combination of the two proposals is not. Katz and Postal (1964) provide syntactic arguments for generating Q and Neg as deep structure constituents. Lyons (1977, pp. 753–68) and Hudson (1975) discuss the syntax and semantics of interrogatives.

Akmajian and Heny (1975), Huddleston (1976) and Burt (1971) all discuss the cycle and rule ordering. The original work on constraints is Ross (1967), followed by Chomsky (1973). The discussion of recursive functions in chapter 11 draws heavily on the article by Hartley Rogers in Hintikka (1969), but other useful introductions to the mathematical side of linguistics are Gross (1972) and Wall (1972). A general account of the psychological and mathematical connections can be found in Lyons (1970).

Chapters 12–15

The extended lexicon is first mentioned in Chomsky (1970, pp. 184–98). Another article on the extended lexicon is Bresnan (1978), but the lexicon employed in this book has most in common with the lexicon of the lexicase model developed by Starosta but not described in any one publication. The analysis of the passive is based on Freidin (1975), and a similar analysis of infinitives and gerunds is in Schachter (1976). The concept of surface filters was introduced by Perlmutter (1971) and has recently been developed by Chomsky and Lasnik (1977), which is not recommended for beginners. The general problem of the relationship between syntax and semantics and the control problem are treated in Jackendoff (1972, especially ch. 1 and 5). An easy introduction to trace theory is in Chomsky (1976, pp 78–117).

Chapters 16–23

Fillmore (1968) and Anderson (1977, ch. 1) give a good account of why the standard model treatment of grammatical functions, cases and prepositions is unsatisfactory. An interesting paper showing the relevance of roles to psycholinguistic theories is Schlesinger (1979).

An excellent coverage of these topics is Lyons (1968, pp. 289–304, 334–99). Chapters 22 and 23 in this book draw on Lyons's account but benefit from work done after 1968. The discussion of agentivity in chapter 17 is based on Cruse (1973). Allerton (1978) contains interesting data and comments on indirect objects and benefactives. Finally, a splendid if complex account of agent and patient, transitive and intransitive verb, and the marking of nouns by affixes is to be found in Dixon (1979). A paper concerned with non-local roles and local relations, like chapter 21, is Starosta (1978).

References

ANDERSON, J. M. (1977), *On Case Grammar*, Croom Helm

ALLERTON, D. J. (1978), 'Generating indirect objects in English', *Journal of Linguistics*, vol. 14, pp. 21–33

AKMAJIAN, A., and HENY, F. (1975), *An Introduction to the Principles of Transformational Syntax*, Massachusetts Institute of Technology Press

BRESNAN, J. (1970), 'On complementizers: toward a syntactic theory of complement types', *Foundations of Language*, vol. 6, pp. 297–321

BRESNAN, J. (1978), 'A realistic transformational grammar', in M. Halle, J. Bresnan and G. Miller (eds.), *Linguistic Theory and Psychological Reality*, Massachusetts Institute of Technology Press

BURT, M. K. (1971), *From Deep to Surface Structure*, Harper & Row

CHOMSKY, N. (1965), *Aspects of the Theory of Syntax*, Massachusetts Institute of Technology Press

CHOMSKY, N. (1970), 'Remarks on nominalization', in R. A. Jacobs and P. S. Rosenbaum (eds.) *Readings in English Transformational Grammar*, Ginn & Co.

CHOMSKY, N. (1973), 'Conditions on transformations', in S. Anderson and P. Kiparsky (eds.), *A Festschrift for Morris Halle*, Holt, Rinehart & Winston

CHOMSKY, N. (1976), *Reflections on Language*, Fontana

CHOMSKY, N., and LASNIK, H. (1977), 'Filters and control', *Linguistic Inquiry*, vol. 8, pp. 425–504

CRUSE, D. A. (1973), 'Some thoughts on agentivity', *Journal of Linguistics*, vol. 9, pp. 11–23

DIXON, R. M. W. (1979), 'Ergativity', *Language*, vol. 55, pp. 51–138

FILLMORE, C. J. (1968), 'The case for case', in E. Bach and R. T. Harms (eds.), *Universals in Linguistic Theory*, Holt, Rinehart & Winston

FREIDIN, R. (1975), 'The analysis of passives', *Language*, vol. 51, pp. 384–405

GROSS, M. (1972), *Mathematical Models in Linguistics*, Prentice-Hall

HINTIKKA, J. (1969), *The Philosophy of Mathematics*, Oxford University Press

HUDDLESTON, R. (1976), *An Introduction to English Transformational Syntax*, Longman

HUDSON, R. A. (1975), 'The meaning of questions', *Language*, vol. 51, pp. 1–31

HUDSON, R. A. (1976), *Arguments for a Non-Transformational Grammar*, University of Chicago Press

JACKENDOFF, R. S. (1972), *Semantic Interpretation in Generative Grammar*, Massachusetts Institute of Technology Press

KATZ, J. J., and POSTAL, P. M. (1964), *An Integrated Theory of Linguistic Descriptions*, Massachusetts Institute of Technology Press

KURODA, S.-Y. (1969), 'Remarks on selectional restrictions and presuppositions', in F. Kiefer (ed.), *Syntax and Semantics*, D. Reidel

LYONS, J. (1968), *Introduction to Theoretical Linguistics*, Cambridge University Press

LYONS, J. (1970), *Chomsky*, Fontana

LYONS, J. (1977), *Semantics*, vol. 2, Cambridge University Press

PERLMUTTER, D. M. (1971), *Deep and Surface Structure Constraints in Syntax*, Holt, Rinehart & Winston

POSTAL, P. (1964), *Constituent Structure: A Study of Contemporary Models of Syntactic Description*, Indiana University Press

REICH, P. A. (1969), 'The finiteness of natural language', *Language*, vol. 45, pp. 831–43. Reprinted in F. W. Householder (ed.), *Syntactic Theory 1*, Penguin 1972

ROGERS, H., Jr., (1969), 'Turing Machine Computability', in J. Hintikka (ed), *The Philosophy of Mathematics*, Oxford University Press

ROSS, J. R. (1967), *Constraints on Variables in Syntax* (Indiana University Linguistics Club), excerpts reprinted in G. Harman (ed.) (1974), *On Noam Chomsky: Critical Essays*, Doubleday

SCHACHTER, P. (1976), 'A non-transformational account of gerundive nominals in English', *Linguistic Inquiry*, vol. 7, pp. 205–41

SCHLESINGER, I. M. (1979), 'Cognitive structures and semantic deep structures: the case of the instrumental', *Journal of Linguistics*, vol. 15, 307–24

STAROSTA, S. (1978), 'The one per sent solution', in W. Abraham (ed.), *Valence, Semantic Case and Grammatical Relations*, J. Benjamins

WALL, R. E. (1972), *Introduction to Mathematical Linguistics*, Prentice-Hall

Index